Energy Aware Computing

Powerful Approaches for
Green System Design

Bob Steigerwald
Chris D. Lucero
Chakravarthy Akella
Abhishek R. Agrawal

Intel
PRESS

ISBN 13 978-1-934053-41-6

Publisher: Richard Bowles
Editor: David J. Clark
Program Manager: Stuart Douglas
Text Design & Composition: MPS Limited, a Macmillan Company
Graphic Art: MPS Limited, a Macmillan Company (illustrations), Ted Cyrek (cover)

Library of Congress Cataloging in Publication Data:

Printed in China

10 9 8 7 6 5 4 3 2

Second printing, December 2011

IMPORTANT

You can access the companion Web site for this book on the Internet at:

www.intel.com/intelpress/tmip

Use the serial number located on the last page of the book to register your book and access additional material, including the digital edition and pointers to development resources.

Contents

Foreword

In the twelfth century, craftsmen imparted their practical skills to apprentices. The parents of a minor would pay a premium for a master craftsman to train their son in return for seven years of indentured servitude. Between hauling charcoal, water, and iron, and pumping billows, a lad would slowly gain the skills of a blacksmith through trial and error. Upon completion at the age of majority, twenty-one, the apprentice became a journeyman earning the right to be paid for conducting smith work.

And so secrets of the blacksmith and other forms of knowledge and trade were passed from generation to generation during times the Italian scholar Plutarch would later dub the *dark ages*. Few were privy to fundamental knowledge during such times. Moreover, violent religious struggles and the spread of deadly diseases often wiped out both people and the conventional wisdom they had accumulated over generations.

Hundreds of years later, the Prussian philosopher Immanuel Kant in his famous late eighteenth century essay on the topic would describe the succeeding *age of enlightenment* as "mankind's final coming of age, the emancipation of the human consciousness from an immature state of ignorance and error." Monumental discoveries of this age included the foundations of reason put forth by French philosopher Rene Descartes and the laws of mechanics described by English physicist and mathematician Sir Isaac Newton.

The age of enlightenment improved our understanding of the world around us and was seen as the culmination of reason. However, mankind has a habit of referring to the current age as the most enlightened generation in history. Even the age of enlightenment seems dark compared to the modern era of the Internet where knowledge and discovery are democratized and economic barriers between countries have been shattered by the emergent global economy. Nevertheless, there is little doubt that at some future date generations from now the current age too will be seen as dark by comparison. This pattern of knowledge and understanding following a path of darkness followed by light is a successive theme throughout mankind's varied history.

Energy aware computing is still in the dark ages. The early years were rife with chaos and struggle as researchers argued over whether energy aware computing was even necessary. In the years that followed, irrefutable evidence mounted establishing energy awareness as critical to sustaining the performance gains mankind has become accustomed to in its computers.

Today, we argue not over whether energy aware computing is needed, but what the best approaches are to ensuring energy efficiency in computer designs. This has motivated thousands of researchers, professionals, and students the world over to improve their understanding of computer efficiency in an effort to tackle the resulting design problems.

Alas, establishing the validity of a new energy aware computing approach is an art reminiscent of smith work during the dark ages. Only a handful of researchers throughout the world are skilled in the art of energy efficiency measurement and management. Fewer still have been able to conclusively demonstrate their energy aware designs in hardware or software work effectively on real systems. Apprenticeship or collaboration with these researchers is required to conduct energy aware computing research.

With only a handful of skilled artisans the world over, the apprenticeship model of the dark ages will not sufficiently address the scale of the energy efficiency problem. While some of the basic concepts of power and energy can be read from textbooks, practical techniques for measurement and management of energy on modern computer systems are currently passed directly from one researcher to the next. These trade secrets are in danger of being lost. The pervasiveness of computers now and in the foreseeable future means the computer energy efficiency problem is immense and will persist. Solving this problem will require the effort and creativity of tens of thousands of researchers in the coming decades.

The time is ripe for the age of enlightened energy aware computing. And this is the book. The authors have written a practical treatise on energy measurement and management that promises to take us on the first step of our journey out of the dark ages and toward enlightenment. What follows is an energy aware computing roadmap for the novice and the practitioner with illustrative examples of energy efficiency in both software and hardware design. Researchers, professionals, and students who want to understand and contribute to the green computing movement without the required years of indentured servitude should immediately add this book to their library.

Dr. Kirk W. Cameron
IEEE Computer Green IT Column Editor
Co-Founder Green500 List
Founding member SPECPower

Preface

There is a growing demand worldwide for resource conservation and sustainability in all walks of life. Computers are no exception. The high tech industry is investing heavily to manufacture and use energy-efficient computers in all applications from embedded systems to enterprise data centers. Taking steps to save energy makes great sense whether it's to create power-friendly embedded systems, extend the battery life of a tablet PC, or save money cooling a data center. This book is intended for systems and software engineers. Our objectives are to lay a foundation for understanding energy aware computing and to provide hardware and software methodologies that system and software engineers can use when designing computing solutions so that they too can contribute to green computing.

Energy Saving Initiatives

Over the past few years while researching and gathering the information to write this book, we have come across interesting stories about efforts to promote and energy efficiency and sustainability in the computing industry. As a prelude to the book we would like to share a few of those to reinforce our conviction that energy efficiency in computing is worth the investment.

Data Centers on Ships

There is an article on ZDNet whose headline reads "Google makes waves and may have solved the data center conundrum" (ZDNet, 2008). Owning the largest data centers in the world and paying a massive energy bill every month would certainly motivate a company to research moneysaving alternatives and we think this idea is very innovative. Google applied for a patent in February 2008 for a *floating* data center powered by wind and wave energy and cooled by sea water.

Google's data centers would sit offshore about 3 to 7 miles in about 50 to 70 meters of water and use a "plurality of motion-powered machines" (Pelamis Wave Energy Converter units) to power a "plurality of computing units." With enough energy converter units, Google figures they can generate about 40 megawatts of power. That could power 100,000 *400-W* servers or 160,000 *250-W* servers. If they were to purchase that energy for U. S. dollars (USD) 0.10 per kWHr, Google would have to pay USD 4000 per hour, USD 96,000 per day, or about USD 35 million per year. Clearly, some serious money can to be saved here. While many challenges present themselves including jurisdiction, taxes, bandwidth, and others, it's a bold and innovative move to both save money and use renewable resources for sustainability. It's also consistent with their core values: "At Google, sustainability is a core value that comes directly from our founders, and we believe being green makes business sense" (Google, 2011).

Beyond wave energy, Google makes use of and sponsors research in wind, solar, and geo-thermal energy as well. (Google, 2011) The other side of the coin is reducing the amount of energy data centers consume. Most enterprises (especially those with large data centers) are trying to find ways to use less energy. One outcome of these efforts has been the Climate Savers Computing Initiative.

Climate Savers Computing Initiative

Started by Google and Intel in 2007, the Climate Savers Computing Initiative (CSCI) is a nonprofit group of eco-conscious consumers, businesses, and conservation organizations whose goal is to increase the energy efficiency of computing equipment, increase the adoption and deployment of power management, and shift user behavior to smart computing practices. As participants in the Climate Savers Computing Initiative, computer and component manufacturers commit to producing products that meet specified power-efficiency targets, and corporate participants commit to purchasing power-efficient computing products. Sponsors of the Climate Savers Computing Initiative include the Climate Conservancy, the World Wildlife Fund, and the Green Computing Impact Organization. Since it was established, more than 675 members, including large commercial enterprises and technology industry stakeholders, have joined the initiative, and thousands of individuals have pledged their support.

While one of the main objectives is to reduce CO_2 emissions from the operation of computers, CSCI is not just focused on the data center. One of the facts on the Web site states: "U.S. college students could save more than 2.3 billion kilowatt hours per year of electricity by enabling power saving features on their desktop PCs. That equals an annual savings of more than [USD] 200 million in energy costs and a 1.8 million-ton reduction of CO_2 emissions from the operation of computers—equivalent to taking more than 350,000 cars off the road." This is one of the reasons CSCI provides detailed instructions on how to use the power management features on desktop and notebook PCs. To find out more about CSCI, see (Climate Savers, 2011).

Rendering in the Cloud

Another company with large data centers is Dreamworks Corp., makers of computer-generated animated films including the *Shrek* series and *How to Train Your Dragon*. According to Bloomberg Business Week magazine (December 6, 2010), Dreamworks "spends over [USD] 100,000 per month powering each of its data centers in San Francisco, Marin County, and Singapore." To give an idea of the computing magnitude required to create these movies, it took 55 million hours of computer time to render the video frames for *Shrek Forever After*—6 hours per frame. To save money, Dreamworks outsourced much of the rendering to Cerelink, a cloud computing company in Corrales, New Mexico. The cost of energy in Corrales is about USD 0.09 per kilowatt-hour compared to USD 0.14 in Los Angeles. Adopting a cloud computing approach has saved Dreamworks on production costs and makes use of a shared resource, contributing to sustainability.

Governments in Action

In 1992 the US Environmental Protection Agency (EPA) introduced Energy Star[†] as a voluntary labeling program designed to identify and promote energy-efficient products to reduce greenhouse gas emissions. While you may have heard of Energy Star, you may not realize that computers and monitors were the first labeled products. Energy Star now covers over 60 product categories (and thousands of models) for the home and office. The products that earn the Energy Star logo deliver the same or better performance as comparable models while using less energy.

In their guide *How to Buy an Energy Efficient Personal Computer* (FEMP, 2000), the Federal Energy Management Program states:

- Executive Order 13123 and FAR section 23.704 direct agencies to purchase products in the upper 25 percent of energy efficiency, including all models that qualify for the EPA/DOE Energy Star product labeling program.

- Agencies that use these guidelines to buy efficient products can realize substantial operating cost savings and help prevent pollution.

- As the world's largest consumer, the federal government can help "pull" the entire U.S. market towards greater energy efficiency, while saving taxpayer dollars.

The important thing to note here is that when governments get involved and make regulations that require the procurement of energy-efficient products, they do, as a very large consumer, influence product features and energy-savings and move the market toward developing energy-efficient alternatives.

Europe is also making changes. In 2008 a few of us were contacted by a representative of the Netherlands Ministry for the Environment. The European Union had just established the Green Public Procurement (GPP) initiative. Green Public Procurement (GPP) is defined as "a process whereby public authorities seek to procure goods, services and works with a reduced environmental impact throughout their life cycle when compared to goods, services and works with the same primary function that would otherwise be procured." In response to the GPP, the Netherlands government set a target for 100-percent sustainable procurement by 2010. This government official that contacted us had the unenviable task of defining the sustainability requirements for computer software and having read our paper on Energy-Efficient Software (Steigerwald, 2010), thought we might be able to help. We provided some guidelines (Larsson, 2010) and hope that they were somewhat useful. We have completed significantly more research since then (hence the motivation for this book) and can envision a future where energy efficiency is a primary criteria for selecting both hardware and software.

How this Book Is Organized

This book is organized in three parts and ten chapters.

Part 1: Principles of Computer Power, Measurement, and Management

Part 1 explains how energy is used, managed, and measured in computer systems. It establishes a foundation to understand and apply energy saving design principles to hardware and provides the necessary background to better understand energy-saving approaches for software.

Chapter 1: Introduction

Chapter 1 provides a brief introduction to power and energy concepts, how power is used in computing devices, and typical power budgets of computers from embedded systems to data center servers.

Chapter 2: Power Measurement in Modern Computing Systems

For a deeper understanding of how energy is distributed and used and how to measure it, Chapter 2 covers power supply inputs and their importance in energy efficient design. We also review the basics of power measurement as a means of understanding the platform power consumption and the methodologies for accurate power measurement at the component, platform, and system levels.

Chapter 3: Power Management in Modern Computing Systems

Central to saving energy in computers are the mechanisms to manage energy. In Chapter 3 we describe power management in the Intel architecture including CPU and system-level power states, system- and facility-level power management, and power management settings within various operating systems.

Part 2: Developing Energy-Efficient Software

Part 2 is focused on designing and developing energy-efficient software. The design decisions that software developers make directly affect the amount of energy a computer will consume.

Chapter 4: Impact of Software on Energy Consumption

Chapter 4 is our first chapter focusing on how software can be energy-efficient. It describes why and how software has an impact on platform energy-efficiency and demonstrates with several examples that software applications can have a significant impact and that software energy-efficiency is a relative metric.

Chapter 5: Writing Energy-Efficient Software

Chapter 5 describes the mechanisms used to save energy in software primarily under workload conditions. It demonstrates techniques that developers can use to improve performance with corresponding energy savings, save energy by limiting data movement, and improve energy efficiency by being context-aware.

Chapter 6: Idle Efficiency

This chapter describes the mechanisms used to save energy in software while idle. It explains techniques that developers can use to keep software quiescent when it should be including methods to achieve deeper C-state residency in the CPU, knowing and working with the states of other platform hardware, and effective use of system timers.

Chapter 7: Evaluating and Measuring Software Impact to Platform Power

It's difficult to chart a path to your destination if you don't know where you are. Chapter 7 explains how to measure the energy impact of software. By knowing the methods and tools available and how to use them, you will be able to measure the differences between your alternative designs and chart your progress.

Part 3: Case Studies in Energy Aware Computing

Part 3 of the book covers case studies in energy-efficient system design from embedded systems to mobile computers to data centers. These examples show what has been done and will motivate you to think of new and innovative ways to develop even more energy-efficient designs.

Chapter 8: Embedded Applications

Embedded systems are processors that are designed to "do a few things well." Chapter 8 provides descriptions of various embedded markets and how power management principles apply to the systems they employ, including telecommunications, military/aerospace, medical equipment, and retail point-of-sale systems.

Chapter 9: Computing on the Go—Smart Phones, Tablets, and Netbooks

This chapter explores what distinguishes small form factor devices from other traditional computing devices, introduces a few specialized tools and methodologies for analyzing power, and presents a set of case studies showing energy-efficiency improvement for computing on the go.

Chapter 10: Writing Energy-Efficient Software for the Data Center

Chapter 10 presents and discusses various techniques software developers can adopt to write energy-aware and energy-efficient software for the data center by presenting two detailed case studies to illustrate a new approach focusing on software energy efficiency. The objective is to empower the software developers to bring their unique and indispensable expertise to the data center.

Acknowledgements

The studies, data, results, and guidelines compiled in the book are the result of years of research from many talented engineers at Intel who have a strong passion for energy-efficient performance. The contributions they have made and the time they have spent, much of it outside their normal duties, deserves to be acknowledged.

For significant contributions to this book for analyses, cases studies, and written content, we'd like to thank these talented engineers:

- A special thanks to Susumu Arai, Jaya Jeeyasalan, Barnes Cooper and Eunice Chang whose work has provided inputs into multiple chapters in the book, especially Chapter 7 on measuring software impact to platform power.

- Rajshree Chabukswar – Chapter 5, Computational Efficiency; Rajshree is an expert in getting the best performance from software and has spent years studying how performance gains lead to energy-efficiency benefits.

- Jun De Vega – Chapter 5, Data Efficiency; Jun has moved a whole lot of data in countless experiments—enough to prove that it's best to keep data close to processing elements, both for performance and for energy savings.

- Manuj Sabharwal – Chapter 5, Context Awareness; Manuj's research on increasing the platform's awareness of its surroundings and activities as well as his idle software case studies have been an invaluable contribution.

- ■ Petter Larsson – Chapter 9 inputs; Petter has a talent for getting the most energy out of small devices such as cell phones and tablets. We appreciate his contributions to Computing on the Go.

- ■ Jamel Tayeb – Chapter 10; Jamel is an expert in energy-efficiency in the data center and in both measuring and tuning data center software for energy efficiency.

We also extend our gratitude to David Clark for his excellent copy editing, making the book more readable and consistent throughout. Thanks to our illustrators, MPS Limited, a Macmillan Company, who took our rough drawings and made them really stand out. And last but not least, we want to thank our program manager, Darren Smith, for getting us started on the right foot and Stuart Douglas for gently pushing us through the writing phase and then on to the finish line.

Reviewer comments and suggestions were extremely valuable. We deeply appreciate those who took the time to provide indispensable feedback on the manuscript including Professor Kirk Cameron, Shekhar Borkar, and Ali Muhtaroglu.

Bob Steigerwald thanks his manager, Arun Kumar, for giving him and many of the engineers the time to research and compile the book's contents. Above all, Bob is very thankful for the support of his wife, Silvi, who showed great patience and gave lots of encouragement over many nights and weekends.

Chris thanks his wonderful children who continue to provide him inspiration for researching new ways to conserve energy for their future and generations to follow. He would also like to acknowledge his peers in the Embedded and Communications Group within Intel for their support and drive to make technology an ever more valuable part of people's everyday lives.

Chakravarthy Akella would like to thank all his teachers, professors, and mentors who have provided guidance and knowledge. Chakravarthy is also thankful to his family who supported and encouraged him through the process.

Abhishek Agrawal would like to especially thank his wife, Nidhi, for her continuous encouragement and support throughout the whole process. Abhishek would also like to thank all his professors and mentors who have provided guidance, his peers for sharing the knowledge, and also his managers at Intel, Bob Steigerwald and Arun Kumar, for giving the time to research and compile the book's contents.

Chapter 1

Introduction

It's not easy being green.

—Kermit the Frog

The objectives of this book are to lay a foundation for understanding *Energy Aware Computing* and to explain powerful hardware and software methodologies that system and software engineers can use to develop energy-efficient computing solutions. By applying these green computing approaches, computer hardware and software professionals can do their part for resource conservation and sustainability.

This chapter will provide a quick overview of topics that will be useful to understand before diving in to the concepts presented in later chapters including some basics of power and energy, batteries, thermal design power, performance per watt, idle efficiency, and finally a primer on computing platforms from embedded to supercomputers.

Introduction to Power and Energy

The primary aim of this book is to explain how to develop systems that are energy-efficient. Since we will be using energy terms quite frequently, it will help to understand some definitions up front.

The first three terms, *newton, joule,* and *watt,* are all part of the International Standard of Units or SI (short for le Système international d'unités).

A *newton* (named for Sir Isaac Newton) is a unit of force. It is equal to the amount of force required to accelerate a mass of one kilogram at a rate of one meter per second per second.

$$1\ N = 1\ \frac{kg \cdot m}{s^2}$$

A *joule* (named for James Prescott Joule) is a unit of energy and represents the amount of work done by a force of one newton moving an object through a distance of one meter. The energy required to lift a 100 gram object 1 meter against the pull of earth's gravity is about 1 joule.

$$1\ J = 1\ N \cdot m = 1\ \frac{kg \cdot m^2}{s^2}$$

A *watt* (named for James Watt) is a unit of power and represents the *rate* of energy conversion. One watt is the rate at which work is done when an object is moved at a speed of one meter per second against a force of one newton.

$$1\ W = 1\ \frac{J}{s} = 1\ \frac{N \cdot m}{s} = 1\ \frac{kg \cdot m^2}{s^3}$$

These standard units help us to define power, energy, and heat.

Power, measured in watts, it is the *rate* at which energy is consumed. Electricity-consuming devices are rated by the amount of energy they consume while in operation. For example, a 100-W lightbulb consumes 100 joules of energy per second that it is lit. A notebook computer might consume energy at a rate of 25 W.

The conventional definition of *energy* is the "capacity to do work". A device that is *energy-efficient* requires less energy for its "work" or task than its energy-inefficient counterpart. For this paper, we use energy to mean the amount of joules required to carry out a specific task. Rather than express the energy in joules, it is typically expressed as a function of watts. Since 1 watt = 1 joule/second, it follows that:

■   1 joule = 1 watt second

■   60 joules = 1 watt minute

■   3600 joules = 1 watt hour (WHr)

■   3,600,000 joules = 1 watt kiloHour or 1 kilowattHour (kWHr)

■   3.6 joules = 1 watt milliHour or 1 milliwattHr (mWHr)

In the US, billing for electricity in kWHr is the standard. The cost is roughly USD 0.15 to 0.20 per kWHr. In this book, the rate at which energy is consumed by the computer or by a computer component will be expressed in watts or milliwatts. The total energy to complete a task or workload will be expressed in wattHours (WHrs) or milliwattHours (mWHrs). For example, a notebook PC (>=2 cores, >=2 GB RAM, discrete GPU) that is Energy Star compliant must consume below approximately 88.5 kWHrs per year based on certain usage parameters.

Defined as thermal energy in transit, *heat* is a natural byproduct of having electricity running through metal pathways. We have all experienced this with the tungsten filaments of light bulbs and of course electric heaters. It should be no surprise that a computer CPU generates a lot of heat. The higher the computational load we put on the computer, the more energy it requires, and therefore the more heat it produces. As we'll see later, *dissipating* the heat is both a design challenge and an additional energy cost we face in striving for energy-efficient computing.

Batteries

Batteries store energy and you expect to get a certain amount of energy from them. The amount they can deliver depends on the battery technology and the battery capacity. Most mobile computing platforms today, including notebook PCs, tablets, and smart phones, use lithium-ion (Li-ion) rechargeable batteries. They tend to have the best energy-to-weight ratios, no memory effect, and minimal leakage (loss of charge) when not in use. The capacity (the energy potential) of a battery is expressed in wattHours (WHrs) or milliwattHours (mWHrs). For example, if you have a notebook computer that has a 60-WHr Li-ion battery and the power demand is a continuous 15 W, you will be able to operate the notebook PC for four hours before you must recharge. Many factors influence the amount of energy being used including the CPU, the GPU, the display, and the disk activity. The Apple iPad[†] is an impressive feat of engineering. It has a battery capacity of 24.8 WHrs and can deliver over 10 hours of high definition video playback on a single charge, all the while sipping less than 2.5 W.

Energy Consumption in Computers

Armed with an understanding of power and energy, let's now look at the energy demands of various computing platforms.

Thermal Design Power (TDP)

TDP (expressed in watts) is a power rating for a computer system, a term used to represent the maximum amount of power the cooling system in a computer must be able to dissipate. It is a designed-in limitation of a computer system that reflects the tradeoffs made for performance and cooling methods. Lower TDPs are typically found in embedded applications and mobile systems and can get by with passive cooling methods such as convection, thermal radiation, or conduction. Higher TDP systems require active cooling methods such as fans, heat pipes, or even liquid submersion. The TDP does not represent the maximum wattage that a processor can withstand (sometimes processors will exceed TDP for a brief period), but rather the maximum power it would normally draw when running the applications for which it was designed. This ensures that the system will operate effectively without exceeding its thermal envelope.

Table 1.1 shows some typical TDP ratings for a range of computer systems.

Table 1.1   Computer System TDP Ratings

Computer System	Thermal Design Power (TDP)	Typical Cooling Approach
Low-power embedded	<5 W	Passive methods
Smart phone	4–5 W	Passive methods
Netbooks and tablets	4–12 W	Mostly passive methods, possibly a fan
Notebook (ultra-low voltage)	10–15 W	Passive methods, possibly a fan
Notebook (mainstream)	45–60 W	Heat sink and fan
High-end desktop (quad core)	90–130 W	Heat sinks, multiple fans, cooling tubes
Small servers	80–165 W+	Heat sinks, multiple fans, cooling tubes
Larger servers up to supercomputers	300 W to thousands	Elaborate cooling solutions depending on the number of processors and the amount of BTUs generated

The important tradeoffs to understand here are that more performance typically means more power required to deliver that performance and more cooling to dissipate the heat that is generated. Therefore in designing systems, we want to find ways to get the most performance for the least amount of power or the best *performance per watt*.

Performance per Watt

With significant consideration being given to the cost of energy in computing environments, performance per watt has become and an increasingly important measure of system value. The cost of energy and cooling (or the battery life) are paramount in decision making. Performance per watt is the quantity of computation that can be delivered by a computer for every watt of power consumed.

Many industry benchmarks are used to measure computer system performance. You may have heard of SPECMark, Whetstone, Dhrystone, Linpack, and many others. Benchmarks for energy-efficient computer performance have also been established, including MobileMark, SPECPower, and SWaP (space, watts, and performance). In general, they consider the amount of energy used to complete various workloads.

One interesting example of how this has been applied to supercomputing is a project by Professors Wu-Chun Feng and Kirk Cameron at Virginia Tech. They decided that rather than celebrate the Top500, the world's fastest supercomputers, they would instead honor the Green500, or the most energy-efficient supercomputers in the world (Cameron, 2011 and Sharma, 2006). They extended the Linpack method of measuring the number of floating point operations per second (FLOPS) to be FLOPS/watt. The Green500 is essentially a reordering of the Top500 list by energy-efficiency. The first list made public (back in 2008) was apparently completely dominated by IBM's Blue Gene supercomputers.

More than a measure of supercomputing efficiency, performance per watt can be an excellent source of feedback for the methods we apply in hardware and software design to achieve better energy-efficiency in all classes of computing devices. In Chapter 5 we'll see a simplified version of this where we measure the power to execute the same compute task using different instruction sets, for example a serial approach versus a vectorized approach using Intel® AVX. The vectorized approach delivers better performance and lower power, essentially superior performance per watt. Also in Chapter 5 we'll show how effective use of multithreading delivers better performance with a corresponding power benefit.

Do Nothing Efficiently

While our computer systems should be designed to work efficiently and deliver the best possible performance per watt during computation, they should also be designed to *idle efficiently*. When there is no work to do, the system should be quiescent, which by definition means "in a state of tranquil repose." Because power has always been an important design consideration in embedded and small form factor devices, they tend to be very well behaved when in an idle mode. Larger form factor devices unfortunately have a long way to go. In Chapter 6, we'll see how software applications running on these devices can be unnecessarily active (when they should be idle) and waste a considerable amount of energy.

In summary, if it is not clear already, you will soon realize that making energy-efficient computers is a very challenging multidimensional design problem with a myriad of tradeoffs. Table 1.2 shows a list of power measurements used as design considerations and as a means to gauge progress in your energy-efficient system designs.

Table 1.2   Power Measurements as Design Considerations

Power Terminology	Description
Thermal Design Power (TDP)	Highest power a platform consumes
Average Power	Average power doing typical work
Idle Power	Power of system doing nothing
Sleep Power	Power in the sleep state
Off Power	Power in the off state
Typical Energy Consumption (TEC)	Yearly energy consumption (WHr)

Introduction to Modern Computing Systems: Intel® Atom™ through Intel® Xeon®

Up to now we have made mention of a few of the more obvious computing devices we encounter in our lives. But we have just scratched the surface. There is a very broad spectrum of compute platforms in the world and they are becoming ever-more pervasive. We believe that the energy-efficient design principles described in this book can be used in all of these applications.

Embedded Systems

Seemingly invisible and in many cases taken for granted, embedded computers are the workhorses behind many of the intelligent devices we encounter on a daily basis. An embedded system can be defined formally as a computer system designed to perform one or a few dedicated functions often with real-time computing constraints. It has also been defined as a computer or set of computers that are part of a larger system whose central purpose is something other than computation. Embedded systems are often designed to operate under extreme conditions of heat, cold, moisture, vibration, and dirt so they can be used in mission-critical computing applications.

In many cases, embedded computers are application-specific integrated circuits (ASICs). Simple ASICs are customized for a specific use, perform a few functions well, and are typically controlled by a fixed firmware program. Typical devices you would encounter controlled by simple ASICs are control panels, simple electronic control systems, and so on.

More sophisticated ASICs that require more flexibility and higher performance are called SoCs, short for System on a Chip. These SoCs may contain a full 32-bit processor (such as the Intel Atom processor) and deliver more flexibility and higher performance for more demanding applications. Examples include retail, industrial robots, medical devices, telecom, aerospace, consumer electronics, and in-vehicle applications. Chapter 8 provides some case studies and more detail on embedded applications.

Small Form Factor Systems?

The line can become blurry between embedded devices and small form factor devices. For example, a cell phone controlled by a sophisticated ASIC might be considered an embedded application, whereas a smart phone capable of executing any of thousands of apps from an app store, provide turn-by-turn navigation, weather, and so on is more a general-purpose and very mobile computing device. Whereas the original meaning of small form factor was ascribed to devices that perform the same functions as a desktop computer, but in a smaller space, it seems to have become more of a buzzword without a standard definition. Rather than get caught up in that, we'll just create categories for Smart phones/tablets and for netbooks/nettops.

Smart Phones and Tablets

This is arguably one of the most exciting segments of computing today. Primarily because they are so visible in the media and in such high demand, smart phones are becoming increasingly more capable and tablets are establishing an entirely new and formidable class of mobile computing device. Admittedly, tablet concepts have been around for a few years but with the release of the Apple iPad, which set a high bar for this class of devices, the segment has exploded with designs with entries from nearly every major computer and cell phone manufacturer. For both smart phones and tablets energy-efficiency is critical for long battery life. Hardware designs in these segments are dominated by ARM, which has long been the standard in low-power designs for cell phones. However, there is growing demand for more capability, which means higher performance, a space in which Intel has been the leader. With both of these (and other) industry powerhouses vying for market share in this space, the winner(s) will be those who can navigate the many design tradeoffs and deliver the best customer experience at the best performance per watt.

Netbooks and Nettops

Introduced in 2007, netbooks and nettops are smaller, relatively inexpensive versions of notebook (laptop) and desktop PCs. At the time they fill an important and untapped market gap between smart phones and PCs; the segment had explosive growth in 2008 and 2009. The light weight, portability, and low cost of netbooks was an instant hit with consumers. Likewise, the low cost and low power consumption of nettops was very appealing to businesses large and small.

The key tradeoff with these devices is performance. Both are satisfactory for most productivity applications (e-mail, word processing, spreadsheets), Internet browsing, and casual gaming, but they are not well suited for compute-intensive applications that include high-end photo and video editing and immersive gaming.

Notebooks and Desktops

Notebooks and desktops are the mainstay of the computer product industry. Since the first personal computers emerged in the late 1970s, amazing advances have been made in line-width, processor speed, memory density, and parallelism, and the industry continues to develop products that follow Moore's law. Developed by Gordon Moore in 1965, Moore hypothesized that number of transistors that could be placed on an integrated circuit would double about every two years. In the 30+ years of PC product-development, the industry has optimized price-performance and delivered innovations that today yield a dizzying array of alternatives. If a friend or family member asks you, "What computer should I buy?" your answer is probably another question: "What do you plan to do with it?" Their satisfaction will be based on tradeoffs in performance, battery life, weight, display size, network connectivity, device connectivity, expandability, and ultimately the user experience.

In recent years, the PC processor space has shifted to a PC *platform* space with more and more of the overall system design coming from the leading chip manufacturers Intel and AMD. For both mobile and desktop, these market leaders and the manufacturers continue to work on energy-efficient designs. In fact, Intel's recent introduction of its 3D transistor technology will provide superior energy-efficiency that could potentially help PC manufacturers consistently deliver on the promise of the all-day notebook PC.

Servers

A server is the class of computer system that we normally equate with a data center. The term server is not necessarily meant to represent size or power, but more its function. As the name implies, its job is to provide services. At the low end, the power and performance of servers is blurred with that of a high-end desktop, but some applications of servers don't even need that to perform their jobs effectively. In fact designs are emerging to create servers with an array of low power processors (such as Intel Atom, ARM, Nvidia, Via) to deliver better performance per watt for certain applications. Typically though, the server space is dominated by processors such as Intel Xeon and AMD Opteron†. At the high end, servers approach the class of supercomputers.

Just as with notebooks and desktops, advances in the server space have led to much better performance at much lower power and much lower cost. Where price-performance tends to drive improvements in PCs, availability and throughput tend to drive improvements in servers. One innovative approach is the *blade computer*. These systems strive to minimize physical space and energy by offloading common hardware and functions to the common physical enclosure or chassis. They have been incredibly effective at reducing the footprint and cooling requirements and have increased the flexibility businesses need to adapt to changing workload demands.

Another technology that has dramatically improved server utilization (and hence lower overall power demand) is virtualization software. A single server can run multiple *virtual machines*, allowing it to provide multiple kinds of services without having dedicated physical equipment for each. In this way, a hosting service provider can be running your business applications on one virtual machine and someone else's applications on another virtual machine, on the same physical device with absolutely no interaction between them.

As the world appears to be embracing a *cloud computing* paradigm (for real this time) we will see far more growth in massive data centers. Keeping them cooled and running at peak efficiency will be increasingly important. See Chapter 10 for more information on getting the best performance per watt in your data center computing applications.

HPC and Supercomputers

HPC stands for high-performance computing. Supercomputers are the largest members of this class. Some of the most well known names and brands of the largest supercomputers can be found in the Top500 (Top500, 2011) list we mentioned earlier and they include Cray Inc., IBM, SGI, Hewlett-Packard, and Oracle. These systems are used for the world's most computationally demanding applications and research and they consume relatively huge amounts of energy to complete their tasks, so much so that these systems have to have very elaborate mechanisms for cooling, including (although rare) submersion in a thermally conductive liquid.

Leading applications for supercomputers include weapons simulations, war games, weather forecasting, climate change, quantum mechanics, fluid dynamics, molecular studies, materials simulations, graph analyses, and cryptology. There are also a host of unsolved problems called "Grand Challenge" problems that have come from the fields of speech, vision, semiconductor design, nuclear fusion and many more.

Some more entertaining applications have been with IBM's Deep Blue, which was programmed to play chess and defeated the world champion Garry Kasparov in 1997 (Mr. Kasparov defeated Deep Blue in 1996), and with IBM's Watson, which defeated the Jeopardy! World champions Ken Jennings and Brad Rutter in early 2011.

Summary

Computers are encountered in nearly all aspects are our lives and there continues to be substantial growth in the application and adoption of computing platforms. From embedded systems to supercomputers, all of these devices require energy. As designers of systems and software, it is our duty be conscientious about energy consumption and sustainability, and as professionals promote the design, development, deployment, and adoption of well-chosen technologies to improve computer platform energy efficiency.

Chapter 2

Power Measurement in Modern Computing Systems

If you cannot measure it, you cannot improve it.

—Lord Kelvin

I n order to contribute to the reduction of overall global power consumption and to minimize a company's own carbon footprint, a company must optimize its hardware and software computing solutions to run more efficiently. The first step in this process is to understand how the power is supplied to the system, followed by the ability to account for every watt that the system consumes. The prerequisite for an energy-efficient design is a strong understanding of power measurement. The ability to measure power and account for power allows designers to examine the cause and effect of the policies employed in their system designs and reach an optimized solution.

The Flow of Power

Every time energy is transformed from one form to another, the transformations are accompanied by certain conversion losses. Similarly, when power is supplied from the source to the components, it goes through a series of transformations (typically step-up or step-down), and each transformation has a conversion loss associated with it. By the time power reaches a component it will have undergone several such transformations. Hence, every watt consumed at the component level is equivalent to a much higher value at a facility level.

For instance, say a component consumes 1 W while performing a certain operation. Say, the power is supplied by a voltage regulator (of efficiency η_{VR}) and the voltage regulator draws power from the board power supply (of efficiency η_{PS}). Finally assume that the building or the facility itself has inefficiency (of efficiency $\eta_{FACILITY}$). So, a component consuming 1 W ends up costing the end user 1 W/($\eta_{PS}\,\eta_{FACILITY}\,\eta_{VR}$), which is typically a much higher number. Since the various efficiencies are multiplied with each other, one inefficient component could greatly impact the entire system.

Hence, in order to build an energy efficient system, it is important to identify and understand each of these transformations. In some cases, it is not possible to change or control various components or devices. However, in other cases a good understanding of systems would allow a better selection of components, which would lead to energy-efficient designs. The subsequent sections explain the flow of power at various levels.

Facility Level

The electric power consumed is generally monitored at the facility level. These consumption levels are what the facility owner pays as utility expenses. So, at the end of the day, the goal of the designer is to minimize the power consumed at the facility level. The definition of a facility is very vague and it could mean a data center or something as simple as an office building.

Providing generic guidelines for an efficient facility design might not be possible as each facility has its own unique need. Nevertheless all the variables should be factored in to get the optimal design point. For instance, setting the data center temperature at a certain value might be a more efficient configuration; on the other hand, an office building might focus on implementing additional power sensing probes to track the overall power usage.

Power Supply Level

The electric power supplied by a facility is generally AC power while most semiconductors operate on DC power. In the context of electronics systems the term *power supply* is generally used for the device that converts the AC power from the facility to the DC power for the consumption of the system. Based on the application, the power supplies can vary in shape, size, and form. Some examples of power supplies are ATX power supplies, a fixed 48-V power supply for networking equipment and even a brick for laptop power supply.

The power supplies generally have the highest inefficiency in the entire system. Hence it is very important to optimize these power supplies in order to minimize the losses. Power supplies that can supply higher power are generally more expensive and can therefore be perceived by some as better than those that have a lower capacity. For instance, if offered at the same price, a lot of users would select a 600-W power supply over a 450-W power supply with the notion that "more is better." However, from an energy-efficiency perspective, users might be better off using a 450-W power supply. This is generally the case as power supplies have a sweet spot where they have the highest efficiency.

Motherboard Level

The motherboard gets the power from the power supply and feeds it to various components on the board. The flow of power is achieved by layers of copper in the board known as the *power planes*. The voltage supplied to the motherboard is generally higher than what most components require. Thus voltage regulators are used to step down the voltage.

Based on the system design, one or more voltage regulators in series might be required to step down the voltage in a given rail. Generally, one regulator is sufficient to step down the voltage to an acceptable value. Major components on the board (such as the CPU and chipset) have multiple voltage rails and therefore multiple voltage regulators. In order to save cost and board space, multiple components use the same voltage regulator for their power needs.

Power Supply

As discussed earlier, the power supply is a device or system that supplies DC electrical power to the platform. The selection of a particular type of power supply over another depends on multiple factors such as the market, form factor, and other design criteria. The power supply efficiency plays a big role in the efficiency of entire platform and the inefficiencies of the power supply account for a huge portion of the energy consumption in the system.

The ATX Power Supply

The most commonly used power supplies are the ATX power supplies (Figure 2.1), which are commonly found in all desktop units. Although various power supplies differ from each other, understanding the ATX power supply's operation in detail provides a good foundation about power supplies in general.

Why is an ATX power supply needed? The ATX power supply serves a dual purpose. Since printed circuit boards (PCBs) use a DC power supply, an ATX power supply converts AC wall power to DC power for the motherboard. In addition to that, an ATX power supply has multiple outputs (12 V, 3.3 V, 5 V, and so on). Some components can be directly powered with these power outputs. For example, most system fans use a 12-V input, and the hard drive can be directly connected to one of the outputs from the power supply without using any additional voltage regulation from the designer's standpoint.

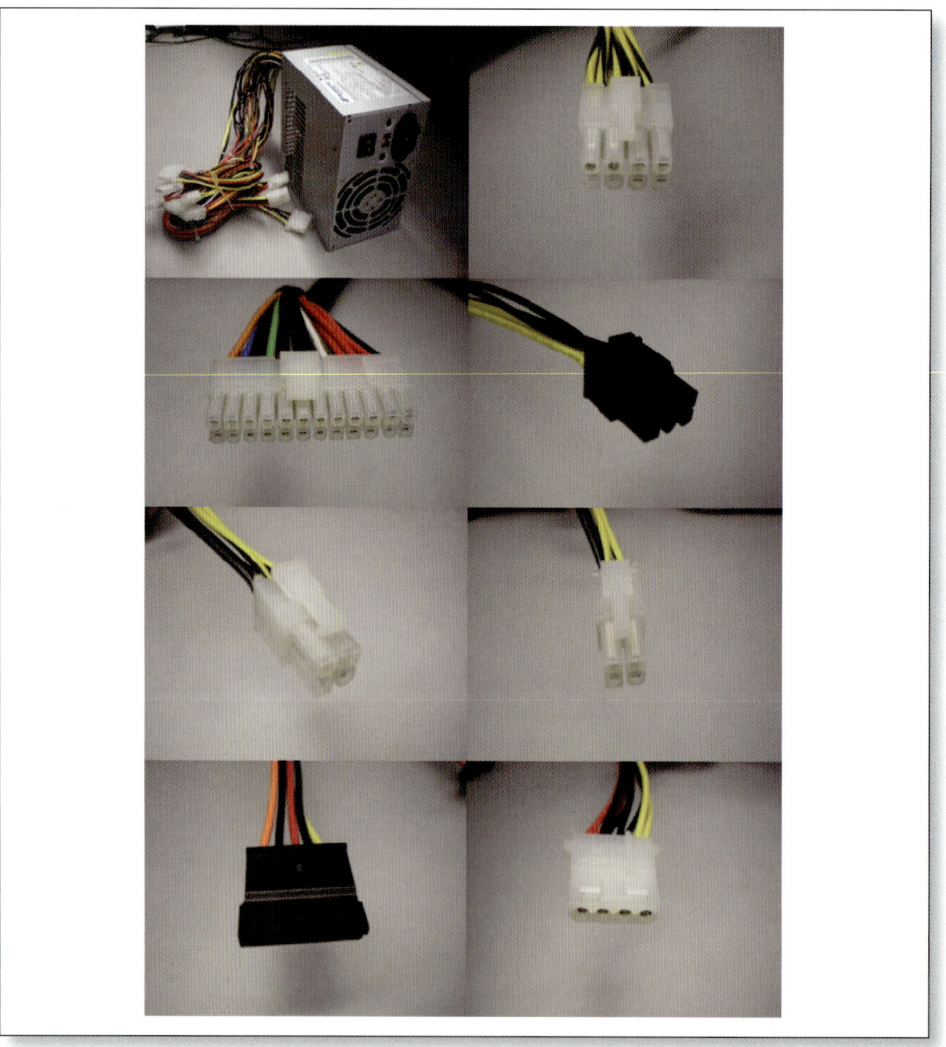

Figure 2.1 ATX Power Supply and Connectors

The primary connector that powers most of the components on the board is the 20- or 24-pin connector. The 20- and 24-pin connectors are identical in shape and functionality with the only difference being the 4 pins (two ground and two 12-V outputs). In several boards the additional 4 pins are detachable, so that the same connector could be used for boards with 20- or 24-pin inputs.

Some of the higher power boards need additional power, especially to the CPU. This power is supplied via additional connectors with 4 or 8 pins that supply additional 12-V input to the board. The CPU consumes most of the power from these connectors, so the power measured on these connectors can provide a reasonable estimate of processor power consumption. This assumption should be used carefully as the power from these rails can generally be shared with other components such as the CPU cooler fan or the DIMMs.

Generally the graphics cards and other PCIe[†] cards receive the power from the PCIe slot they are plugged into. However, for some high performance graphics cards, this power is not sufficient and they require a dedicated power supply, which is supplied using a dedicated 6-pin connector. The hard drive has additional connectors (Molex connector and SATA connector).

Color coding: the power supply rails are color-coded representing the voltage of the power rail, as listed in Table 2.1.

Table 2.1   Color Coding for Power Rails

Color	Voltage
Green	Power On
Grey	Power Good
Black	Ground
Orange	+3.3 V
Brown	+3.3 V Sense
Red	+5 V
Purple	+5 V Standby
Yellow	12 V

The Power Supply Efficiency

The efficiency of a power supply is determined by dividing the total system DC output with the system AC input power. So, if the summation of all the

DC outputs from the power supply is 55 W and the total AC power supplied is 70 W, the power supply is $(55/75)\% = 73\%$ efficient. The efficiency of the power supply is not fixed as it varies based on the output load. Figure 2.2 shows a typical efficiency curve of an ATX power supply.

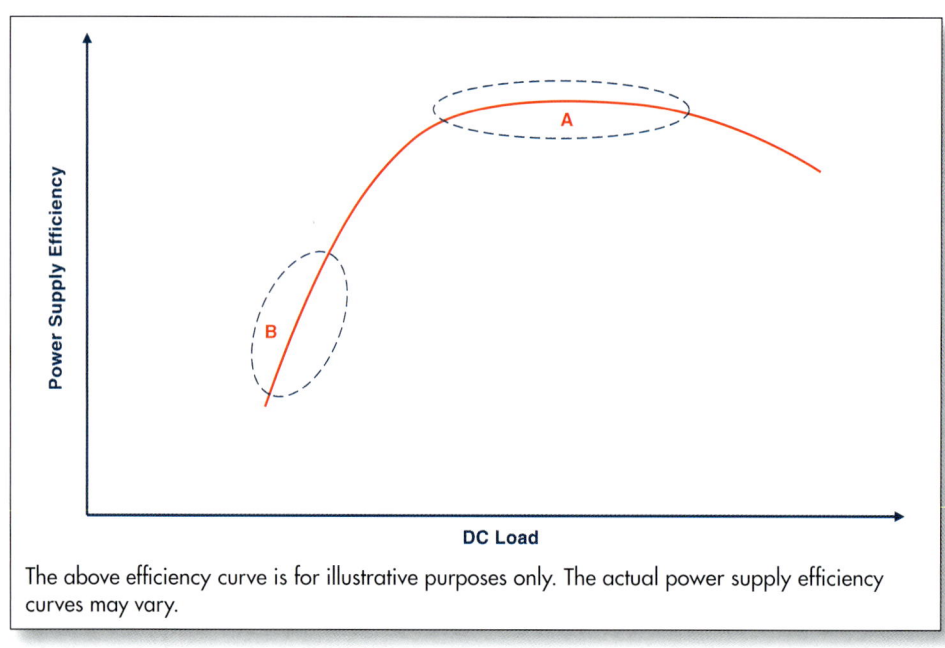

The above efficiency curve is for illustrative purposes only. The actual power supply efficiency curves may vary.

Figure 2.2   Power Supply Efficiency Curve

The power supply efficiency changes based on the output load. A typical power supply has an operation range (shown as Region A in Figure 2.2) with highest efficiency. As the power exceeds this value the efficiency of the power supply goes down. Similarly as the power decreases the efficiency of the power supply steeply drops. In other words, generally speaking when the platform is under idle or near idle conditions the power supply is most likely to be least efficient. Since the efficiency drops so rapidly, it is not uncommon to operate under non optimal points. The technology used in power supply design has been improving and new standards like "80 plus" have pushed the efficiency higher. The term *80 plus* in the context of a power supply efficiency implies that the power supply is more than 80-percent efficient at 20 percent, 50 percent, and 100 percent of the rated output. This spreads out the Region A in Figure 2.2 to allow a greater range of operation at high efficiency.

Let us look at an example where a user expects that the system will consume about 110 W for 20 hours and 250 W for 4 hours in a given day. The user has three 80-plus-certified power supplies at comparable costs to choose from with the peak output load 200 W, 500 W, and 600 W. Out of the three power supplies, the user has to weed out the 200 W power supply because the power supply can't be used reliably to supply the peak load of 250 W. Now, the 600-W power supply would be over 80-percent efficient between the range $600 \times 0.2 = 120$ W to 600 W. While the 500-W power supply would be efficient between $500 \times 0.2 = 100$ to 500 W. Hence for this use case the 500-W power supply would be the better choice.

Although the real-life design choices are more complicated, a similar approach can be used to make a proper selection. For instance in the above example, although the 600-W power supply is not more than 80-percent efficient at 110 W, its efficiency might still be close to 80 percent, which might still be acceptable in some designs. So in most cases, actual power measurements on the power supplies can provide vital information that could be used in the design process.

Voltage Regulators

A voltage regulator as the name suggests is an electrical device designed to regulate the voltage to supply a desired voltage level to components. In the context of a printed circuit board, a voltage regulator generally steps down the voltage from the input power supply to the voltage required by the components. The past few years have seen an increase in design complexity of components, thereby increasing the need for multiple sources of power at various voltage levels. In order to assist with such complex designs, power management multi-channel integrated circuits (PMIC) are generally used. These PMICs offer greater flexibility in power supply design and a single chip can provide multiple power supplies.

There are several kinds of voltage regulators and they can be classified based on their design and application. The most commonly used voltage regulators are linear regulators and switching regulators.

Linear Voltage Regulators

A linear voltage regulator is the simplest form of voltage regulator. The name linear regulator is derived from the fact that the devices operate in a linear region. Due to the linear nature of operation, they are very good when a steady output is needed. These are comparatively less expensive and generally less efficient. These regulators are generally not energy-efficient, but they are very popular due to the simplicity and cost.

The simplest way to understand how a linear voltage regulator works is by comparing a linear regulator to a variable resistor. The resistor causes the input voltage to drop from a high value (say 12 V) to a desirable value (say 2 V). As the input voltage fluctuates, the resistance of the regulator automatically adjusts itself to provide a fixed voltage at the output. The operation of linear voltage regulator is very simple; however, there is a huge penalty associated with it. Going back to our example, assuming 1 ampere flowing through the circuit, the value of resistance needed to drop the voltage from 12 V to 2 V would be $(12 - 2)/1 = 10$ ohms. This would result in the joule heating of the regulator equal to $(1)^2 (10) = 10$ W. The power converted into heat not only makes the board less energy-efficient but additional power needs to be supplied to cool the system. For this reason linear regulators are generally not used for big voltage drops or for high power drawing components.

Figure 2.3 shows how a linear pass element, in this case a variable resistor, takes the incoming 12-V rail, drops 10 volts, and delivers 2 volts to the load. The concept is easy to understand, but in real life two things are different: an additional ground terminal is used, and the variable resistor is replaced with a variable (or linearly controlled) transistor.

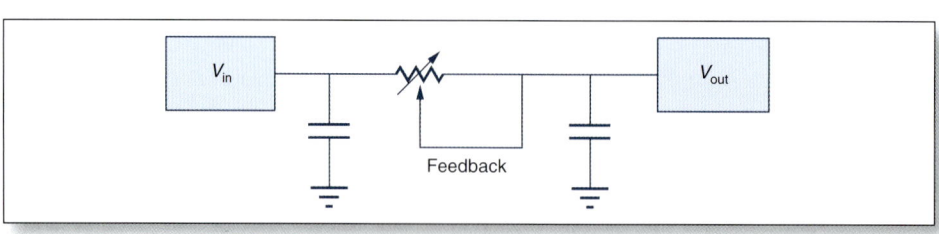

Figure 2.3 Linear Voltage Regulator

One can purchase a wide variety of three-terminal voltage regulators that might serve any purpose and could make one think "why do we need anything else?" The answer to that question is efficiency, or lack of efficiency, in the case of these simple regulators. Here's the explanation: in the example above the power source delivered 12 V at 1 amp, the load received 2 volts at 1 amp. Therefore to deliver 2 watts to the load required 12 watts of input power. The efficiency is less than 17 percent and 10 watts of power must be dissipated as heat. As the difference between the input voltage and the output voltage increases, the more inefficient linear voltage regulators become.

Switching Voltage Regulators

A switching voltage regulator or a buck regulator is one of the most commonly used voltage regulators. The switching regulator works on the concept of switching on and off in order to achieve a desired output, hence the name switching power supply. The process of switching on and off occurs at a very fast rate; some of the fastest regulators operate in the order of 1 MHz. Since the regulator switches off (as opposed to varying resistance like a linear regulator) it provides a very efficient way of regulating the power. The switching power supplies are more complex and need to be designed properly. Switching power supplies often require filtering to provide a cleaner output.

In other words, with a switching power supply, the electronic switch alternates being connected to either Vin or 0 V. The rate at which the switch alternates can vary, but 300 kHz is a typical switching frequency. The inductor "smoothes out" the alternating switch voltage and provides a DC voltage to the load that is equal to the average voltage coming out of the switch. If we assume for now that the switch and the inductor are ideal components, then an interesting thing comes out of the efficiency calculations. The switch either has current flowing through it but no voltage drop, *or* a voltage drop across it but no current through it. In other words at no time is there current flowing through the switch *and* a voltage drop across the switch, as shown in Figure 2.4. The result is no power loss!

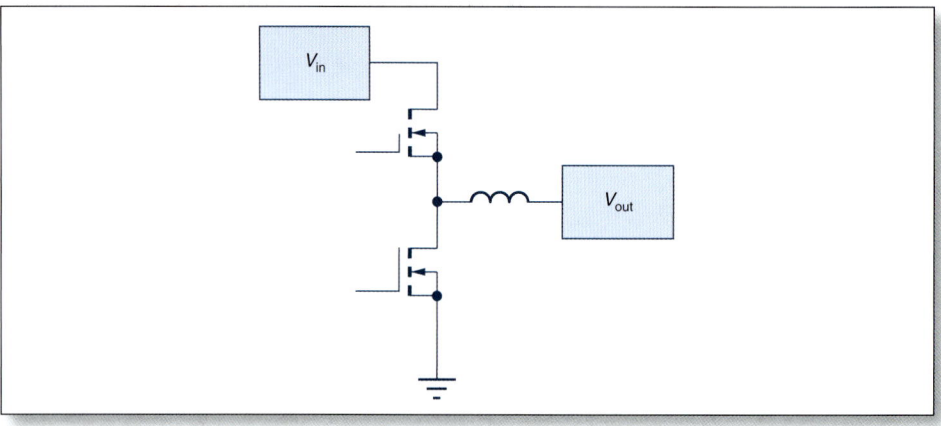

Figure 2.4   Switching Regulator

Unfortunately even this model is simplified; a more complete schematic would include the metal-oxide–semiconductor field-effect transistor (MOSFET) drivers, and the voltage regulator controller. Often the controller has integrated MOSFET drivers; sometimes the controller even includes the main switching transistors. Figure 2.5 shows a real-life switching voltage regulator circuit.

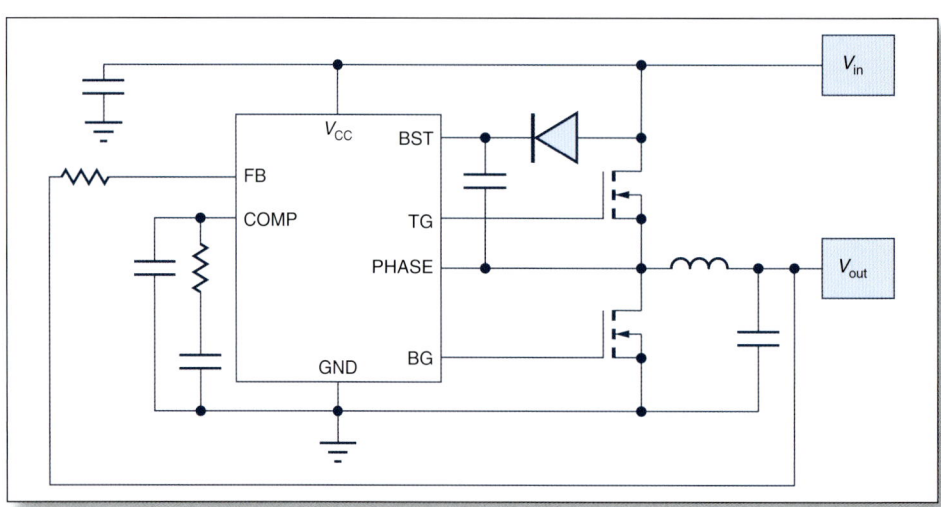

Figure 2.5   Real-Life Switching Voltage Regulator Circuit

Of course this is still a very simple model. In Figure 2.5 the switch is replaced by a pair of transistors, and this is what is at the heart of any synchronous buck regulator used on virtually any computer motherboard today. To vary the output voltage of a switching regulator you simply vary the amount of time the switch spends at 12 V versus 0 V. This is known as a variable duty cycle or pulse width modulation. Switching power supplies are more complex than a similar linear power supply, but the higher efficiency often makes them the only practical solution.

Of course switching voltage regulators do not use perfect components but efficiencies over 90 percent can be obtained. Some disadvantages of using switching voltage regulators are the noise issues, radio frequency interference, and even higher failure rates compared to the linear voltage regulators.

Power Measurement

Power measurement has been of great value and interest to system designers as it helps in gauging the benefits of various power management policies and other energy efficiency policies in place. However, very few tools and instructions are available to measure power consumed in a platform. The subsequent sections attempt to explain the fundamentals allowing the reader to comprehend methodology on how to measure power in a system with ease. The contents of this chapter are arranged in such a way that a person with little or no power measurement experience can learn about the process and steps involved. What approach you might use for power measurement can differ based on several factors. In some cases simple and inexpensive devices can be used for the measurement, while in several cases, special data acquisition systems (DAQs) might be needed. The following section explains how to deal with different kinds of power measurement.

System AC Power Measurement

Generally, the system AC power is the easiest to measure. The equipment used for AC power measurement can range from devices that cost a few dollars to a few thousand dollars based on the features and accuracy. The process of AC power measurement generally involves connecting an AC power meter between the source and the system. For the sake of discussion we can break down the AC meters into two key categories, namely the simple AC meters and sophisticated AC meters. Both kinds of AC meters seem to provide similar

AC power numbers as an output; however they greatly differ in functionality and capability. Figure 2.6 Shows both kinds of AC meters. Although the AC meters shown in Figure 2.6 are for a standard US wall outlet, similar meters are available for outlets throughout the world.

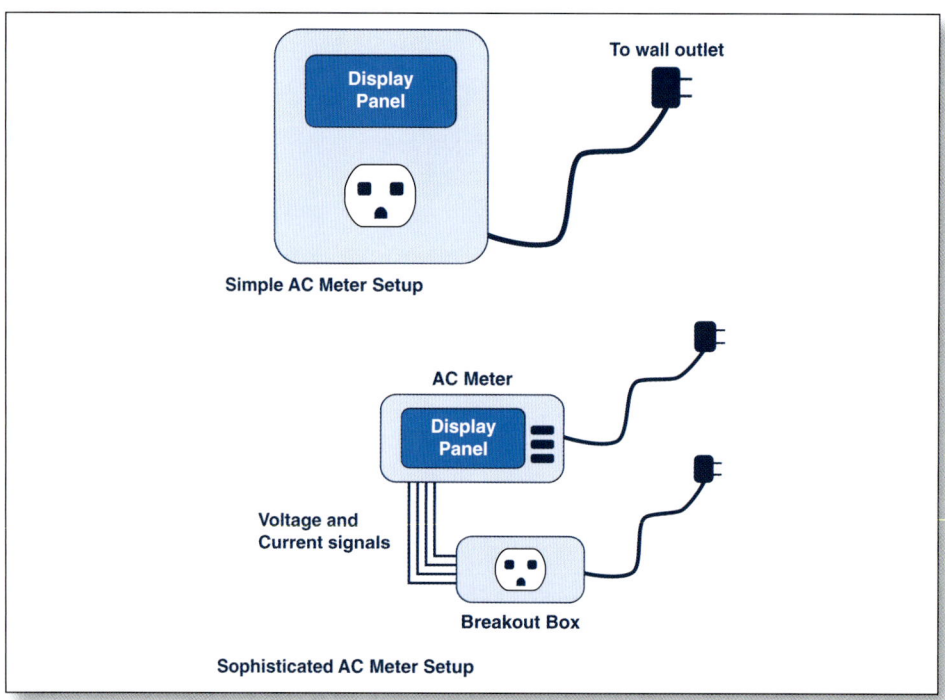

Figure 2.6   AC Meters

Simple AC power meters generally have a power cord that is connected to the wall outlet while the unit itself has a socket when the system under test can be connected. These devices are the cheapest and quickest way of measuring power. These devices however have several drawbacks:

■   *Integration with other devices*—Most of these devices can't be integrated with other data acquisition systems or with other standard data acquisition software. As a result these AC meters are generally used as standalone devices.

- ■ *Sampling rate*—The sampling rate of these simple AC meters is very low so they might not be suitable for power measurements when the AC power fluctuates greatly. For instance, these devices might not be sophisticated enough to capture any spikes that may arise during the boot sequence of a platform.

- ■ *Resolution*—One of the key drawbacks is that a lot of these devices have a very low resolution and might not be suitable for measuring small changes in the power consumption.

- ■ *Range*—The simple AC power meters have a small range for power consumption, so they may not be suitable for measuring power under many uses cases. For instance, it might not be possible to use these devices to measure the standby power of a platform; similarly these devices might not be suitable to measure power of a server rack with multiple platforms as it might exceed the range.

The simple AC meters have several practical uses, as they require very little setup time. Generally these devices are very compact and easy to use thereby making them ideal for quick validations. With improvement in technology these devices are getting more sophisticated.

The more sophisticated AC meters have an additional box generally known as the breakout box. The breakout box acts as a hub between the system under test and the wall power. The power cord from the breakout box is what is connected to the wall and the unit under test is connected to the outlet on the breakout box. The AC meter is a separate unit that has its own dedicated power supply unlike the simple meters. The breakout box communicates with the AC meter through four cables, two for voltage measurement and two for current. The sophisticated AC meters are generally bulkier and need additional programming to make them to work. However, these are the preferred devices for testing and benchmarking purposes.

Apart from the cost, complexity, and bulkiness, these devices offer several advantages. These AC meters offer better integration with other data acquisition systems and standard data acquisition software. These units generally have a very fast sampling rate and a very high resolution. These devices have a wider range of operation or can be configured to measure a wide range of power; for instance these devices can measure power in the milliwatt to kilowatt range (and even megawatts in some cases). It should be noted that all AC meters can't be clearly classified as simple or sophisticated meters. So, it is possible to find a few AC meters that have more features than the simple meters and fewer features than those found in the sophisticated meters.

DC Power Measurement Basics

The AC power measurements provide information about the complete system and are very useful, in analyzing system designs. However, the AC measurements are not capable of providing the insight about how power is consumed within the system. The DC power measurement process is generally more complex; however it allows the user to probe into the system and it provides a useful breakdown of the power consumed by various components and sub-components. For instance, DC measurements can show if a particular hard drive is consuming more power than another or if one set of memory modules are more efficient than another. The DC power measurements on a platform have several limitations and dependences. Hence it is very important to understand the platform schematics in order to proceed with DC measurements. The DC power can be measured in multiple ways, such as with scopes and multimeters, but the easiest way of measuring DC power is by using automated data acquisition systems (DAQs). Before we proceed with understanding DC power measurements, it is worthwhile to understand how the DAQs operate. Subsequently, it will be useful to understand how the various sensors and resistors operate.

Understanding DAQs

Data acquisition systems (DAQs) sample analog signals and convert them into digital signals that can be processed by a computer. DAQs can measure small voltage drops at a very high sampling rate making them ideal for automated power measurements. The DAQs have several inputs known as channels. Since a voltage is the potential difference between two points, for each voltage measurement two inputs are required: one to represent the ground (or the low side) and another to represent the voltage (or the high side). These measurements are also known as differential measurements because they indicate the difference between two inputs. An alternate way of measuring voltage would be the single-ended measurement. In a single-ended measurement, the high side is the input provided to the DAQ via one of the input channels but the reference ground (or the low side) is selected by the device based on its own ground. The single-ended measurements are less accurate because the ground of the DAQ may not be same as the ground of the device under test. However, the advantage of using the single-ended measurements is that they use only half the channels, which require fewer wires and connections. This also frees up the DAQ's resources to measure additional channels or perform faster sampling.

The DAQs generally interface with the computer via standard connections like COM ports and GPIB. In recent years the USB port has become the interface of choice for many DAQs. Generally, most DAQ manufacturers provide software to be used along with the hardware or have recommended data acquisition software that can be used. The user interface of the DAQ shows the voltage measured on each channel corresponding to the hardware connection made on the system. This helps a lot in real-time tracking, analyzing, and storage of the data.

Understanding Sensors

The DAQs allow users to measure electrical signals; however; most of the parameters that have to be measured in the real word are not electrical signals. The sensors sense the parameter of interest and convert the value into an electrical signal that can in turn be measured by the DAQs. Figure 2.7 shows how a typical measurement system operates. Every measurement system has a parameter that has to be measured, that gets converted into an electrical signal through a sensor. This information is gathered by a DAQ and relayed back to the computer system.

Let us take the example of measuring pressure. A pressure transducer is an example of a sensor: it converts pressure into an electrical output. The output of the pressure transducer can be connected to a DAQ and as the pressure changes, the output voltage changes proportionally. The change in voltage can be monitored using a DAQ. Once the user knows the relation between the input and output of a sensor, the user can measure the physical parameter.

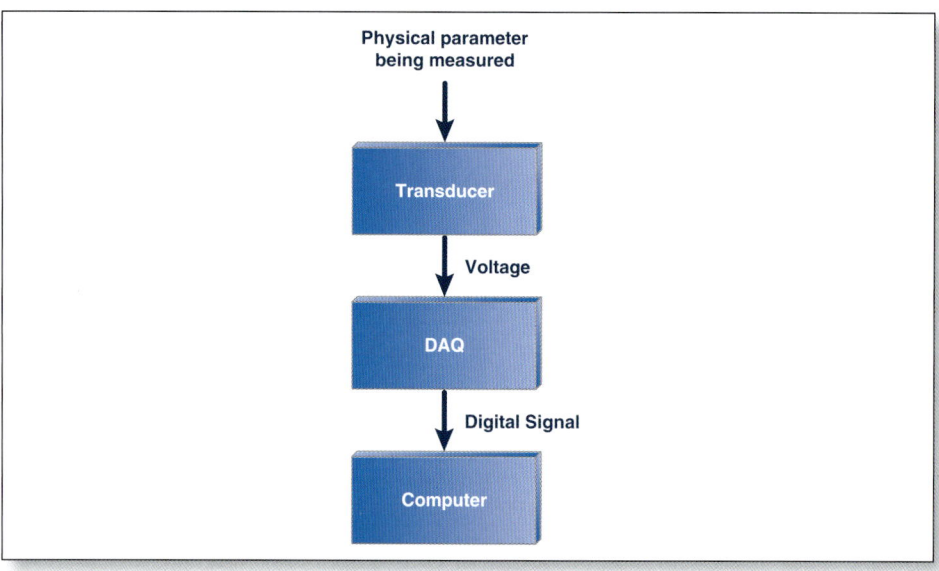

Figure 2.7   A Measurement System

A sensor need not be a big complicated device. The simplest form of a sensor is a sense resistor. Sense resistors are generally small resistors that are used for measuring the current. As current flows through these resistors it creates a voltage drop. This voltage drop can be measured using a data acquisition unit. Once the voltage drop information is known, the current can be calculated by using the following equation:

$$I = \Delta V/R$$

where I is the current flowing through the circuit in amperes, and ΔV is the voltage drop across the resistor in volts and R is the resistance of the resistor.

In order to measure the power in a circuit, the following relation can be used:

$$P = VI$$

where P is the power consumed in watts, V is the voltage in the circuit and I is the current measured above. It should be noted that there is a big difference between voltage V and the voltage drop ΔV. The voltage V is the potential difference of a point with respect to the ground, whereas ΔV is the voltage drop across the resistor. Typically, in printed circuit boards the value of V is of the order of 1 through 12 V, whereas the value of ΔV is a much lower value dependent on the resistor and can be a very small value of the order of a few millivolts or even microvolts.

It should be noted that as the resistors cause a voltage drop, they generate heat. So, in order to avoid overheating, the sense resistors should be selected carefully. The sense resistors have a power rating and this value should not be exceeded. The selection of the sense resistors should be done based on the following equation

$$P' > Imax^2 R$$

where P' is the power rating of the sense resistor, Imax is the maximum expected current in the circuit being measured, R is the resistance of the sense resistor. Advances in resistor technology have enabled new sense resistors that are capable of withstanding higher levels of power dissipation. However, sense resistors are generally not used for measuring higher power parts.

The following case study will allow a better understanding of how a sense resistor works.

Case Study: Measure the Power on 12 V Rail Output From an ATX Power Supply

As described in the earlier section, the ATX power supply has multiple outputs and in this case we will investigate the process of measuring power on one of the 12-V rails. In order to measure the power the following steps need to be followed. Understanding this process can help the user understand the basics of sense resistors.

Step 1 The first step involved is to identify the 12-V rail. The rail can be identified by its color (yellow), as shown in Figure 2.8. There can be multiple 12-V rails on a system and this process shows the steps involved in measuring one of the rails. The procedure can be repeated across other rails if desired. If you do not want to make changes to your power supply cables, you can get an extension to the 24 pin cable and apply the rework on the extension.

Step 2 Once identified, cut the cable and solder a sense resistor (say 0.001 ohm) in series with the wire. The voltage drop will be measured across points 1 and 2 where 1 is closer to the power supply and 2 is closer to the motherboard.

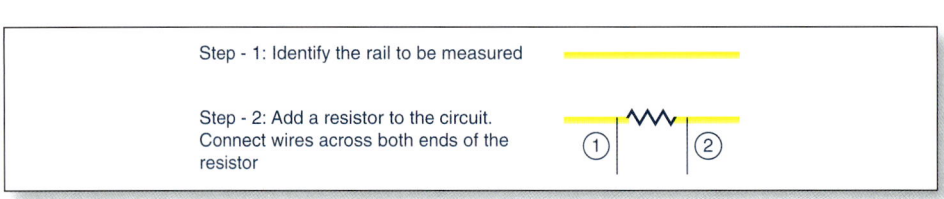

Figure 2.8   Instrumentation of a 12-V Rail

Step 3 Identify the ground connection on the power supply and solder a wire to the ground wire, as shown in Figure 2.9. Please note that there are multiple ground wires and you can pick any of the ground wires in order to do the measurement.

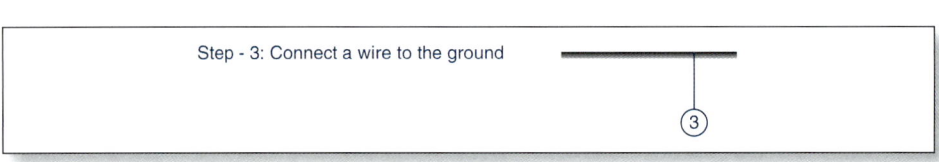

Figure 2.9   Instrumentation of a Ground Rail

Step 4 In order to measure power, four channels of DAQ are needed, two to measure the voltage drop across the resistor and two channels to measure the voltage. Let us call the channels of the DAQ CH1 through CH4. Connect wires from Figure 2.8 such that 1 is connected to CH1 and 2 is connected to CH2. The DAQ can be configured so that it reports the differential voltage drop such that 1 is the high side and 2 is the low side. In several DAQs the high and low sides are clearly indicated and cannot be configured, so care should be taken in such cases to connect the wires properly. If wires 2 and 1 are swapped, the net output will be a negative number with the same magnitude.

In order to measure the voltage, connect the wire 3 (from Figure 2.9) to CH3 and connect wire 2 to CH4. Please note that 2 indicates the low side for current calculations and high side for the voltage calculations. For low values of R the voltage from wires 1 and 2 would be very close.

Hall Effect Sensors

The Hall Effect sensors provide a change in output voltage response when subjected to a magnetic field. One of the many uses of these sensors is current measurement. When placed in series in an electrical circuit, these sensors provide an output voltage proportional to the current flowing through the circuit. Compared to sense resistors, the hall effect sensors have negligible voltage drops. Thus, the Hall Effect sensors are often referred to as lossless.

The Hall Effect sensors are generally preferred when the system is sensitive to voltage drops. The Hall Effect sensors are more expensive than the sense resistors and are more difficult to set up and operate. Nevertheless, their wide range of operability make them a popular current measurement device.

Peripheral Devices

Components such as DIMMs and PCIe cards also contribute to the system power. The biggest challenge in designing energy-efficient systems with these components is that the power consumed varies from one device to another similar device. Even components having similar performance characteristics could have very different power consumption values. Consider the case where two identical systems have identical performance, the only difference between the systems being the brand of the memory modules used. Assuming four DIMMs consuming 5 W each on the first platform and four DIMMS with 3 W each on the second platform, the difference in the power could be as high as 8 W at DIMM level. This kind of difference between the power consumed in DIMM modules is not very uncommon. It should be noted that the 8 W of power delta at the component level could translate into a higher power at the system level once the efficiency of the power supply and AC to DC conversion losses are considered.

In order to characterize the power of these components, a riser card with a current sensing option can be used. A riser card seats between the device and the motherboard. Generally, the riser cards that have a current sensing option available on them have one or more resistors in series with the power rails. Using the methods described earlier in the chapter, the power consumed by the peripheral device can be measured. It should be noted that riser cards are generally used only for testing and validation purposes. Use of such cards in production devices might not be desirable unless the system is designed to accommodate them.

The system fans and the heatsink fan can also contribute significantly to the overall power consumed in the system. For the same volumetric airflow, certain fans consume lower power than others. Multiples fans should be evaluated and the most efficient fan must be picked in order to design an energy-efficient system.

Summary

This chapter provides an overview of how the power flows from one component to another and the efficiencies associates with it. The key factors to be considered in an energy-efficient design are explained along with common pitfalls. At the end of the chapter the user is expected to understand the basic concepts and operation of voltage regulators, sensors, DAQs, and the power measurement process. The ability to account for every watt within a system would be very useful in the design process. Armed with this information a user can measure power as they optimize the system.

Chapter 3

Power Management in Modern Computing Systems

Give me six hours to chop down a tree and I will spend the first four sharpening the axe.

—Abraham Lincoln

A s modern computing became power-sensitive, several power management features were introduced in the processors, followed by similar features in peripheral devices. The term *power management* is broadly used to describe various features that intelligently change the system behavior to reduce the system power consumption.

Intel processors support several power management features that help in reducing the power consumed at a processor, system, and facility level. Each power management feature has a unique benefit and this chapter describes the features and the associated benefits. Understanding how these policies behave and interact with each other will help system designers in picking a policy that best suits their application.

Power Management Overview

Power management policies can be broadly divided into two categories. The first area includes all the policies that could impact the power consumption of the CPU without influencing other components on the platform. This approach is useful in in many cases because the CPU is one of the key elements in the platform. The second area includes the policies that impact the entire system. These policies can influence the power consumed in a single platform, multiple interconnected platforms, or an entire facility. Power management can also be used to address several unique challenges in the system design. The following examples show some areas where power management can be used to solve a specific challenge:

- *Failure of a thermal solution.* Power management can be used to reduce the power in order to avoid overheating of a part following the failure of a thermal solution. In such cases the key objective is to reduce the power even at the expense of performance loss. Power management policies applied during such situations are often very aggressive and result in a disproportionately high performance loss. These types of power management features are generally applied in emergency situations.

- *Energy-efficient designs.* System designers intending to design systems with highest energy efficiency (performance per watt) can use power management features in their system designs. The policies employed would intelligently turn off unused components within a system and change behavior such that the system consumes the least number of joules to perform a given task or a group of tasks.

- *Battery life.* During several applications, it is crucial for the system to be operational. For instance, a user traveling in an airplane would prefer the system to be operational through the duration of the flight even if it means a slightly lower performance. In these cases the ability of the system to be functional holds precedence over its performance. Such situations are most common in devices operating on battery power. In these cases power management can ensure that the system resources are utilized carefully.

Other Considerations

Energy-efficient optimization has to be done on a case-by-case basis. In some cases it is possible to improve the energy efficiency of the system by completing a task faster and going to a lower power state, while in other cases it could make more sense to operate at a lower frequency for a longer duration. These case-by-case optimizations are possible with a proper understanding of power management. Power management ends up being one of the key factors in a tradeoff involving multiple variables in a system design. The system can be optimized by hardware controls, software controls, and smart system designs.

ACPI Power States

Advanced Configuration and Power Interface (ACPI) is an open industry specification co-developed by several companies (ACPI, 2004). ACPI establishes industry-standard interfaces enabling OS-directed configuration, power management, and thermal management of platforms.

ACPI supports several power management states. It is a common misconception that ACPI compliance is a prerequisite for power management. The presence of ACPI compliance generally implies that the system supports the power management states. However, systems can still have elements of power management without having ACPI compliance. Secondly, ACPI compliance by itself does not assure a user of the most energy-efficient design, because several power management tuning capabilities are beyond the ACPI domain.

C-States

In most real-life applications, the CPU pauses several times during the execution process as it awaits inputs either from the system or the user. This happens more frequently during idle or low intensity applications. This provides an opportunity to shut down the CPU or individual cores within the CPU while the system sits idle waiting for inputs. The CPU C-states (except C0) are states when components within the CPU are shut down; hence the C-states are also known as the CPU sleep states or low power state. It should be noted that during C-states the CPU sleeps but the rest of the platform is unaffected and continues to operate normally. The state C0 is the normal operational state and the numbers C1, C2, C3 … Cn indicate sleep states. A higher value of n in Cn indicates that more components in the CPU are shut off and the CPU is in a deeper sleep state. A deeper sleep states imply lower power consumption and higher latency.

When certain processors have multiple cores, the C-states can be applied either at a package level or at a core level. For example, an instance of a single-threaded application on a quad-core processor could exercise the first core, while allowing the second, third, and fourth core to be in low power states. When the first core completes the execution of the task, it enters a low power state. Since all the four cores are in the lower power state, the package enters the low power package state.

P-States

A few years back all CPUs ran at a fixed frequency and voltage setting. However, before long it was observed that the rated frequency and voltage settings might be overkill for certain applications. This lead to the birth of *performance states* or *P-states*. A value of P1 indicates a nominal operational frequency and voltage and any other value P*n* indicates a lower operational voltage and frequency. ACPI currently supports up to 16 P-states. Each processor has unique number of P-states enabled on it. P-states are an attractive option as the system continues to execute and there is negligible latency associated with switching to a different P-state.

Turbo

Turbo is a unique case in which the frequency and voltage are stepped up. In many ways turbo can be seen as an opposite of P-states because the frequency and voltage are increased as opposed to decreased in other P-states. The CPU enters turbo state if it is operating below certain specifications that provide the processor some headroom to boost the performance while still following design specifications. A few parameters are: number of active cores, estimated current consumption, estimated power consumption, and processor temperature. If the processor operates below these limits and the workload demands additional performance, the processor frequency will dynamically increase until the upper limit of frequency is reached. Turbo has multiple algorithms operating in parallel to manage current, power, and temperature to maximize performance and energy efficiency. Turbo is beneficial if the goal is to complete the task sooner and enjoy the lower idle power later, a method commonly known as HUGI (hurry up and go idle) or race to idle.

T-States

Most processors have thermal protection mechanisms available that prevent damage to the part in case of overheating. In such cases the processor throttles when the trigger point is achieved in an attempt to reduce power. This throttling is achieved by turning the processor clocks off and then back on with a predetermined duty cycle. Since the throttling is primarily done to reduce power for thermal reasons, the states are known as T-states.

Since the key goal of such a protection mechanism is to reduce power, the performance implications are generally ignored. The T-states provide greater control because they can be applied to individual cores.

System Configurations

Most of the power management features that were discussed so far in this chapter deal with power management at a processor level. However, processors only contribute to a part of system power and it is very important to consider the entire system. There are several power management features and policies currently available that benefit the user at a system level. Since more components are affected by the system-level features, the energy savings get scaled out. The system-level power management features are application-specific and not every feature is applicable in a given use case. It is however very important to understand how these features operate because the rapid changes in technology might improve the existing features, and a feature that previously was deemed inapplicable could now be vital. System-level power management can be performed by using power states that are specifically architected to reduce system power or they can be a combination of existing features or software intelligently used to reduce power.

Sleep States or S-States

System sleep states are the power management states at a system level where most components on the system are switched off. Users often employ the term *sleep states* interchangeably to denote both the processor sleep states (C-states) and the system sleep states (S-states). The system sleep states provide greater power savings than the processor sleep states, but they generally have a higher latency penalty compared to C-states. Similar to other ACPI states, each S-state has a different level of activity and latency associated with it.

■ *S0.* This state is the nominal operation point of the system. It should be noted that although the system is considered to be active, individual components of the system might choose to go to a low power state or be shut down. For instance, the processor can choose to go to a C6 state and be sleeping while the system is in S0 state.

■ *S1.* This is the shallowest of the system sleep states currently available under the ACPI framework. This state is also known as *Stopgrant*. While the system is under this state the power to processor is maintained, but no instructions are executed. The processor stops its processing activity and shuts down many of its internal components.

■ *S2.* In S2 state, the system goes one level further into sleep by shutting off the processor. It should be noted that as technologies evolve some power management states become less important than others and some get phased out. Over time, other sleep states have been chosen over S2 and this sleep state is not commonly used anymore.

■ *S3.* The S3 state is known as *Suspend to RAM* and this state is very similar to the S2 state. In this state all power to the processor is shut off and the information that was previously stored in the registers is sent to RAM, which stays on. Since the registers are transferred to DRAM, the system context is maintained. Many noncritical circuits and certain clocks are shut down.

■ *S4.* The S4 state is known as *Suspend to Disk* and is one level deeper than S3. As the name indicates the memory and the system context is now saved on the disk and most of the system is shut down. Since the system context is stored on the hard drive, the resume time from this state is dependent on the performance of the hard drive. For instance, the use of solid state drives (SSDs) can greatly reduce the resume time from S4 state.

■ *S5.* This is the deepest sleep state currently available and is also known as *Soft Off*. Under this state the entire system is shut down except certain devices that might need to generate a wake event. The wake event can be triggered in multiple ways; for instance, LAN, GPIO, or USB could be used to trigger the wake event.

Intel® Intelligent Power Node Manager

Intel® Intelligent Power Node Manager is a technology that is used in optimizing and managing power and cooling resources in data centers. The Intel Intelligent Power Node Manager technology provides two core capabilities, it reports system-level power consumption and it limits system power—utilizing policies defined by IT management. These features provide key information and control to enable the data center to be more energy efficient. Data center managers have traditionally determined the number of servers to provision into a rack by dividing the total power available to the rack by the power supply nameplate data or a de-rated value.

The Intel Intelligent Power Node Manager technology provides accurate, immediate information about how much power a server consumes while running a workload. Knowing actual consumption helps in power budgeting and increasing server density. This technology monitors the power and increases accountability at a platform level to ensure that every watt consumed in the data center is accounted for.

Using intelligent energy management at the platform level helps IT administrators squeeze extra value and performance out of the existing rack space while reducing the total cost of ownership by better managing power and cooling operational costs. Administrators can improve business continuity by dynamically capping power to avoid overcooling systems thereby reducing downtime and allowing critical operations to continue even during power or thermal events. They can also balance resources by dynamically moving power from one part of the data center to another, depending on where the need for power or cooling is greatest.

Virtualization Power Management

Virtualization is a technology where virtual machines are created on systems in order to have multiple environments on the same system. This technology has several advantages, but the one that is most applicable in this chapter is its ability to create energy-efficient systems.

In several use cases, multiple systems are warranted for handling peak usage. However, the system could be below peak usage for extended periods of time. Assume the case where there are four systems as shown in Figure 3.1, each of them operating at a low utilization rate. Using virtualization it is possible to consolidate all the workload into a single system (or two systems) and put the unused systems into S-states. It should be noted that there is some penalty associated with the workload migration process and it should be considered while conducting the operation. Secondly, although the illustration shows geometric addition of workload, in real usage that is not the case. In fact it works to the advantage of the user because overhead associated with keeping the operating system on is no longer present.

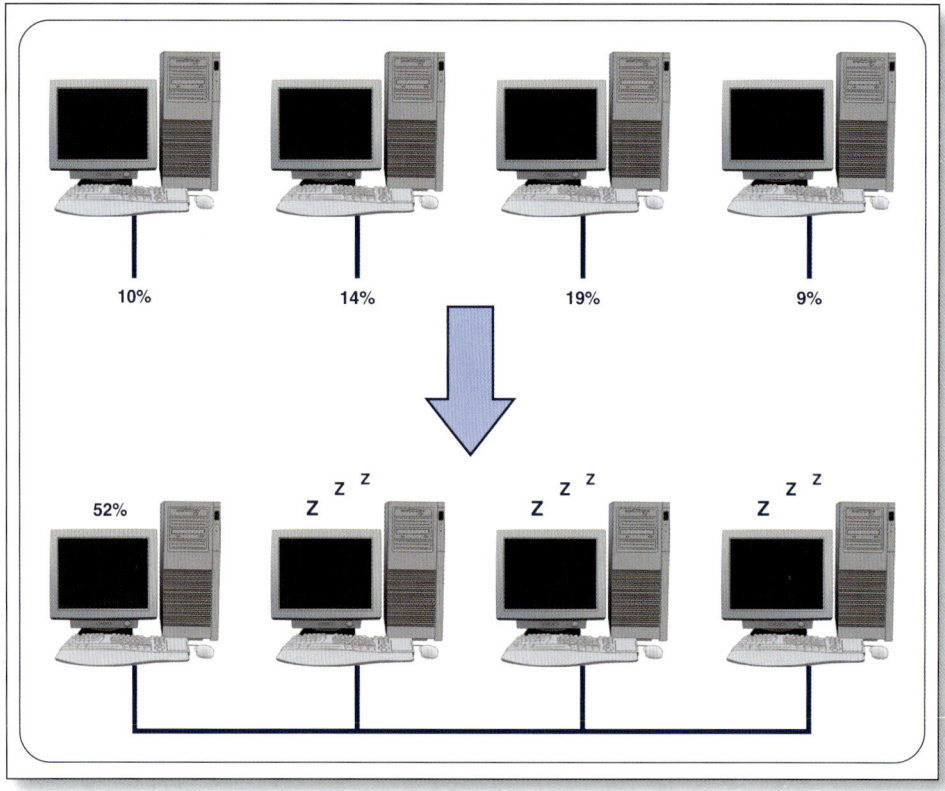

Figure 3.1 Using Virtualization for Power Management

Display Power Saving Technology

The Display Power Saving Technology (DPST) feature is currently supported only on mobile processors. This technology helps in saving backlight power while continuing to maintain a good visual experience. This is accomplished by adaptively enhancing the displayed image while decreasing the backlight brightness simultaneously. The goal of this technique is to provide equivalent end-user-perceived image quality at a decreased backlight power level.

The original (input) image produced by the operating system or application is analyzed by the Intel® DPST subsystem. An interrupt to software is generated whenever a meaningful change in the image attributes is detected. A meaningful change is when the Intel DPST software algorithm determines that enough brightness, contrast, or color change has occurred to the displaying images that the image enhancement and backlight control needs to be altered.

The Intel® DPST subsystem applies an image-specific enhancement to increase image contrast, brightness, and other attributes.

A corresponding decrease to the backlight brightness is applied simultaneously to produce an image with similar user-perceived quality (such as brightness) as the original image. Intel® DPST 5.0 has improved the software algorithms and has minor hardware changes to better handle backlight phase-in and ensures the documented and validated method to interrupt hardware phase-in.

Memory Power Management Technology

Power management policies that are applied to the processor such as sleep and throttling can also be extended to memory, although with a slightly different implementation. The term memory power management can apply to many technologies, each finding a unique application. Generally, these features are provided by the processor and implemented on compatible memory modules.

Dynamic Clock Enable (CKE) is one such technology that reduces the idle power of the memory module with latencies in the order of nanoseconds. If memory stays idle for extended durations additional power management states can be applied. The memory standby provides significant savings with latency generally less than 100 ms. Memory offlining provides the greatest savings and the power consumed in the memory approaches a very low value (could be considered close to 0W for most practical purposes). It should be noted that the power management technology is changing rapidly and by the time you would be reading this the latencies of these states would have decreased significantly. The user should thereby reassess these power management states from time to time to investigate if any of these are suitable for their application.

In addition to the above memory power management states there are several other states available for the designers. Some of these states are variants of the previously discussed states while others are totally different. The Intel® Rapid Memory Power Management (Intel® RMPM) (also known as CxSR) is a technology that puts rows of memory into self-refresh mode during the processor sleep states to allow the system to remain in the lower power states longer. Memory throttling is another tool available to the designer to reduce power consumption if a memory module gets overheated due to a poor system design or system fan failure.

System Level Performance per Watt Optimization

With the numerous power management tools available, a system designer can get overwhelmed. It is very likely that the end user might not optimize the entire system for energy efficiency. The key objective of the designer should be to maintain the peak performance per watt. In order to get a grasp of performance per watt the first principle that should be well understood is the difference between the bandwidth of the system and the application ratio.

In simple words, the bandwidth of the system represents how busy a system is, while the application ratio represents how hard the system is working. Would you believe that the CPU is fully stressed if on running an application the system task manager shows the CPU as being fully utilized (100 percent)? A lot of people incorrectly assume that the CPU is stressed to its peak. If the task manager shows full utilization, it simply implies that the CPU is busy. There can be other applications that could stress the CPU further and extract more work out of it. One way to monitor the intensity of an application is to measure the CPU power. Generally higher intensity applications result in higher power numbers and better performance/watt numbers. For example, while running an application or a benchmark, if the CPU power increases by changing some hardware or software in the system, then there is a strong possibility that the performance increased simultaneously resulting in a net increase in performance per watt. This happens if the CPU bottlenecks were cleared by changing system hardware or software. On the other hand if power increase does not result in performance increase it would imply that the change resulted in an overhead to the processor. Hence, changes in power should be monitored along with the performance to understand if the changes resulted in increase or decrease of system energy efficiency.

The applications can be broadly divided into two categories. The first category of workloads is time bound and the second category is fixed task over variable time. Activities such as video streaming could be considered time bound, that is, the task takes the same time duration irrespective of the processor performance. The second kind is running a complex finite element code where a faster processor would mean quicker execution of the task.

While considering the energy efficiency of the tasks that are time bound, the key goal is to reduce the overall power without losing any performance. For instance, if a time-bound task can be performed at a lower frequency without losing any performance, then it is energy-efficient. On the other hand the tasks that are not time bound should be treated differently. Let us consider an example where a system designer has a choice of operating the system at

100 W for 5 hours or at 200 W for 2 hours for completing a task. Clearly, finishing the task in 2 hours seems more energy-efficient. This holds true in most cases where the scenarios with the highest power has the highest energy efficiency. The system designer has one final question to answer before making the recommendation, "what does the system do from hour 2 to hour 5 while the second system continues to operate?"

If the user has the option of shutting down the system then no additional energy is consumed. However, if the system stays on awaiting user instructions then the idle power of the system should be considered. Generally it is possible to shut off the system in most devices and our original assumption still holds true. But if the device being optimized remains switched on 24×7 then idle power becomes critical in the decision-making process.

Power Management in Linux

Most of the major operating systems have the key power management features enabled in them. However, since the operating systems tend to cater their software to a wide set of end use applications, certain assumptions are made by the operating system vendor in configuring the default power management setting. Unfortunately each user and each application has a specific requirement that cannot be met with the default configuration, making some level of customization necessary. Linux, being an open source program, provides a lot of knobs and features that allow power management customization.

P-States

Linux allows the users to alter the processor P-states on demand. It is possible to change the P-state using certain scripts based on system requirements. The user can configure multiple settings including setting the upper and lower limits and even fixing the processor to run at a certain state.

In order to make changes the first step is to log in as root and open the folder `/sys/devices/system/cpu`. This folder should show all the cores on the system under the names CPU0, CPU1, and so on. For the sake of this discussion, let us consider the CPU0 folder. If the power management features are correctly enabled on the system, the user would see a folder named `cpufreq`. The user can determine the different frequencies available on the system by using the command

```
cat scaling_available_frequencies
```

The output should show the different frequencies supported reported in hertz (Hz). The upper and lower limit can be set in the operating system by using the command

```
echo -n xxxxx > scaling_max_freq
```

where xxxxx stands for frequency in Hz. Similarly

```
echo -n xxxxx > scaling_min_freq
```

can be used to set the lower frequency. This process has to be repeated for all the cores to ensure that the entire system is controlled.

A couple of things should be noted at this point. If the maximum and minimum frequencies are equal, the system is locked at the set frequency. If the user enters a value for maximum frequency that is lower than the minimum frequency value previously entered, then the system will return an error. Similarly if the user tries to input a value for minimum frequency that is higher than the highest frequency value previously entered, then the system will return an error. If such a situation arises, the user can always return to the default mode by entering the lowest frequency in `scaling_min_freq` and the highest frequency in `scaling_max_freq`. Alternatively the system restart clears all the above power management settings.

P-State Settings

From the root login enter the `cpufreq` folder.

```
[root@localhost ~]# cd /sys/devices/system/cpu/cpu0/cpufreq/
```

The `cpufreq` infrastructure contains various frequency policy changing governors, which determine the CPU frequency based on various criteria such as CPU utilization. The following are the governors that are commonly available:

- *Performance governor.* This governor keeps the CPU at the highest possible frequency within a user-specified range.

- *Powersave governor.* This governor keeps the CPU at the lowest possible frequency within a user-specified range.

- *Userspace governor.* This governor provides information about the available frequencies to the user. The user can then choose of control the CPU frequency.

■ *Ondemand governor.* This governor chooses the P-state policy for the end user based on the frequencies and workload.

The following command shows the various power management governors available:

```
[root@localhost ~]# cat scaling _available_governors
```

The output should look like

```
ondemand userspace performance
```

The user can view the governor currently being used by using the following command:

```
[root@localhost ~]# cat
/sys/devices/system/cpu/cpu0/cpufreq/scaling_governor
```

In most cases the ondemand governor is the most commonly used governor and the same would be reflected in the output.

The user can see the current frequency by entering the current command in the Linux terminal window:

```
[root@localhost ~]# cat
/sys/devices/system/cpu/cpu0/cpufreq/scaling_cur_freq
```

Linux provides the user the ability to see the various frequencies supported by the processor with the following command:

```
[root@localhost ~]# cat
/sys/devices/system/cpu/cpu0/cpufreq/scaling_available_
frequencies
```

The system displays all the supported P-states on the system. For the sake of this example let us assume that the system displays the following frequencies:

```
2800000 2200000 1600000 1200000
```

Example 1: Changing the settings such that the system always stays at the highest frequency (which is 2.8 GHz in this case). The user sets the maximum frequency by using the following commands:

```
[root@localhost ~]# echo 2800000
>/sys/devices/system/cpu/cpu0/cpufreq/scaling_max_freq
```

```
[root@localhost ~]# echo 2800000
>/sys/devices/system/cpu/cpu0/cpufreq/scaling_min_freq
```

The above commands would ensure that the highest and lowest permissible frequencies are both 2800000 Hz, which means that the system is locked at the given frequency. It should be noted that this operation should be repeated on all the cores by going to corresponding folders cpu1, cpu2, and so on.

Example 2: Changing the frequency so that it is locked at intermediate level (say 1600000). If the user has to reduce the frequency from the previously locked value of 2800000 to the new value of 1600000, using the same commands as above would result in an error. This would be because the last command executed in example 1 would set the minimum frequency at 2800000 and now the user is requesting a smaller value for maximum frequency. The system sees this as a conflict.

Hence the first step involved is to clear the previous configurations. This can be accomplished by setting the highest frequency to the highest permissible frequency and the lowest frequency to the lowest permissible frequency:

```
[root@localhost ~]# echo 2800000
>/sys/devices/system/cpu/cpu0/cpufreq/scaling_max_freq

[root@localhost ~]# echo 1200000
>/sys/devices/system/cpu/cpu0/cpufreq/scaling_min_freq
```

Once the above commands are executed, it clears the previously configured maximum and minimum values and the user can set the required value:

```
[root@localhost ~]# echo 1600000
>/sys/devices/system/cpu/cpu0/cpufreq/scaling_max_freq

[root@localhost ~]# echo 1600000
>/sys/devices/system/cpu/cpu0/cpufreq/scaling_min_freq
```

With the above commands, the user can configure the system and set limits for highest permissible frequency, lowest permissible frequency, and so on.

T-States

The T-states can be very useful in Linux as they provide very precise control over cores. Generally the intent of using T-states is to reduce power even if it means a huge performance penalty. Therefore, these states should be used carefully for targeted applications. Generally time-bound applications would be ideal targets for T-states. The first step would be log in using root account, and then type the following command:

```
cd /proc/acpi/processor/CPU0
```

As in the previous case with the P-states, the process has to be repeated for each desired core. The number of T-states supported can vary by platform; the states available on a system can be determined by the following command:

```
[root@localhost~]# cat /proc/acpi/processor/CPU0/throttling
```

The output should show the current state and the various T-states supported:

```
state count:              8
active state:             T0
states:
    *T0:                  00%
     T1:                  12%
     T2:                  25%
     T3:                  37%
     T4:                  50%
     T5:                  62%
     T6:                  75%
     T7:                  87%
```

In the above example there are eight states supported with increments of 12.5 percent each. Certain systems may have 16 states with increments of 6.25 percent per state.

In order to throttle the cores the following command can be used:

```
[root@localhost~]# cat /proc/acpi/processor/CPU0/throttling
[root@localhost~]# echo -n > throttling
```

Where, n would be the targeted T-state. In this example there are eight T-states starting from T0 to T7, hence a number between 0 and 7 would be acceptable values for x. Let us assume that we entered the value $x = 6$. In order to confirm our choice was accepted, use the following command:

```
[root@localhost~]# cat /proc/acpi/processor/CPU0/throttling
```

The output should be similar to that shown below:

```
state count:              8
active state:             T6
states:
T0:                  00%
T1:                  12%
T2:                  25%
T3:                  37%
T4:                  50%
T5:                  62%
*T6:                  75%
T7:                  87%
```

As seen from the example, T-states are very easy to use and configure. These states are not commonly used for power management as they have very limited application. In order to avoid the misuse of this state, Linux has discontinued the support of software control of T-states. The interface for controlling T-States is no longer present in Linux Kernel 2.6.38. However, the functionality is still present in the CPU and can be accessed via CPU registers.

I/O Power Management

I/O power management includes efficient use of devices that receive or send information to the system, such as SATA ports, Ethernet, or Bluetooth[†]. Using features like WOL (Wake on LAN) on a network card causes the network card to stay on even when the system is shut off. Unless the I/O features are being used by the end user in their application, turning off these features can result in lower power consumption. In order to shut off WOL on a port eth0 the user can use the following command:

```
ethtool -s eth0 wol d
```

Another potential area of saving for Ethernet is by reducing the link speed. The 1-gigabit/second speed consumes more power than the 100-megabit/second link speed. If there are times during the day when the network traffic is expected to be slow, the link speed can be reduced to save power. The following command is used to drop from a 1-gigabit/second to a 100-megabit/second link speed:

```
ethtool -s eth0 autoneg off speed 100
```

In order to revert back to the original settings the following command can be used:

```
ethtool -s eth0 autoneg off speed 1000
```

Similarly, the power consumed on other input output devices can be controlled and tweaked. Power Management features are available for wireless radios such as Wi-Fi[†] and Bluetooth that save power during periods of inactivity as well as during use. The SATA controllers have a feature known as Aggressive Link Power Management (ALPM) that allows the device to go into a lower power mode if there is no traffic. Certain hard disks support additional features that can be accessed by using the following command:

```
hdparm -i /dev/sda
```

The command

```
man hdparm
```

provides additional insight into the hard disk power saving options.

Power Management in Windows[†]

Windows 7 has several enhancements over the Windows XP operating system in the area of power management. One of the key improvements in Windows 7 over the older versions is the resource utilization during the idle time. If fewer resources are utilized during periods of inactivity, the CPU can stay in sleep states for extended periods of time uninterrupted, leading to lower power consumption. Another enhancement in Windows 7 is the capability to limit background activities and invoke them only when there is a specific need.

Some other enhancements include better use of the device states to send unused devices into lower powered device states. For instance, when the network cable gets disconnected from the system, the network card is automatically placed in the device state. Similarly when Bluetooth is not being actively used, the system sends the device to a low power state.

Windows Performance Analyzer

A Windows-based system can be optimized using the Windows Performance Analyzer (WPA). This tool provides information on system- and application-level resource usage. The WPA tool provides information about the CPU usage, I/O counts, disk utilization, and other practical information.

The WPA is comprised of two key programs: Xperf.exe, which is a command line tracing tool, and Xperfview.exe, which is a graphical trace tool. Detailed implementation information is provided by Microsoft.

Timer Coalescing

Longer idle durations provide the greatest power savings and in turn the highest energy efficiency. Long idle durations are not possible if the processor gets pinged by multiple software programs requiring its attention frequently. In an ideal case, most software programs would start and finish simultaneously, which would allow the CPU to take uninterrupted planned breaks. In real life, it might not be practical to start and terminate all the programs simultaneously, but for certain periodic software it is possible to terminate software simultaneously by synchronizing their timers. This activity of synchronizing timers of periodic software activity is known as *timer coalescing*.

Wherever possible, periodic activity should be replaced by on-demand invoking of processes. However, if periodic activity cannot be avoided, timer coalescing should be used. The `SetWaitableTimerEx` function can be used for timer coalescing and the WPA tool can be used simultaneously to monitor the impact.

Configuring Settings

The Powercfg.exe script can be used to configure power management settings during the logon of the system. The command

```
powercfg -list
```

provides all the power schemes available in a given system environment. The system administrator has the option to view the contents of each scheme and make modifications, if required. Using the command the user can probe various devices to see which devices support which sleep states.

Another simpler way to manage power management settings in Windows 7 is by using the Improve Power Usage troubleshooting tool. To access this tool, go to the control panel, select Troubleshooting and within System and Security access the Improve Power Usage tool. In a system that is not optimized, this tool would provide suggestions to improve the efficiency. Certain changes can also be made by accessing the Power Options button on the control panel.

Windows XP and Other Older Operating Systems

Windows XP and older operating systems had limited controls in terms of power management. Most of the power management settings were limited to the controls available in the control panel. In order to access these settings the user should open the control panel and select the Display option, followed by Screensaver and the Power option. The user is provided with alternatives of selecting from a limited list of options available. These schemes only apply at a macro level and cannot be customized per application or for smaller time domains.

Chapter 4

Impact of Software on Energy Consumption

They always say time changes things, but you actually have to change them yourself.

—Andy Warhol

Software causes computers to consume energy. This is no surprise; our computers should be doing useful work and in doing so they consume energy. But how much energy should they use? Have you ever wished that the battery in your laptop, tablet, or mobile phone would last longer than it does? Wouldn't it be great if your business could save money on the electricity required to cool the data center?

Much of computer energy used (and saved) is based on the effectiveness of hardware energy-efficiency and the hardware power states that were described in Chapter 3. Software has an impact as well, in two ways: while running a "workload" and while "idle."

Workload Energy

A *workload* is any active computation performing useful work such as playing a DVD (video decode), playing a game, editing photos, web browsing, sending e-mail, or uploading a video to YouTube[†]. Enterprise examples include handling database transactions, print requests, managing email, web servers, and credit checks. The workload energy is the amount of energy used during the execution of the workload over and above the amount of energy the computer uses when it is idle. Some workloads are very demanding and use all of the available CPU and/or GPU capacity, while other workloads use very little of the available system resources. An important design goal for system and software engineers should be to have the energy used be proportional to the actual workload. Figure 4.1 shows a typical platform's power relative to its CPU utilization. The upper bar depicts the platform power and the lower, curved bar indicates the energy-efficiency—a function of the useful output per energy used or performance per watt.

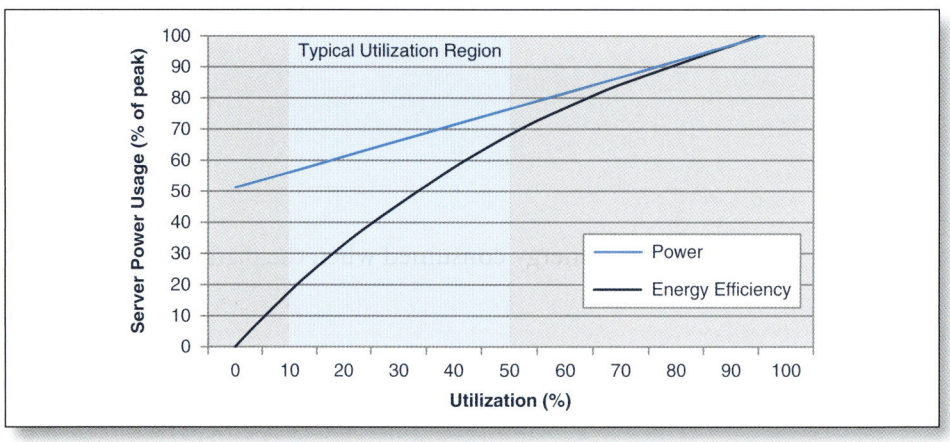

Figure 4.1   Current Typical Platform Efficiency

What is very startling about this chart is the left side, which depicts the high energy cost of just keeping the server up and running, ready and waiting to do something. It's not very efficient. The behavior we would really like to see is shown in Figure 4.2. The line for total power is directly proportional to the utilization, so as the system workload becomes more demanding, power increases. Likewise, if there is little to do, the energy use is very low.

The green bar in Figure 4.2, showing energy efficiency, leads us to believe that we can achieve efficiency beyond the proportional power line, that is, that there are software techniques that will give us hyper-efficient results. In Chapter 5 we'll go over software development methods that help systems achieve this kind of performance: computational efficiency, data efficiency, and context awareness.

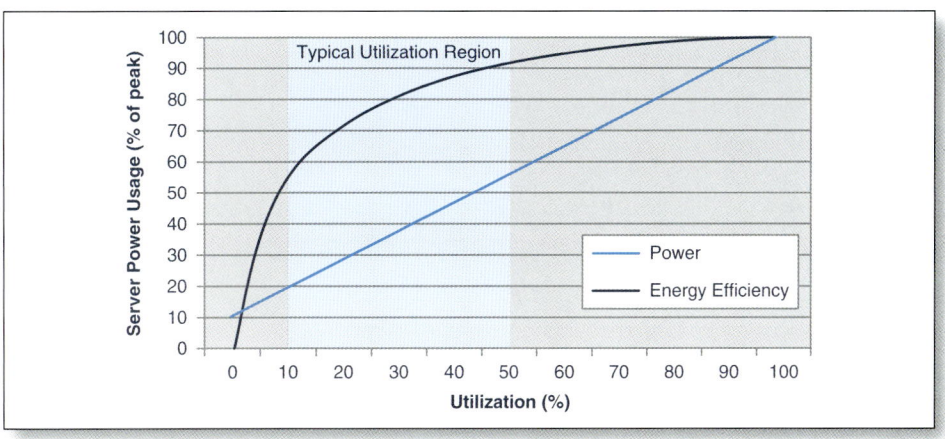

Figure 4.2 Desired Platform Efficiency

Idle Energy

Idle Energy is the energy consumed when the platform is not performing useful work (apparently); that is, you are not actively using the system or in the case of the server, no transactions are occurring. In Figures 4.1 and 4.2, the power at idle is on the left edge. Clearly the behavior of the platform in Figure 4.2 is a better situation to be in: when system utilization is very low, energy use should be very low.

One example we are all familiar with is our home electronics. If you have ever walked around your home with a power meter and measured the power draw of appliances and electronics that are "off," you might be surprised how much energy is being used. What is the value of this energy use? In many cases, it's "instant on" or system responsiveness. We don't want to wait—so we keep the components in our devices energized so that when we hit the power switch there is instant gratification. If you are willing to wait and save some money on energy costs, your newer electronics, especially TVs and digital video recorders, have low power modes that you can set. Bottom line: there is a tradeoff between your time and your money.

In all computer platforms, the same tradeoff exists. System responsiveness comes at a price. A high-energy, ready state provides lower *latency*—better system responsiveness. But does the idle state have to be a high-energy state? To answer that question, let's examine the *idle floor*.

The Idle Floor

The idle floor is the lowest power state that the platform reaches when it's not performing useful work. As we showed in Chapter 3, modern CPUs have energy-saving states (C-States), so that they can save energy when idle. Platform components are improving as well to provide low-energy idle states and low-latency responsiveness. Much investment and improvement has been made on the hardware side to try to reduce the power at system idle.

Figure 4.3 shows energy measurements taken while a notebook computer was running a popular benchmarking application that measures battery life. The idea is to run the software until the battery dies to determine how much useful life the notebook PC can deliver from a full charge. It's a great way to compare multiple notebook PCs for their energy-efficiency.

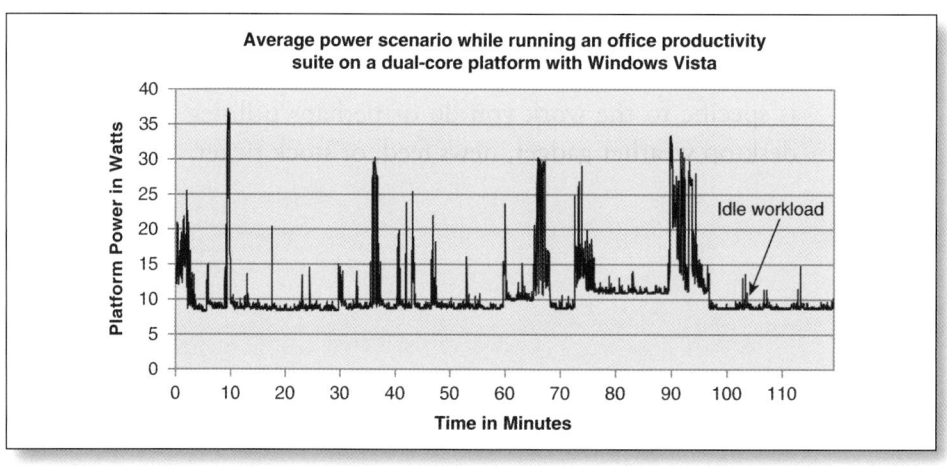

Figure 4.3   Typical Mobile Platform Power Profile in ACPI S0 State

The entire time this test is running, the system is in S0—an active state. It's interesting to note, however, that most of the time the system is in a state we call *active-idle*, which we'll refer to as $S0_i$. From a user perspective, an active-idle state is happening when you are, for example, reading the contents of a Web page or even editing a document. Energy is being consumed, but the system isn't doing much work. In Figure 4.3, active idle is easy to spot.

Simply draw a horizontal line that intersects approximately 8 watts on the Y-axis. This line you have just drawn represents the *idle floor* of this system. For some reason, even when idle, this system does not burn less than about 8 watts. Of course any active system is going to consume energy, but what we really want to know is how we can *lower* the idle floor and still have the system be responsive. The challenge is to determine what system components are active and what stimuli are keeping them active. Unfortunately, much of the stimulus can come from software.

The IT Build

A real-life example of the software impact to system idle is the enterprise IT build. The *IT build* is all of the software that the corporate IT department places on a new system before issuing it to a new employee. You get office applications, virus protection, system state monitoring, and utilities that give you a system that makes you productive and also helps the IT department manage your computer. After you get it, you probably add more software that is specific to the work you do or perhaps utilities you are fond of, such as a desktop weather gadget, news feed, or stock ticker.

We are particularly interested in the battery life of the enterprise notebook. Many people are mobile professionals who spend their time on the road or simply going from meeting to meeting. We know from marketing studies that consumers (and IT departments) are willing to pay more for improved battery life. Unfortunately the "all-day notebook computer" continues to elude the mainstream.

In 2009, an engineer at Intel performed a study to determine just how much the added software contributed to the battery drain of an IT-provided notebook computer. Table 4.1 shows the results of the study.

Table 4.1   Power Impact of IT Build and User Applications

Configuration	Battery Life	Idle Power
OS + Minimum Drivers	6:32	8.6 W
+ IT Build	4:43	11.9 W
+ User Applications	4:17	13.1 W

Note: Measured in 2009 with actual OEM Notebook PC, 56-WHr battery, and corporate IT build

As the focus of this part of the book is on software, this is a great study because the only thing that changed on the system was the addition of software. In Table 4.1, we show the results of three experiments. The top row is the base case. In this case, the engineer started with a brand new OEM notebook computer with the battery charged at 100 percent. The system was powered up and left at idle until the battery ran out. The LCD display remained on at minimum brightness with no screen saver, and the system did not go into standby or sleep. The system was connected by an Ethernet cable to the corporate LAN. After 6 hours and 32 minutes, the battery ran out and the system turned off. Since we started with a 56 WHr battery, a quick calculation tells us that the average power draw was 8.6 W.

After adding the IT build and using the same process, the battery life was clocked at 4 hours and 43 minutes—1 hour and 48 minutes less—nearly 28 percent less battery life by adding software and letting the system sit "idle"! As you can see from the third experiment, adding more user applications, starting them up, and letting them sit idle yielded even lower battery life. By just adding software and letting it sit idle with no user interaction, the battery life of a brand new notebook computer went from 6½ hours down to 4¼—a reduction of over 33 percent. By adding software, the idle floor of the system jumped from 8.6 W up to 13.1 W. What is the *idle* software doing to reduce battery life by 33 percent?

Before you go charging into your local IT department to demand an explanation, consider that most of the software they have added was probably purchased and that they have little control, except to ask their software suppliers to do a better job. What this experiment really shows us is that software *does* have an impact. This raises the next question: can software really be designed to be energy-efficient at idle?

Idle Impact of Application Software

In the case of the IT build study above, we learned that a collection of software applications added to the system increased the idle power draw by over 50 percent (from 8.6 W to 13.1 W). Thinking more deeply about this, it's reasonable to wonder if all applications have some sort of equivalent impact or if certain applications are having more impact than others. Most people familiar with an IT build would conclude that the virus checker and system monitoring applications are going to be more active on what appears to be an idle system—much more so than a browser open to a static Web page or an office word processing program. What we would really like to know is how each of these applications compares to others in their same category. After all, energy-efficiency is relative. To answer the question, we conducted a study of application idle impact for a broad range of applications—30 applications in 7 categories—to understand the relative impact of those applications to platform idle power. The application categories and the number of applications in each category were as follows:

- Chat/VOIP applications (6)

- Browsers (4)

- Runtime libraries (4)

- Media players (5)

- Virus scan applications (3)

- Photo editing applications (3)

- Productivity applications (5)

The study was conducted on a prototype notebook PC instrumented to measure total platform power draw. For all 30 applications, we used the following process:

1. Start by installing a fresh operating system—we built up a clean operating system and made a system image. We then reloaded this image onto the solid-state-drive before each application measurement.

2. Install and configure the application.

3. Reboot the machine.

4. After boot, start the application and let idle for 5 minutes to get past any start-up activity.

5. Capture power draw for 15 minutes.

6. Repeat steps 3 through 5 to obtain three 15-minute idle power measurements.

7. Compute the average of the three measurements and log the result.

With the installed operating system (Windows 7[†]) running and the system at idle, we took a baseline measurement. On this particular system the baseline (idle floor) was 9.6 W. We then followed the above process for the 30 applications.

Figure 4.4 shows the results for 12 of the applications in the study that had the worst impact. The chart shows two things, the average power over baseline (in watts) and the percentage impact of that power draw over baseline. For example, the leftmost application when running at idle caused the platform power draw to increase by 2.4 watts or 24 percent higher than system idle without the application running. Likewise, the rightmost application (a media player) increased platform idle power by 4.6 watts or 48 percent. The other 18 applications did not raise the power over baseline by more than 5 percent and many had close to zero impact (Sabharwal, 2010).

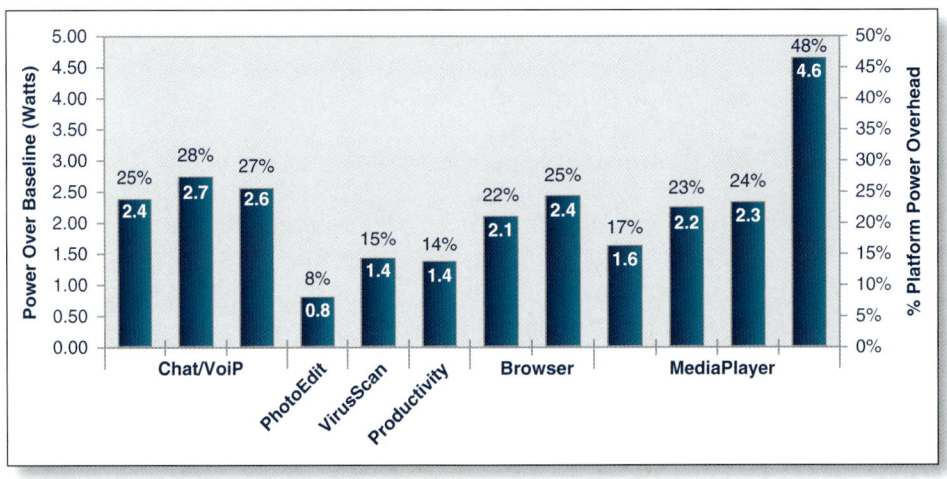

Figure 4.4   Relative Application Idle Impact to Platform Power

The most important conclusion to make from this study at this point is that software applications, even within the same category, exhibit dramatically different idle behavior. If they wanted to, the applications not shown in the chart above could claim to be *energy-efficient software* relative to their competition.

Because computers spend much of their time in an idle state and we can see from the above studies that software has an impact on platform idle power, Chapter 6 will go into much more detail about the design decisions that lead to this impact how to adjust those decisions improve idle efficiency.

Summary

Software influences computer platform energy-efficiency—from embedded systems all the way up to supercomputers. When the computer platform is engaged in useful work, under *workload*, techniques can be used to complete the task more quickly and get the system back to its lower-power idle state. But software also impacts the system's idle floor, leading to wasted energy and in the case of mobile systems, lower battery life. There are techniques for software developers that can help them create energy-efficient software. Chapter 5 describes methods that help software achieve better energy-efficiency under a workload and Chapter 6 describes methods to improve software idle behavior and idle efficiency.

Chapter 5

Writing Energy-Efficient Software

Many strokes, though with a little axe, hew down and fell the hardest timber'd oak.

—William Shakespeare

In his article "Harnessing Green IT: Principles and Practices," San Murugesan (Murugesan, 2008) defines the field of green computing as "the study and practice of designing, manufacturing, using, and disposing of computers, servers, and associated subsystems—such as monitors, printers, storage devices, and networking and communications systems—efficiently and effectively with minimal or no impact on the environment." *Using* a computer means that it is powered on and either in an idle state or performing some compute task. In either case, software instructions and data are coursing through the electronic pathways and therefore causing energy to be consumed.

This chapter takes a deeper look into how software influences energy consumption and how engineers can develop software that uses less.

Computational Efficiency—Hurry Up and Get Idle

In Chapter 4, we saw a profile of energy used during a run of MobileMark '07. The idle floor was somewhere in the neighborhood of 9 watts, that is, when the processor was not actively working on something, the system consumed 9 W in its idle state. When the system was actively processing a workload, the power use varies, but could be as high as 30 to 40 W. Since we know the computer is not always working and there is a big difference between active power and idle power, it makes sense to conclude that the sooner we complete the compute task or *workload*, the sooner the system will get back to idle and the more energy we'll save. Computational efficiency is achieved by improving an application's performance and achieving a very beneficial side effect of saving energy.

Computational Efficiency Saves Energy

The idea of computational efficiency is to reduce the amount of time that the system is in a high power state. In other words, if we can improve the performance of the application so that it processes its workload more quickly, the system should return to its idle state sooner and therefore consume less energy overall. We call this concept "*race to idle*"—get the work done as quickly as possible so that the system can return to a low-power state.

Let's look at a hypothetical example. Suppose you have a sorting algorithm that has efficiency $O(n^2)$ and another sorting algorithm that has efficiency $O(n \log n)$, shown in Figure 5.1. By our reasoning, the $O(n \log n)$ algorithm will deliver better performance and in doing so, save energy.

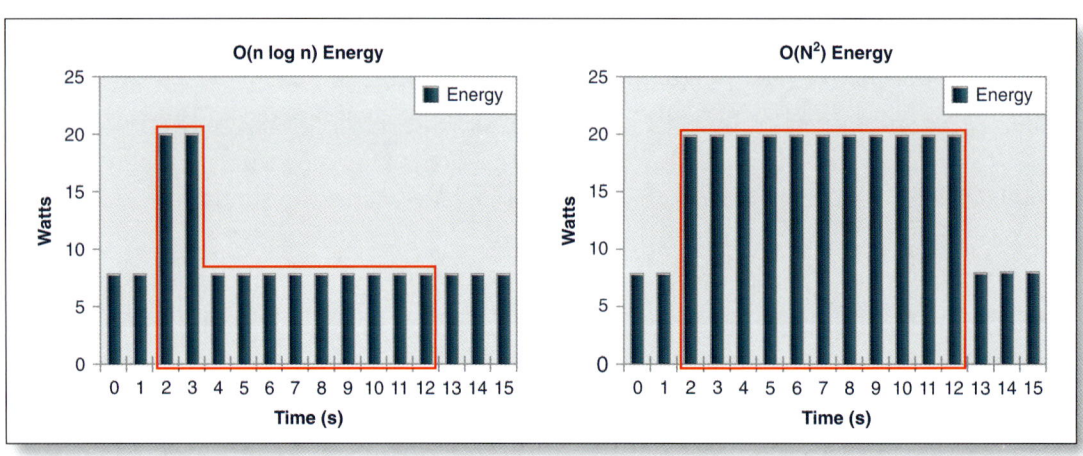

Figure 5.1   Relative Efficiency of Two Algorithms

Let's examine some data. Suppose our platform has an idle floor of 8 W and the platform, while executing the $O(n^2)$ algorithm on a set of data, consumes 20 W over a period of 10 s. The total energy consumed for the task is 200 joules (20 J/s $\times$ 10 s = 200 J). Our $O(n \log n)$ algorithm, by definition, is more efficient so let's assume it takes only 2 seconds to complete the same sorting task. If we assume it also consumes 20 W over the workload period, the total energy to complete the sort is 40 joules. (20 J/s × 2 s = 40 J). To be fair, we need to also add the energy consumed at idle up to a period of 10 seconds, using the same duration as the first test case. So the idle energy consumed is 8 s × 8 W or 64 joules. Total energy for *0* (*n* log *n*) case is therefore 40 J + 64 J = 104 J. Using a more efficient algorithm has saved us 96 J (200 − 104).

Computational efficiency saves energy! That's the theory anyway. Of course the big hole in our logic above is the assumption that both algorithms push the system to consume an identical 20 W. But what if the more time-efficient algorithm has a complexity that drives the system to consume *more* power than the slower algorithm? Could the total energy for the more time-efficient algorithm be worse? The answer is probably yes, but we believe in the vast majority of cases, the *race to idle* yields favorable results and in the rest of this chapter, we'll show a number of examples that demonstrate why we believe that.

Using Computational Efficiency to Reduce Power Consumption

With recent advances in power technology, power consumption has become as important as performance. Energy-efficient software plays a key role in exploring the latest hardware power savings offered by current generation architecture. Poorly-written code can prevent a system from taking advantage of new hardware features.

With mobile platforms, given the limited time that a battery can operate, power consumption becomes even more important. A mobile platform consists of various components such as a CPU, LCD, HDD, DVD, and chipsets, which individually contribute to the power drain of the notebook. Understanding the power contribution of each major component in the platform provides a better view on the total power usage and can provide guidance on optimizing power consumption.

Methods to Achieve Better Computational Efficiency

This section describes some techniques for tuning software for both power and performance. Many of the methods are generic power optimization techniques that can be used on any computing platform. Others, such as vectorization using automatic vectorizing extensions (Intel® AVX), are specific to Intel's recently released microarchitecture codenamed Sandy Bridge. These features will help you optimize software for performance and achieve corresponding power benefits.

Algorithmic Efficiency

Algorithms and data structures are a long-standing area of research in computer science. Considerable effort has gone into research to find more efficient means to solve problems and to investigate and document the corresponding time and space tradeoffs. Theory (and experience) tells us that the choice of algorithms and data structures can make a vast difference in the performance of an application. For a particular problem, a stack may be better than a queue and a B-tree may be better than a binary tree or a hash function. The best algorithm or data structure to use depends on many factors and suggests that a study of the problem and a careful consideration of the architecture, design, algorithms, and data structures can lead to an application that performs better and consumes less energy.

For example, in an audio processing application we observed that some sine and cosine functions were repeatedly called on fixed values inside a very high count loop. This unnecessarily increased the computations inside the loop by quite a bit. Since the values on which transcendentals were called remained constant throughout the loop duration, they could have easily been computed prior to entering the loop. Using this approach yielded a 1.3x improvement (30-percent performance gain) on an Intel® Core i7™ system, which led to power savings as well.

In another application we identified a high rate of last-level cache misses in a very large and active loop. Further analysis using various performance counters indicated that three loads in the loop were from constant locations and due to this, useful data was getting thrown from other loads out of the cache when the next iteration needed that data, resulting in a high rate of cache misses. We solved the issue by moving the fixed loads out of the loop, which delivered a 1.1x improvement for this application.

Compiler Optimizations

A relatively easy way to achieve better performance is to use an optimizing compiler. Most compilers have settings to optimize code. We have done most of our optimization work with the Intel® Compiler (Intel, 2011, Tools), which provides various switches to optimize for specific Intel architectures for Windows and Linux platforms. On a few real customer video/audio applications, we have obtained performance gains ranging from 1.1x–1.5x because the Intel compiler generates code that is much more efficiently executed on Intel architecture and hence leads to performance benefits with corresponding power savings.

Reducing Active Cycles through Multithreading

A well threaded application that uses all available resources will usually finish faster than running single-threaded. A well balanced, threaded application is more likely to provide better power and performance benefits than a poorly threaded application. Choosing the right synchronization primitives also has significant impact on both power and performance.

The graph in Figure 5.2 shows the result of a study performed to compare processor power consumption of single-threaded workloads with their multi-threaded equivalents. These applications show 12–60 percent energy savings based on how well they are threaded on a quad-core processor.

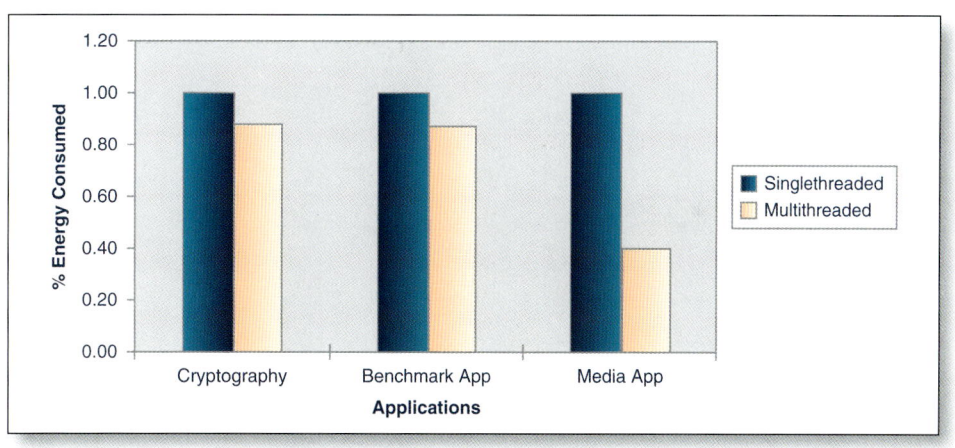

Figure 5.2 Power Impact of Multithreading

The cryptography workload has a 2x performance gain, the multithreaded benchmark application shows 3.9x performance gain, and the media application, with multithreading and other optimizations, shows a 10x performance gain over baseline.

As we did in the sorting example above, the power consumption measurements are normalized to the longest runtime. (That is, in case of workloads finishing faster in multithreaded version, we measure the idle power to match a single-threaded runtime). As the data indicates, the power saving depends on how fast the application can finish the task at hand. In case of the cryptography workload, only two threads were doing the real work, so not all four cores were being used. Hence we see less energy savings between single-threaded and multithreaded version. The media application used all four cores more efficiently and so the energy savings were much greater.

Reducing Active Cycles through Vectorization

Code that performs the same operation on multiple independent data elements is a great candidate for *vectorization*. Modern processors from Intel and AMD provide advanced SIMD (single-instruction, multiple data) instructions (called SSE—SIMD Streaming Extensions) that can perform many simultaneous floating point operations. Intel's latest Sandy Bridge processor has registers that are 256 bits wide and a set of SIMD instructions called Intel AVX (automatic vectorizing extensions) that can perform *eight* 32-bit floating point operations simultaneously. These vectorization techniques are typically applied to applications that loop on floating point operations over a set of data. There is a little bit more overhead to get the data ready for the AVX instruction but the efficiency of the instruction more than makes up for that.

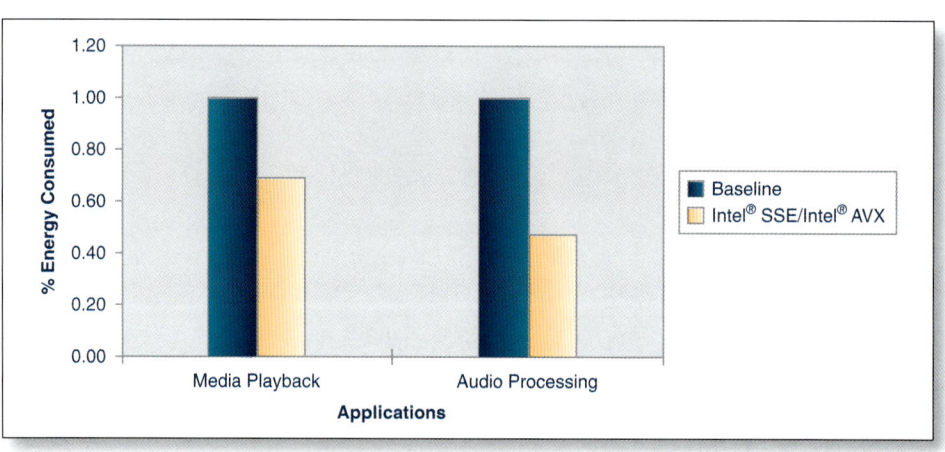

Figure 5.3   Power Impact of SIMD

The graph in Figure 5.3 shows the results of optimizing a media playback application with Intel SSE2/4 instructions, yielding a 2.15x performance improvement and 30-percent less energy consumption. An audio processing application optimized with Intel AVX achieved 5x better performance and

55-percent lower energy. It's easy to see that SIMD used well delivers significant performance and power benefits.

SpinWait Loops

SpinWait loops are commonly used by programmers for locking and synchronization. A SpinWait loop essentially puts the processor into a very tight loop for a specified count. The duration of the wait depends on the speed of the processor. Upon exiting the loop an application typically checks for the availability of a lock (to get access to shared data) and if it's not available it reenters the SpinWait loop. SpinWait loops can suffer a severe performance penalty when exiting the loop because the processor detects a possible memory order violation and flushes the core processor's pipeline.

To alleviate the problem, there is a PAUSE instruction that improves the performance of SpinWait loops. It provides a hint to the processor that the code sequence is a SpinWait loop and the processor uses this hint to avoid the memory order violation and prevent the pipeline flush. In general, one should try to keep SpinWait loops with PAUSE as short as possible.

Reduce Time Spent in Privileged Mode

User mode is the processing mode in which applications run most of the time whereas *privileged* or kernel mode is the processing mode that allows code to have direct access to all hardware and memory in the system. Unless they are graphics-intensive or I/O-intensive (such as file and print services), most applications should not be processing much work in kernel mode.

Applications that spend significant time in privileged mode lead to excessive energy use for example from a high system call rate or I/O bottlenecks. Developers can use Windows[†] Performance Monitor (perfmon) to get an estimate of privileged mode time.

A high system call rate as measured by system calls per second indicates that the software is causing frequent kernel mode transitions. That is, the application jumps frequently from Ring3 (user mode) to Ring0 (kernel mode). A very common example of this is using an expensive synchronization call such as the Windows OS `WaitForSingleObject()` API. This is a very important synchronization API, especially for inter-process communication. However, it enters kernel mode irrespective of whether the lock is achieved or not. For multithreaded code with no or a short period contention on the lock, you can use `EnterCriticalSection` with a spin count. The advantage of this

API over `WaitForSingleObject()` is that it does not enter kernel mode unless there is a contention on the lock. Hence, when there is no contention, `EnterCriticalSection` with spin count is much cheaper to use and reduces the time spent in privileged mode.

We performed experiments on this with a small test application that had four active threads on a Sandy Bridge microarchitecture system. The locks in the test case were implemented using `WaitForSingleObject` and `TryEnterCriticalSection`. There was no contention on the lock, so each thread achieved the lock at the first attempt. As shown in the graph in Figure 5.4, even when there is no contention, using `WaitForSingleObject()` has negative impact on both power and performance as compared to using `TryEnterCriticalSection()`. Using `TryEnterCriticalSection()` provides a 10x performance gain and over 60 percent energy reduction. For more details on this study see (Chynoweth, 2009).

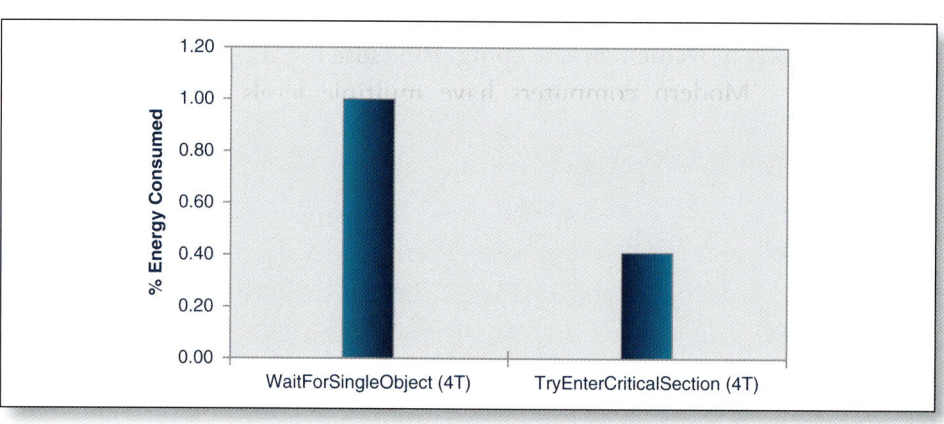

Figure 5.4   Power Impact of Locking Mechanisms

Performance Tuning Tools—References

Various tools can be used to identify performance bottlenecks within an application. One of the tools that can be used to get insight on in the Windows OS is Windows perfmon, included with the OS. This tool will help identify application bottlenecks at a high level. Looking at statistics such as CPU utilization, process utilization, user mode / privileged time, system call rate, context switch rate, page faults/second, and average disk I/O length can help identify the primary bottleneck of an application. See MSDN documentation for more details (Microsoft, 2011, MSDN).

Once the primary bottlenecks are identified and particularly if the workload is CPU-bound, various Intel performance analysis tools can be used to identify and drill down on performance bottlenecks. Intel® VTune™ Amplifier can help identify the top time-consuming modules and drill down all the way to the source code. Developers can use a combination of various performance counters (such as branch mispredicts and cache misses) to identify what is causing a performance bottleneck in a particular section of code. VTune also helps identify areas such as loops that can be good candidates for threading/vectorization for optimizations. For more information on VTune, see (Intel, 2011, VTune).

Data Efficiency—Keep Data Close to Processing Elements

Most applications process data during execution. Efficient data processing leads to better performance, which translates into lower energy usage. Developers can improve system/processor performance and energy efficiency by limiting data movement and keeping data close to processing elements.

Modern computers have multiple levels of storage configured into a memory hierarchy (see Figure 5.5). The data required when running a program will be found somewhere in this hierarchy starting with system cache, followed by system or main memory (RAM), then solid state memory (flash), and finally virtual memory or hard disk. The farther the data is from the processor, the longer it will take before it can be processed. This may cause processing delays (an I/O bottleneck), which may lead to a performance penalty and greater energy use. While there are some algorithms and programming techniques to keep data in the processor cache or RAM, this is not feasible for many applications. This section describes techniques for efficient I/O processing and algorithms plus various disk I/O methodologies that can save energy.

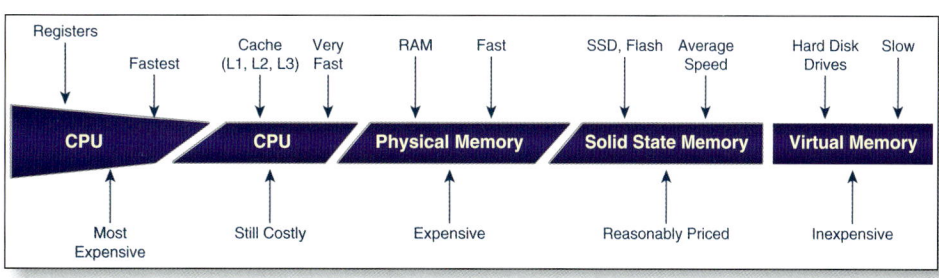

Figure 5.5　Computer Memory Hierarchy

Efficient I/O Processing and Algorithms

An optimized algorithm for your program's I/O component can significantly improve the processing performance of the system and thus reduce overall system energy use. Some recommendations to improve I/O processing are described below.

Asynchronous I/O

Various APIs for I/O operations are provided in the Win32 interface, but all of the read/write calls are eventually routed through ReadFile()/WriteFile() APIs from kernel32.dll. Applications can perform I/O in either synchronous mode or asynchronous mode, which tends to be more efficient. Win32 also provides various flags, control over file-system buffering, and passes on hints to the operating system regarding the type of I/O being employed such as sequential or random.

For asynchronous mode, the application submits the read/write request and continues processing while the I/O operations happen in the background. Once the background I/O operations are complete, the operating system sends a notification of I/O completion to the application. Overlapped I/O could be implemented in various ways, such as signaled file handles, signaled event objects, asynchronous procedure calls (APCs), and I/O completion ports.

We recommend using asynchronous I/O whenever possible to minimize the I/O latency, which is always slower than what the CPU can process. While this may add some complexity to the application, improving the I/O process will improve CPU performance and in turn save system energy. For more information on implementing asynchronous I/O in Windows see (Microsoft, 2011, Synchronous) and for Linux, see (IBM, 2011).

Unformatted Files

Unformatted files are any data such as a text file that do not have various properties such as a consistent structure with regard to record length and order of data elements. To improve performance and save energy, use unformatted files whenever possible. Unformatted I/O of numeric data is more efficient and more precise than formatted I/O. Native unformatted data does not need to be modified when transferred and will take up less space on an external file. On the other hand, when writing data to formatted files, formatted data must be converted to character strings for output, less data can transfer in a single operation, and formatted data may lose precision if read and converted back into binary form. To write the array A (25, 25) in the FORTRAN statements below, S1 is more efficient than S2:

```
S1          WRITE (7) A
S2          WRITE (7, 100) A
100    FORMAT (25(' ',25F5.21))
```

Write Entire Arrays or Strings

Write entire arrays or strings at one time rather than individual elements at multiple times to avoid unnecessary overhead. Every item in an I/O list generates its own calling sequence. This processing overhead becomes most significant in implied DO loops. Use the array name instead of using implied DO loops when accessing entire arrays.

Use Memory for Intermediate Results

Storing intermediate results in memory rather than storing them in a file on a peripheral device can improve performance. The exception to this recommendation is when there is a disproportionately large amount of data in relation to physical memory on your system. Excessive page faults can dramatically impede virtual memory performance (Intel, 2008, I/O Perf).

Disk I/O Methodologies

As computer processors become increasingly faster, hard disk I/O can become the main performance bottleneck in the system. For applications that continually access disk for read/write operations, it is imperative that the software behave in an optimal way to conserve battery power (Intel, 2008, Disk I/O).

Disk Characteristics

When focusing on I/O for performance tuning, it best to understand how the characteristics of the hard drive affect performance. These characteristics include spin rate in revolutions per minute (RPM), seek time, rotational latency, and the sustainable transfer rate. RPM is the rate at which a hard drive spins and directly impacts the performance. Among the fastest today in notebook PCs are 5400 and 7200 RPM drives. Seek time and rotational latency relate to the time taken by the disk to position the read/write head from its current track to the track and sector where data is to be read/written. The actual throughput of the system is also dependent on the physical location of the data on the drive. Since the angular velocity of the disk is constant, more data can be read from the outermost perimeter of the disk than the inner perimeter in a single rotation. When a read request is placed by an application, the disk may have to be spun up first, and the read/write head must be positioned at the appropriate sector. The data is then read and optionally placed in OS file system cache and copied to the application buffer.

Applications performing disk I/O should take into consideration that the average power during spin-up is significantly greater than the power during actual data transfer like a read/write operation. We recommend processing disk I/O in larger chunks with fewer disk accesses.

Impact of Block Size on Sequential Reads

In this section, we'll examine the impact of read block sizes on sequential reads, regarding overall performance and power. For this analysis, we created a large file (around 1 GB) and read the entire file in blocks of various sizes. As a general rule of thumb for any disk I/O, we rebooted the system between runs to avoid any file-system cache interference. The following shows the code flow for the read experiment (Microsoft, 2004, Sequential File).

```
HANDLE hFile = CreateFile(szLargeFile, GENERIC_READ, 0,
NULL, OPEN_EXISTING, FILE_ATTRIBUTE_NORMAL | FILE_FLAG_
SEQUENTIAL_SCAN, NULL);

unsigned int filesize = GetFileSize(hFile,(LPDWORD)0);

totalread = 0;
nrem = filesize;

for (totalread = 0; totalread <filesize; totalread +=
chunksize)

{
if (nrem >= chunksize)
{
ReadFileChunk(hFile,pAlignedBuf,chunksize);
}
else
{
ReadFileChunk(hFile,pAlignedBuf,nrem);
}
nrem -= chunksize;
}
```

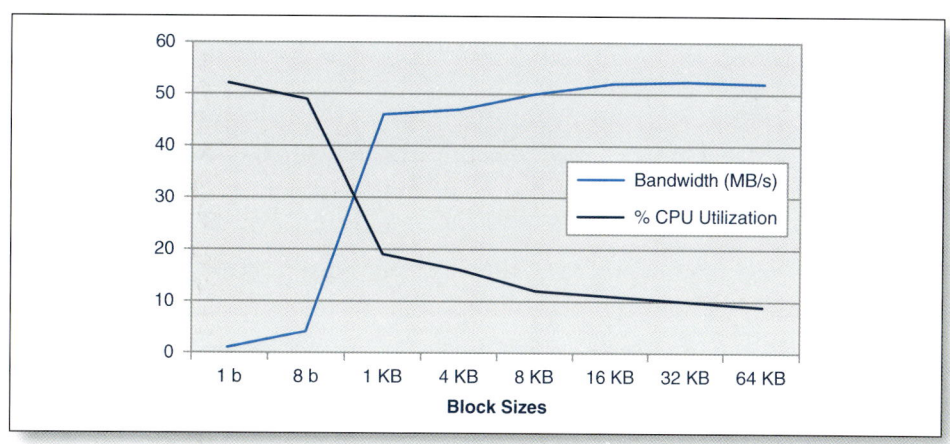

Figure 5.6   Block Size Impact on Performance

Figure 5.6 shows the impact of various block sizes on sequential I/O bandwidth and CPU utilization. Note that as we change from smaller block sizes to larger ones, the data bandwidth (or transfer rate) significantly increases while the processor utilization decreases. Table 5.1 compares the total energy consumed for reading the large file with various block sizes (energy measured for the duration of the total read times using the NetDAQ[†] network data acquisition unit).

Table 5.1   Block Size Impact on Energy Use

Block Size	CPU ENERGY (mWHr)	DISK ENERGY (mWHr)
1 b	9658.77	1056
8 B	1336.18	192.32
1 KB	24.93	13.76
4 KB	24.05	13.56
8 KB	23.27	13.23
16 KB	22.46	12.98
32 KB	22.49	12.85

There is a significant difference between 1-bit and large block reads, but the difference is not as pronounced between various large block reads. This is due to the fact that the energy numbers have been calculated in milliwatt-hours (mWHr) and the workload itself runs for a small amount of time with larger blocks. In general, it is clear that the larger blocks are ideal for both power and performance. A good rule of thumb is to use 8-KB block transfers for the best performance. This may mean buffering more data or consolidating multiple reads for processing in certain applications such as media playback. This also reduces frequent spin-ups that may be needed when the data is read in smaller chunks. Larger chunks have a significantly longer spin-up time and more energy is associated with each spin-up. The transfer rate may not show a noticeable difference beyond a certain threshold (8 KB in this case). Choosing a huge block size (in megabytes) is not recommended.

Impact of File Fragmentation

File fragmentation occurs when the contents of a file are not located in contiguous clusters on the disk. When a file is created for the first time, it is highly likely that the operating system is able to allocate contiguous clusters of storage, but as more content is added by incrementally appending data, the file may end up with fragmented clusters since neighboring clusters may not be available for storage. Most everyone who uses a computer for a long period of time has experienced a slowdown of their desktop or notebook system due to fragmentation, which is precisely why Microsoft provides the "disk defragmenter" utility as one of their system tools.

The following code shows an example of how fragmentation occurs. Two files are being appended with data in 64-KB blocks, one after another. Since both the files are being appended in successive calls and the operating system allocates clusters in a specific order, both the files end up being fragmented on 64-KB boundaries.

```
for (int i=0; i>MAX_SIZE; i += 64KB)
{
AppendFile("Fragmented_File0",64KB,...);
AppendFile("Fragmented_File1",64KB,...);
}
void AppendFile(char *szFilename,...)
{
...
HANDLE hFile = CreateFile(szFilename,
FILE_APPEND_DATA,
FILE_SHARE_READ,
NULL,OPEN_ALWAYS,
```

```
FILE_ATTRIBUTE_NORMAL,
NULL);
(void)SetFilePointer(hFile, 0, NULL, FILE_END);
WriteFile(hFile,...);
CloseHandle(hFile);
...
}
```

File fragmentation causes serious problems from a performance point of view, as well as how it affects the user's experience. Let us first look at performance impact.

Sequentially reading a fragmented file takes much longer than reading a defragmented file. This is due to the seek time and rotational latency penalty incurred while gathering data from noncontiguous clusters. This latency is greatly minimized in a defragmented file since the data is in contiguous clusters. Figure 5.7 shows the performance impact of reading a 256-MB file that was initially fragmented and later defragmented. It took more than twice as much time to read a fragmented file and caused a significant increase in total energy for the same task (Figure 5.8).

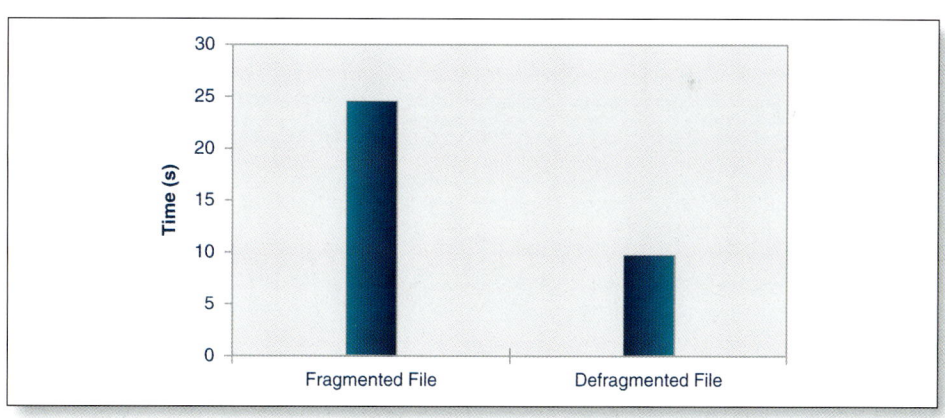

Figure 5.7   File Fragmentation Performance Impact

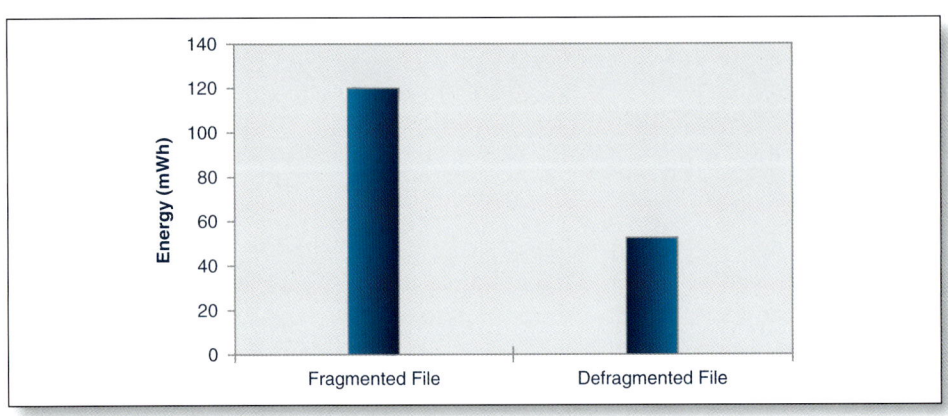

Figure 5.8   File Fragmentation Power Impact

Fragmentation when extending files can be avoided by pre-allocating large sequential files when they are created. The idea is to estimate the size of file in advance and let the file system optimally pre-allocate the largest possible cluster so that the content of the file will be held in contiguous locations. If you are using .NET[†] framework, the SetLength() method can be used as follows:

```
FileStream fs = new FileStream(filename,FileMode.OpenOrCreate);
fs.SetLength(256*1024);
```

The cost of fixing a fragmented file once far outweighs the energy penalty associated with multiple access times. One user-level option to fix would be to use back-end defragmenters more effectively and periodically. Microsoft Windows provides a few undocumented interfaces to detect if a given file is fragmented or not, and even to defragment a fragmented file. NtFsControlFile() is the key function that can be used to detect the number of clusters in a given file, the logical cluster numbers (LCNs) to locate and allocate free large clusters, and move a fragmented file. Developers are advised to use these APIs at their own risk since these are undocumented by the operating system.

Impact of Native Command Queuing on Random Reads

Native command queuing (NCQ) is a disk drive command reordering technique that can often yield significant performance and power benefits.

NCQ is often referred to as the "elevator algorithm." Like an elevator that picks up all passengers on its way to the lobby (regardless of when the button was pressed at each floor), NCQ reorders the read/write commands received in an optimal order to reduce seek/rotational latencies. The drive uses the current location of the read/write head to determine the most efficient path for executing the next commands, much like the elevator. Without reordering, the disk will honor the commands in the order received, and may end up making suboptimal rotations and seeks that cause a decrease in performance and an increase in power consumption.

To take advantage of NCQ, the read operations have to be queued. Synchronous I/O will not take advantage of NCQ since each I/O call is blocked and the read/write operation will be honored in the order received. To test our hypothesis that NCQ saves energy, we simulated the effect of NCQ. The following code shows a snippet of code that chooses a random file and random offset:

```
int chunksize = 64*1024;
for (int i=0; i>nFiles; ++i)
{
HANDLE hFile = CreateRandomFile();
ReadFile(hFile,...); //blocked I/O
}
HANDLE CreateRandomFile()
{
...
int n = GetRandomNumber(0,file_max-1);
.
HANDLE hFile = CreateFile(szFilename[n], GENERIC_READ,
0,NULL, OPEN_EXISTING,
FILE_ATTRIBUTE_NORMAL,NULL);
int filesize = GetFileSize(hFile,0);
int  offset = GetRandomNumber(0,filesize-chunksize);

SetFilePointer(hFile,offset,NULL,FILE_BEGIN);
...
return hFile;
}
```

For our analysis, we chose a random set of files and started reading 64KB from a random offset of each file. The code above shows the case when synchronous I/O was used. In the sample below, the same read requests are queued up initially and later wait on the I/O completion port until all the read requests are complete:

```
int chunksize = 64*1024;
HANDLE gPort;
for (int i=0; i>nFiles; ++i)
{
HANDLE hFile = CreateRandomFile();
QueueRead(hFile,gPort,...); //blocked I/O
}

While (nRead > nFiles)
{
GetQueuedCompletionStatus(gPort,...);
...
++nRead;
}
```

In both cases the same set of data is being read, since the random numbers are seeded the same way. Figure 5.9 shows that when NCQ is utilized, the total time to read the data is reduced by approximately 15 percent. There was a similar reduction in total energy for the task.

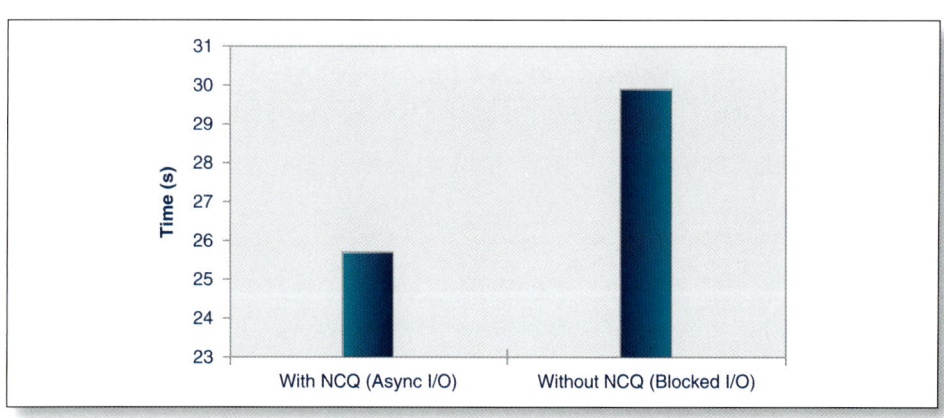

Figure 5.9   Performance Impact of NCQ

Applications that deal with random I/O or I/O operations with multiple files should use asynchronous I/O to take advantage of disks that support NCQ. Queue up all the read requests and use events or callbacks to determine if the read requests are complete. This method can potentially yield a platform power benefit of approximately 15 percent and a performance improvement of about 2x.

While the experiments were conducted on a SATA NCQ drive, similar benefits are expected with other reordering protocols as well. For more in-depth coverage of NCQ, see (Intel, 2003).

Disk I/O in Multithreaded Code

Now let's take a look at the effect of I/O on multithreaded code and the best strategy for I/O when multiple threads require data from the disk. For this analysis we developed an in-house bitmap-to-JPEG conversion program based on the IJG library that will convert a set of BMPs to JPEGs. The block diagram in Figure 5.10 shows the serial version of the application. The "read" box refers to reading the bitmap file in block sizes of 64 KB (the same block size while writing the .JPG files out). The read/write time contributes approximately 41 percent and BMP2JPEG conversion contributes approximately 59 percent of the total runtime. The output JPEG files are quite small compared to the read files (the BMP files were about 10 MB each); therefore, most of the read/write time was consumed by reads.

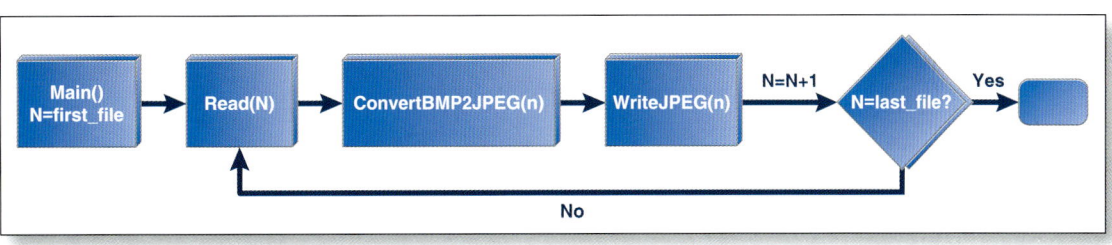

Figure 5.10 Flow Diagram of Serial BMP to JPG Conversion

Next we'll take a look at three multithreaded variations of the same algorithm. The first variation spawns two threads, with one thread taking ownership for odd-numbered files and the other taking ownership for even-numbered files, as shown in Figure 5.11.

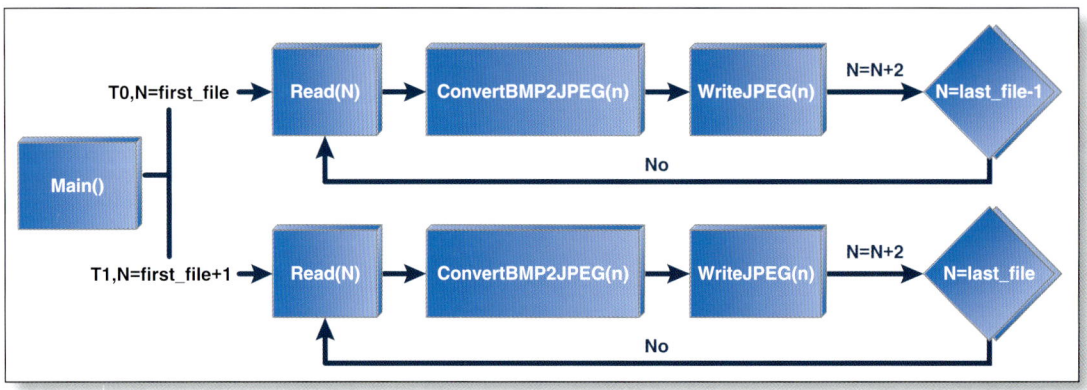

Figure 5.11 Flow Diagram of Multithreaded BMP to JPG Conversion (Variation 1)

Another variation performs the buffer read/write on one thread, and assigns the computationally intensive convert operations to multiple compute threads, as shown in Figure 5.12.

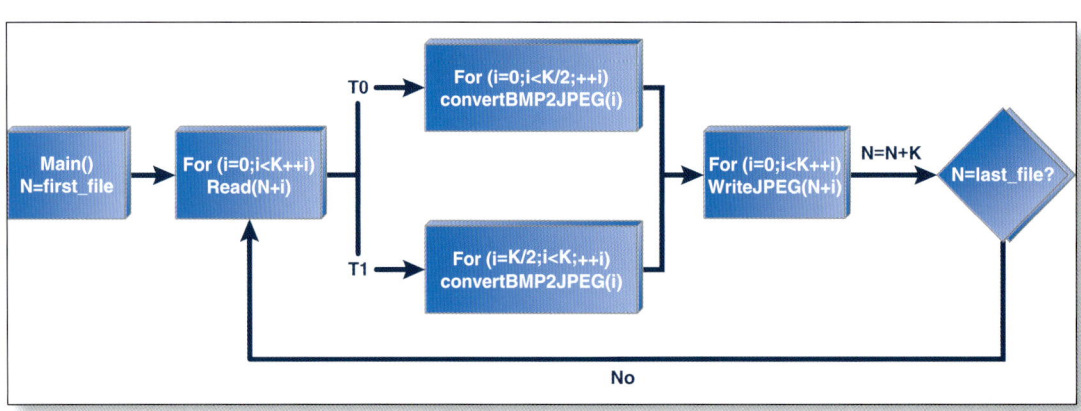

Figure 5.12 Flow Diagram of Multithreaded BMP to JPG Conversion (Variation 2)

For the final variation, shown in Figure 5.13, we will include queued I/O. We created an I/O completion port where all of the read requests are queued, and multiple threads wait on the completion port until the read requests are complete. The conversion operation is initiated and the entire output file is buffered and written out, finally, in one thread. This method provides load balancing of the system along with the possibility of scaling the number of threads easily.

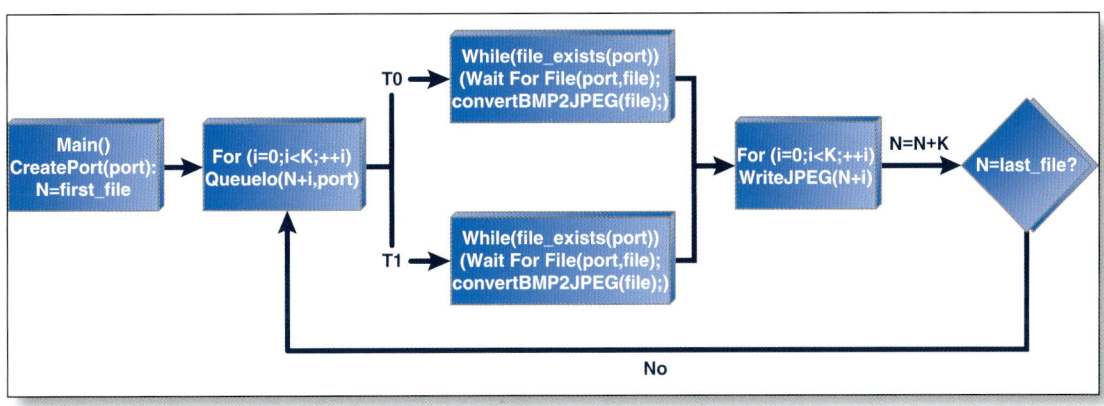

Figure 5.13 Flow Diagram of Multithreaded BMP to JPG Conversion (Variation 3)

Figure 5.14 shows the performance of the single-threaded versus the multithreaded variations.

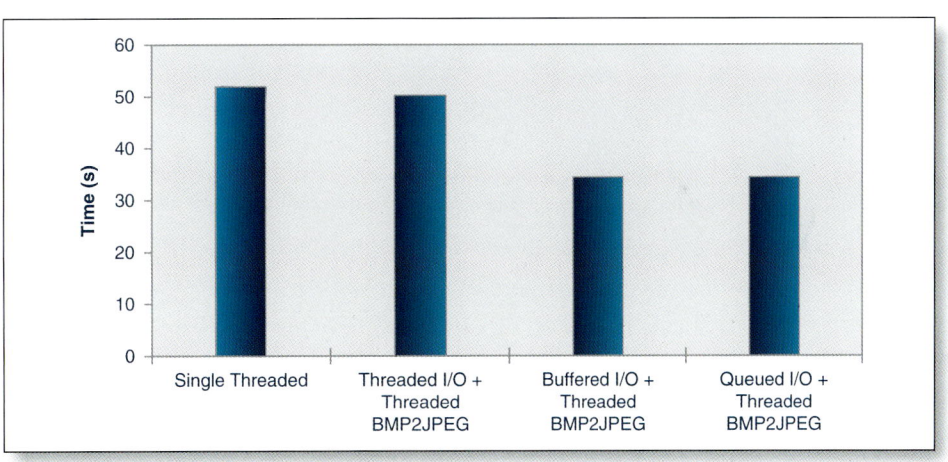

Figure 5.14 BMP2JPEG Workload Time

The performance when using multithreaded implementations with buffered I/O and queued I/O show approximately 1.52x–1.56x scaling over the single threaded case, whereas performance does not scale when the I/O operations are performed in both threads. This performance benefit of threading is lost due to disk thrashing by the competing threads. When both of the threads are running and the disk tries to read 64-KB chunks of data simultaneously, a severe seek/rotational penalty is incurred in the hard drive. Since requests from both the threads need to be serviced, the read head has to be repositioned after every read of buffer block. This causes suboptimal disk rotations and an increase in overall read time; it also masks the performance benefit of multithreading. Figure 5.15 shows the power measurements of the methodologies and confirms that buffering or queuing strategies deliver better energy-efficiency as well.

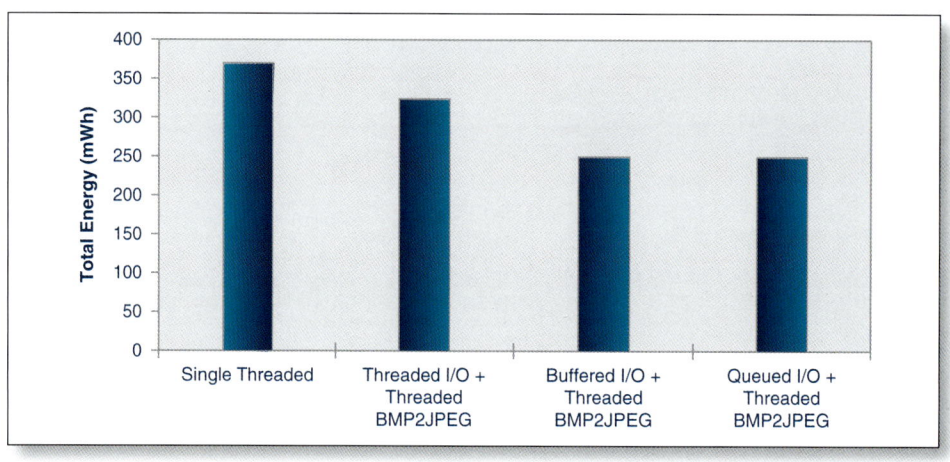

Figure 5.15 Energy Cost with I/O Strategies

If your application has multiple threads competing simultaneously for disk I/O, one option you have is to queue the I/O calls and utilize NCQ. Reordering may help in optimal ordering of the requests from multiple threads and improve performance. If multiple threads competing for the disk causes significant disk thrashing, consolidate all the read/write operations in a single thread; it will reduce read/write head thrashing and reduce frequent disk spin-ups as well.

Profiling Disk I/O Performance

If you suspect that your data processing application may be stalling the CPU, that is, your application performance is *I/O-bound*, you can use built-in tools in Windows to profile and analyze the disk activity and performance.

Perfmon and Process Explorer

Perfmon (Windows performance monitor) and utilities like Process Explorer can help you understand disk I/O activity and identify issues. Perfmon is included with Windows and some of its disk counters are useful for I/O analysis. One counter that is particularly useful is Disk Bytes/sec—the rate bytes are transferred to or from the disk during write or read operations. This counter can be used to understand the data throughput.

Processor counters such as %DPC, %interrupt, and %privilege time can provide some hint if there is significant time processing I/Os when the privilege time consists mostly of DPC and interrupt time.

The % DPC Time counter tracks the percentage of time that the processor has spent receiving and servicing deferred procedure calls (DPCs) during the sample interval. DPCs are interrupts that run at a lower priority than standard interrupts. The % DPC Time counter is a component of % Privileged Time because DPCs are executed in privileged mode. They are counted separately and are not a component of the interrupt counters.

The % Interrupt Time counter tracks the time the processor spends receiving and servicing hardware interrupts during sample intervals. This value is an indirect indicator of the activity of devices that generate interrupts, such as the system clock, the mouse, disk drivers, data communication lines, network interface cards and other peripheral devices.

The % Privileged Time counter tracks the percentage of elapsed time that the process threads spent executing code in privileged mode. When a Windows system service in called, the service will often run in privileged mode to gain access to system-private data. Such data is protected from access by threads executing in user mode. Calls to the system can be explicit or implicit, such as page faults or interrupts.

Process Explorer is a free system monitoring tool from Microsoft with functionality similar to Windows Task Manager but with a more rich set of features (Microsoft, 2011, Process Explorer). With it, you can monitor the I/O Delta Total Bytes and identify any process causing significant I/O activity. To enable the "I/O Delta Total Bytes" column in Process Explorer, click Select Columns from the View menu, click the Process performance tab, and check the box "I/O Delta Total Bytes" (see Figure 5.16). This will give you the total amount of all operations (read, write, other) caused by this process (in bytes) in real time.

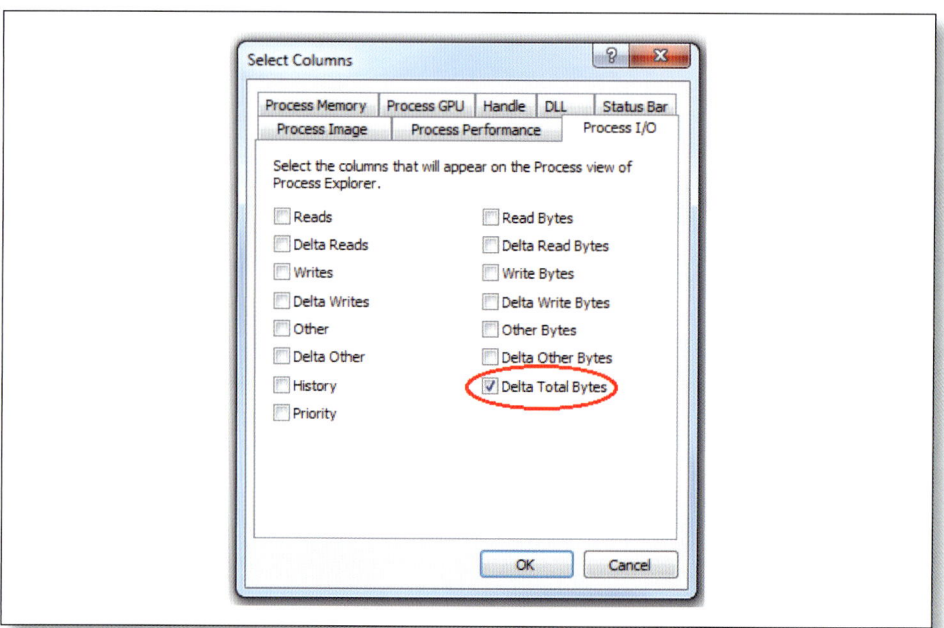

Figure 5.16 Selections Provided by Process Explorer

Identify Whether I/O Is Causing a CPU Bottleneck

Using perfmon or other system profiling tools can provide some clue as to whether the I/O activity is causing the CPU to wait or stay idle while waiting for I/O operations to complete. As seen in the Figure 5.17 the %processor time is somewhat inversely proportional to the disk transfer/sec activity. This particular profile indicates some performance issue since the CPU is stalled or waiting due to I/O activity.

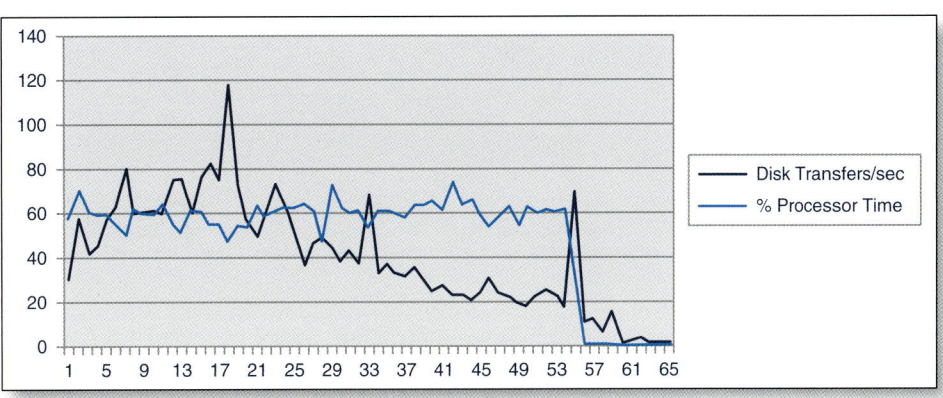

Figure 5.17 Disk and CPU utilization

Other Examples of Data Efficiency

There are a few other examples of data efficiency that we have researched that deliver meaningful energy savings, including buffering data during large file reads and transferring files over a wireless link.

Buffering Data

Buffering data reads can also save energy. In this case study, we show how buffering data for MP3 playback allows the hard drive to rest, saving overall energy during playback. A typical MP3 player application reads several small portions of the file from the hard disk (in chunks of approximately 2 KB for the 4-MB test file) when playing an MP3 music file. The hard disk is kept busy doing lots of small reads that keep the hard-disk average power to above 1.25 W as seen in Figure 5.18.

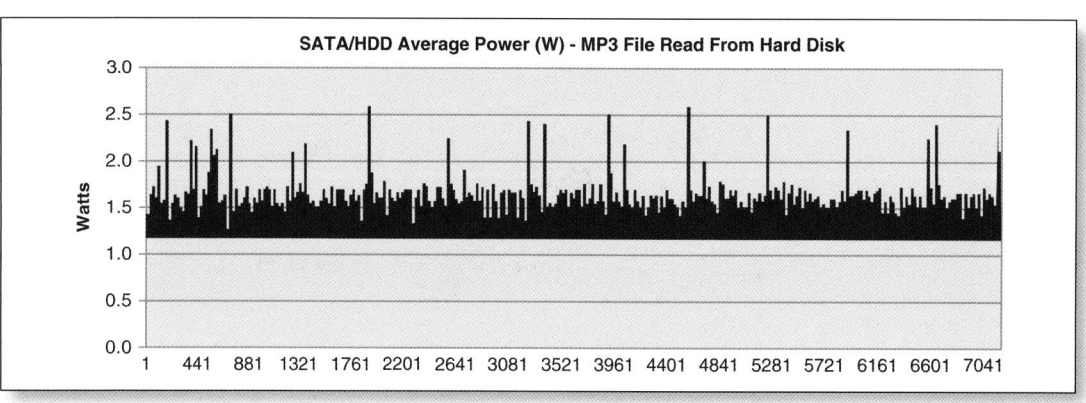

Figure 5.18 HDD Average Power—Data Read from Disk

Buffering larger amounts of data by consolidating multiple reads will lead to better energy-efficiency, in this case by buffering the MP3 file to a RAM Disk (memory). In Figure 5.19, you can see that the initial buffering of the MP3 file to memory kept the hard disk quite busy, but once the data is all read from memory and buffered, the hard disk remains idle and significantly reduces its average power to 0.8 W.

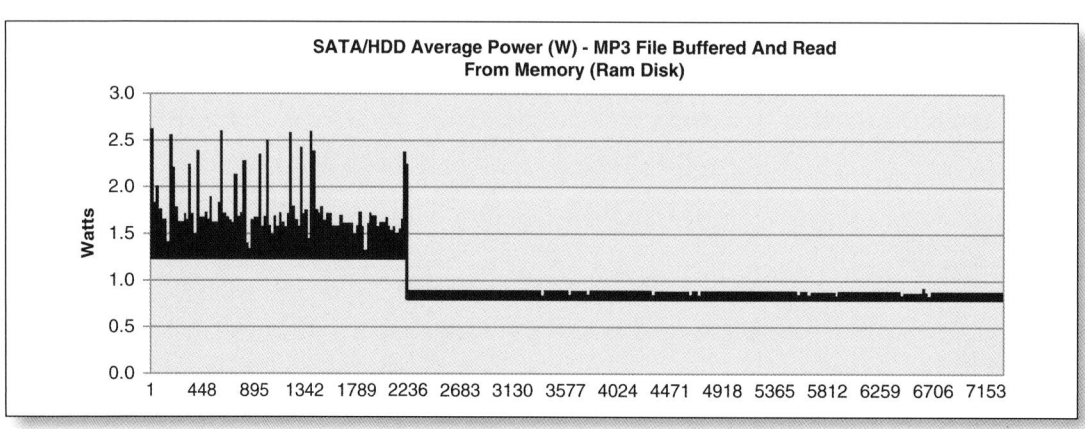

Figure 5.19 HDD Average Power—Data Buffered and Read from Memory

File Transfer over Wireless

Another case study examines the energy cost of transferring files over a network. The hypothesis is that if files are compressed before being transferred, the energy cost will be lower. The more you reduce the amount of transferred bytes by compressing them, the less bandwidth you will need to accomplish the task. There is an up-front energy cost to perform the compression, but at a certain point, that cost would, in theory, be less than the amount of energy saved in the data transfer of fewer bytes. CPU usage climbs as the amount of compression does but you save more energy by reducing total time to transfer the data (Intel, 2008, Data Transfer-WLAN).

The power consumption of a laptop while transmitting data over a wireless network can vary depending on several factors. The study focuses on how the compression ratio or size of the file affects power consumption and not on the performance of a particular compression algorithm or wireless component. The study was performed only on the client side (laptop) and did not include the server side. We would like to determine the most energy efficient usage model for a laptop when transferring data over wireless LAN and answer questions such as:

- For upload, is it better to compress the data before transmission or leave it uncompressed?

- Should a file be compressed before download?

- How will the wireless adapter, CPU utilization, data compression ratio, and transmission time affects the laptop power consumption?

The general methodology used was to transmit compressed "txt" and "tif" files with varying compression ratios (using Gzip 1.2.4) and uncompressed data with varying file sizes and measure platform power with a Fluke NetDAQ. To achieve reproducible and consistent results, we used a controlled network in an isolated environment to reduce noise and interference with only a single client transmitting data. We selected Gzip 1.2.4 as the compression algorithm since it is open source and easy to customize. While we realize that different compression algorithms can affect the compression ratio, this study only focused on the size of compression ratio rather than the algorithm. The differences between Gzip and other compression algorithms were not considered.

Test runs were scaled to maintain workloads long enough (in duration) to minimize errors in platform power measurements. Power consumption per run was computed as the average value of 100 iterations.

The compression ratio of a given data set plays a significant role in determining whether to send/receive uncompressed data or to use compression before transmitting the data. Five different data sets were used, with the corresponding data size and compression ratios shown in Table 5.2.

Table 5.2   Data sets for file transfer

Data Sets	Original Size (KB)	Compress Rate Gzip 1.2.4*	Description
Tulips.tif	1179	1.2x	Medium size file, very low compression ratio
Book1	751	2.45x	Medium size file, low compression ratio
World95.txt	2935	5.06x	Large size file, high compression ratio
Pic	502	8.96x	Small size file, high compression ratio
Frymire.tif	3708	14.04x	Large size file, very high compression ratio

Note: Data sets were from Jeff Gilchrist Archive Compression Test (ACT)†, which are a set of benchmarks for data compression. (Gilchrist, 2002)

To perform the tests, we network-mapped (via access point) the test system to the server's file system and used the Windows XP internal copy command to transfer the data from the client to the server and vice versa over the wireless network. As mentioned above, we measured average energy over 100 runs.

Each of the data sets was transmitted as follows:

■ Upload the uncompressed file to the server

■ Compress the file and upload the compressed file to the server

■ Download the uncompressed file from the server

■ Download the compressed file from the server and then uncompress on the client

Before we examine the final test results, it's important to understand where most of the power is used, which is in the wireless adapter (for data transfer) and in the CPU (for data compression). Table 5.3 lists the test platform's power profile when wireless adapter is disabled, on with no connection, on and connected to an access point, and on but searching for signal.

Table 5.3   WLAN Adapter Average Power Consumption

Scenario	Average Platform Power (W)	Average WLAN Power (W)	Total Average Power (W)
WLAN Radio Off	13.2	0	13.2
WLAN Radio On (no AP connection)	14.1	0.35	14.45
WLAN Radio On (AP connected)	14.2	0.45	14.65
WLAN Radio On (searching for AP)	15.7	1.6	17.3

The wireless adapter used most power when actively looking for an access point (AP) although this is typically just a brief period of time. When the "radio is on" and the system is connected to the network but not transmitting any data, the average power consumption is approximately 450 mW, whereas when searching for an AP, the power consumption is approximately 1600 mW.

As for the CPU, the utilization is high when compressing and uncompressing the data (99–100 percent when compressing and 84–100 percent when uncompressing). It drops to 4–7 percent when transmitting the data regardless if it is compressed or not. As expected the processor frequency goes to maximum (highest Performance Frequency State) when compressing and uncompressing. For transmitting the data over network the processor remains at a lower Performance Frequency state since the CPU utilization is low (4–7 percent).

In various runs, we compared the total power consumption of uploading uncompressed data by first compressing and then uploading the data. Figure 5.20 shows these comparisons. The secondary Y axis in the figure plots corresponding compression ratio for the given data set. Note that the data sets with higher compression ratios (higher than 1.2x) show benefit for power consumption when compressing first and then uploading the data set. For the data set with the lowest compression ratio (1.2x in this case), uploading uncompressed data is more energy-efficient by a small amount.

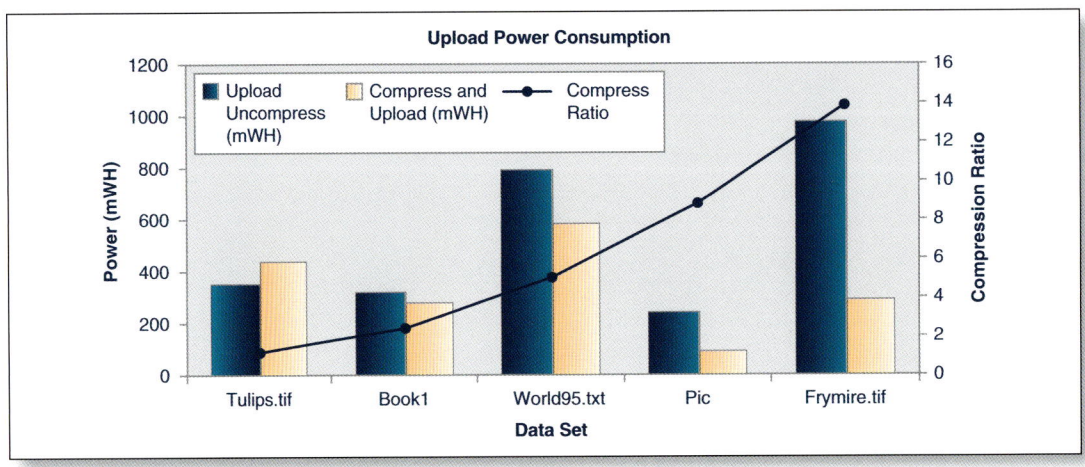

Figure 5.20 Upload over WLAN Total Energy

Similarly, Figure 5.21 shows the power consumption for the same data set during download. Once again, it indicates average power consumption for each data set as well as the compression ratio on the secondary Y axis. For data sets with higher compression ratios, downloading compressed data and then uncompressing is more energy-efficient than downloading uncompressed data. For the data set with the lowest compression ratio (1.2x in this case), downloading uncompressed data is more energy-efficient. For the Book1 data set (compression ratio 2.45x) the power consumption of downloading uncompressed data versus downloading compressed data and then uncompressing yields minimal difference.

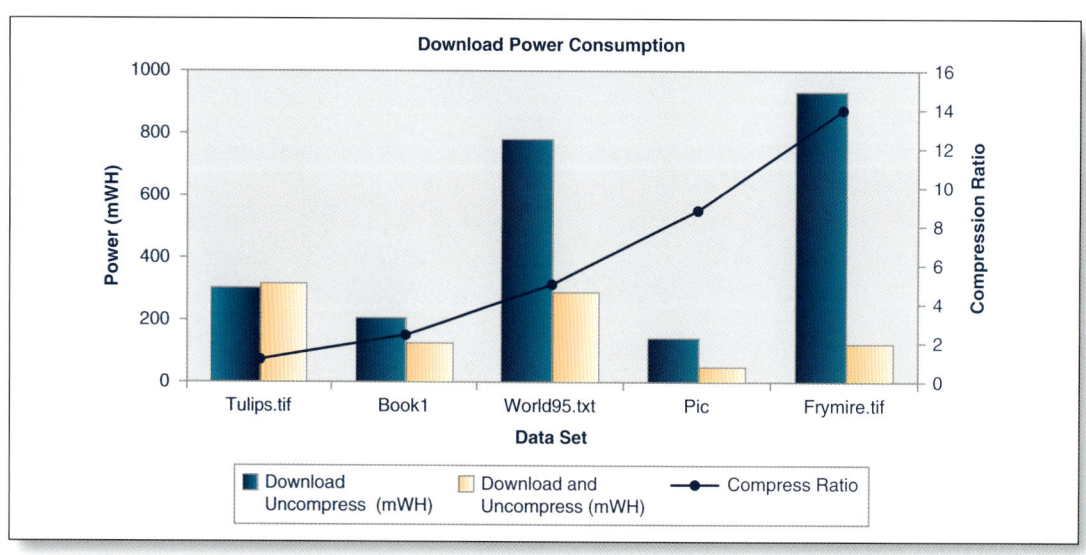

Figure 5.21 Download over WLAN Total Energy

The size of a data file being transferred over a wireless network directly affects the elapsed time to transfer and therefore the power consumption used not only for the wireless adapter but the entire platform. For improved data efficiency and energy efficiency, we recommend the following:

■ For data sets with higher compression ratios (more than 3.0x), uploading/downloading compressed data provides better power savings as compared to transmitting uncompressed data. It is beneficial for applications to transmit compressed data for data sets having higher compression ratios.

■ For data sets with compression ratio around 2.5–3.0x, there is a minimal difference in the power saving when uploading/downloading compressed data versus uncompressed data.

■ For data sets with lower compression ratios (about 1.2x in this case, which is hardly compressed), compressing the data before uploading/ decompressing after download adds extra overhead. We recommend uploading/downloading uncompressed data in these cases.

Context Awareness—Know Your Environment

"Context is any information that can be used to characterize the situation of an entity. An entity is a person, place, or object that is considered relevant to the interaction between a user and an application, including the user and applications themselves" (Dey, 1999).

Humans naturally use context to understand our world, makes decisions, and adapt to the environment. In the English language, the pronouns he, she, we, them, that, it, and others are used contextually. They assume a shared understanding of current events and make our communication more efficient. In journalism, writers must take care that when quoting someone, the original meaning is not lost by "taking it out of context." Our individual reactions to changes in our physical environment, such as heat, cold, and noise are also examples of being context aware. We use our context awareness to understand our current circumstances and make decisions.

Context Aware Computing

Context aware computing means that computers can sense the environment in which they are operating and react to changes in the environment. A simple example most have experienced is the warning you get from the operating system when the battery on your mobile phone or notebook PC is getting quite low. Embedded systems are particularly context aware because in many cases, they are designed specifically to monitor environmental conditions from sensor data and react to them. The use of sensors is growing rapidly in smart phones and tablets and includes light sensors, gyros, accelerometers, GPS receivers, near-field communications, and others. Here are some examples of context aware behaviors in computing devices:

- A PC or smart phone warns you when your battery has reached a very low energy state.

- A notebook PC responds to a change from AC to DC power by automatically dimming the display.

- A tablet PC or smart phone responds to ambient light level and adjusts display brightness.

- A notebook PC quickly parks the hard drive heads when sensors detect that the device is falling—to avoid a head crash.

■ A handheld device writes cached data to flash memory when the battery is getting critically low.

Context awareness makes our devices "smarter." How smart they are (or how smart users perceive them to be) depends on how well the applications take advantage of the data available to them. Smarter devices tend to deliver a better user experience. The quality of the user experience will depend significantly on the design decisions you make. The remainder of this section describes active versus passive context awareness, user-configurable options, and then focuses in on the use of context awareness to save energy.

Passive versus Active Context Aware Behavior

In reacting to a state change, the behavior of our software applications can be passive or active. A *passive* response occurs when the system or application asks the user what action to take ("Switch to power-save mode?") or asks the user to acknowledge that the state change has occurred ("You have 10% battery left. OK?"). An *active* response occurs when the system or application takes action automatically either as a default feature (dim the display in a dark room) or as a user configurable application option (skip full-system virus scan when on battery).

Being passive about an event does not mean the system or application ignores the event. There is a stimulus and the application senses it. The passivity is in letting the user decide what action to take or in simply requiring the user to acknowledge that the event has occurred. As a user experience, some of these passive responses can become annoying. For example, do you ever tire of having your phone or tablet ask you if you want to join the Wi-Fi[†] network that was just detected? To deliver a better user experience, many systems and applications provide user-*configurable* settings. Both passive and active application behaviors can rely on these user settings to determine when to react and what to do.

Offering User-Configurable Options

User-configurable options allow the user to *personalize* their system or applications and their experience. When deciding what kind of user experience options to provide, designers and developers face many choices that come with many tradeoffs:

■ What application behaviors will be passive?

■ What application behaviors will be automatic?

■ What configuration options should be offered?

■ What should the default settings for the options be?

■ How can we make users aware that the configurations options are available?

Let's turn back to this book's focus on power and energy and examine some of the user settings that are available from a power perspective. Most of us are familiar with the power settings available on Windows computers. The familiar control panel for power in Windows 7, shown in Figure 5.22, lets you choose between different power options or policies. As a user, you can configure the system power plan by choosing one of the plans Windows provides (Power Saver, Balanced, High Performance) or define your own using the advanced settings.

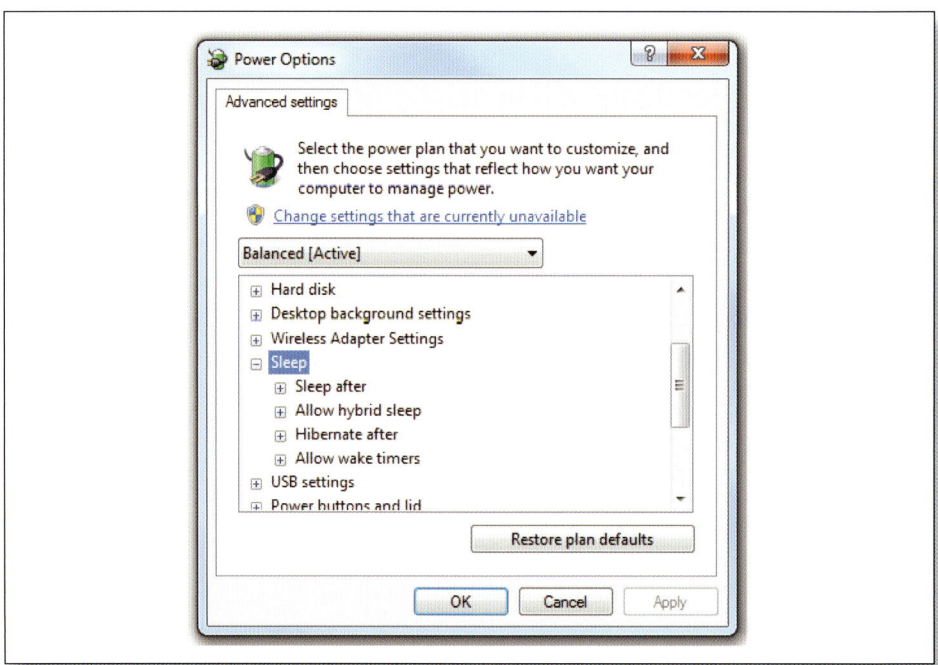

Figure 5.22 Windows 7 Power Options Control Panel

These user configurable options drive system-level context aware behaviors that are designed to save energy. Whether it's turning off the hard drive, dimming the display, or going into sleep mode, the system faithfully watches the clock and takes action. The combination of user-chosen settings determines how energy-efficient the platform is. For example, Figure 5.23 shows the impact of using a screen saver to display high-definition photos versus simply blanking—an increase in energy use of about 400 mW.

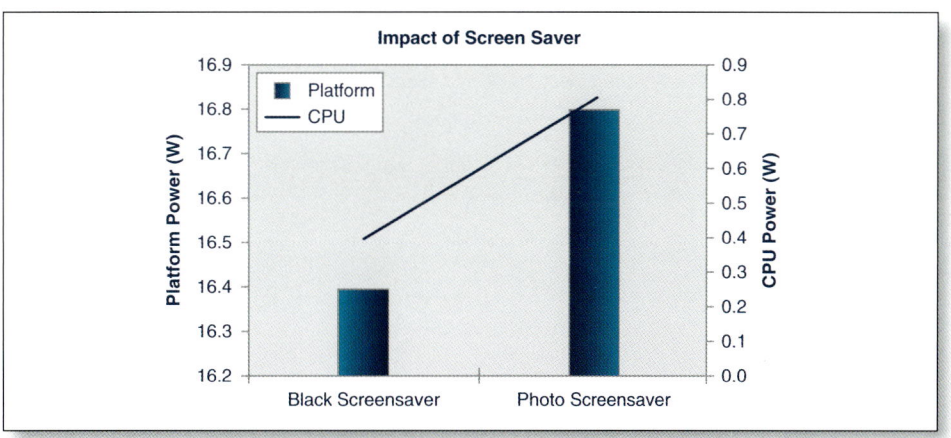

Figure 5.23 Effect of Screensaver on Platform Power Consumption

Throughout the evolution of Microsoft Windows (as well as other operating systems) the number of options and the amount of control over system level power behavior have improved dramatically. Windows Vista and Windows 7 provide advanced mechanisms for enterprises to change and enforce group policies and achieve power savings over thousands of devices.

While use of context awareness for power management at the operating system and platform levels is well established, context-awareness for energy-efficiency at the application level is still new. To add these capabilities to applications, developers can access the contextual data in one of two ways: by querying for the information specifically or by registering for an event notification when a state change occurs. The next sections describe how to use each of these techniques to add context-aware application behaviors.

Querying for Power-related Information

To query for system state information, the developer should use the system APIs provided by the operating system or a software developer kit that provides abstractions of the lower-level system details. This section describes how to get information about the platform power sources, the power policy, the CPU, and other system devices.

On AC or DC?

Does it benefit an application to know if a notebook PC is plugged into an AC power source or operating on battery? Here are some scenarios to consider:

- Should your virus checker start a full system scan when you are running on battery?

- Should your Blu-ray[†] movie player application provide you some options to deliver longer playback when operating on battery, possibly sacrificing some quality?

- Are you willing to give up some special effects in games (particles, physics, smoke, fire) to get more game play on a single battery charge?

If you answered yes to any of these questions, then it's important for the application to determine when the platform is plugged in and when it's on battery. In Windows, you can achieve this by querying a unique GUID called GUID_ACDC_POWER_SOURCE (Microsoft, 2007). Armed with this information, you can adapt the application's behavior and possibly deliver extended battery life for the usage. The following code tracks the changes in AC/DC and used by application globally for notification on Windows Operating system.

```
// Application can track the change in AC and DC power input
// and react when a power event notification occurs.

DWORD PowerSource;

LRESULT
CALLBACK
UserWindProc(
    HWND hWnd,
    UINT uMsg,
    WPARAM wParam,
    LPARAM lParam)
{
    POWERBROADCAST_SETTING *PowerEventInformation;
    switch(wParam) {
        // Handle power management messages
```

```
      case WM_POWERBROADCAST:
        switch(LOWORD(wParam)) {
          // Handle power event notifications
          case PBT_POWERSETTINGCHANGE:
            // Inspect the power event information
           //
            PowerEventInformation = (POWERBROADCAST_
            SETTING *)lParam;
            // This is the AC/DC transition that we
            registered
            // for. Derive the power source for later
            processing.
            if (IsEqualGUID(PowerSetting->PowerSetting,
              GUID_ACDC_POWER_SOURCE) &&
              (PowerSetting->DataLength ==
              sizeof(DWORD))) {
            // Update our global
            PowerSource = (DWORD*)PowerSetting->Data;
            }
          break;
        }
      break;
    }
}
```

Battery Capacity Remaining

It may also be important for an application to know what the current battery capacity is. For example, a video playback application may want to compute the number of minutes of viewing time available given the current battery capacity and power settings and potentially offer to change some settings to increase viewing time.

To determine the battery capacity remaining, a developer would use the GUID_BATTERY_CAPACITY_REMAINING event GUID:

```
// Registration handle for battery capacity changes.
HPOWERNOTIFY BatteryCapacityNotificationHandle;
// Register for system power source change notifications.
BatteryCapacityNotificationHandle =
RegisterPowerSettingNotification(GUID_BATTERY_PERCENTAGE_
REMAINING,DEVICE_NOTIFY_WINDOW_HANDLE);
```

Current Power Policy

Windows provides a method to query for the current power policy. Similar to the query for the ACDC and battery threshold settings, the application would query a GUID called GUID_POWERSCHEME_PERSONALITY. With the knowledge of what the current power policy is, the application may want to change it. To do this, the application must first determine if the system will allow a policy change and then make the change if desired. When the application is finished it's a best practice to return the power policy back to its original state. To change the power policy, call the Win32 API `PowerSettingAccessCheck` to determine if the user has access rights to override the power settings. This API call queries for a group policy override for specific power settings.

```
DWORD WINAPI PowerSettingAccessCheck (
                __in POWER_DATA_ACCESSOR AccessFlags,
                __in_opt  const GUID *PowerGuid);
```

The API will return the active power settings identified by the GUID, allowable values and default values for AC and DC. For more information on how to use this API, please see (Microsoft, 2011).

CPU Parameters

Obtaining specific information about the CPU may be important for the application. For example, you may want to know if the CPU supports a particular instruction set (such as Intel AVX) so that the application can take a higher performance and more energy-efficient code path. You application may also want to know the number of cores in the CPU to set an appropriate thread count.

On Intel processors, the CPUID opcode queries the processor for information about the supported features and CPU type. There are many utilities on the Web that can help you implement a solution that can take advantage of CPUID information. For more information on CPUID, see (Intel, 2009).

To find the number of logical cores on a Windows machine, an application could use a Win32 API as follows:

```
SYSTEM_INFO sysinfo;
GetSystemInfo( &sysinfo );
numCPU = sysinfo.dwNumberOfProcessors;
```

On Linux or non-Windows machines, an application might use:

```
numCPU = sysconf( _SC_NPROCESSORS_ONLN );
```

Other Context Awareness Information

Developers may also want to consider the status of other components on the platform and use that information for intelligent application behavior and energy savings. It might be useful to know information about the status of components such as network cards, Bluetooth†, USB devices, and monitors. For example, should an application continue to render video if the monitor has turned off due to a timeout or if the application window is minimized?

Another set of devices to consider are LAN cards and radios. Networking increases energy consumption not just because the LAN card uses energy for transmitting and receiving, but also because they remain in active state for long periods of time on the chance that some useful network communication may occur. PCs and set-top boxes are the most notable examples of this. The Microsoft System Event Notification Service (SENS) can help alleviate this and other mobile application issues. The SENS API (Microsoft, 2011, SENS) provides a simple function call for checking if the network connection is alive and another that will ping a specified address for you. In addition to these simple functions, you can also register with the service to receive events when a connection is made or lost, to ping a destination, or even as an alternative method to detect when the system changes power states (battery on, AC ON, or battery low). Some of the events available from SENS are:

- `NetworkConnectionChange`—The network connection status or network type has changed.

- `BatteryLevelChange`—The battery power level has changed.

- `BatteryStatusChange`—The battery status has changed.

- `BatteryLifeChange`—The projected remaining battery life has changed.

- `OnBatteryLow`—The battery level is below 33 percent. The `On` prefix is used to prevent name confusion with the `ISensOnNow`. `BatteryLow` method.

- `PowerChange`—The power status has changed (from AC power to battery or the reverse)

Registering for Power-related Events

An important characteristic of context aware behavior is knowing when something has changed so that the system or application can respond. The best way to implement this is to register for event notifications.

Registering for Power Events

Applications can better adapt their behavior to the current power state of the computer by registering for power events. In Windows, there is a function called `RegisterPowerSettingNotification` that applications can use to receive PBT_POWERSETTINGCHANGE notifications. For interaction applications one can use WM_POWERBROADCAST messages sent to a window. For service applications, you would use the `HandlerEx` callback function registered with `RegisterServiceCtrlHandlerEx`. The `lParam` parameter of the WM_POWERBROADCAST message or the `lpEventData` parameter sent to the `HandlerEx` callback function will be a pointer to a structure called POWERBROADCAST_SETTING.

The structure of `RegisterPowerSettingNotification` is:

```
HANDLE RegisterPowerSettingNotification(
    LPCGUID PowerSettingGuid,
    DWORD Flags);
```

The return value for `HANDLE` is of type `hRecipient` and provides the handle to the event registration so that it can be unregistered later using `UnregisterPowerSettingNotification`. The code sample below shows how to register for system power source notifications that indicate whether the system power source has changed:

```
// Registration handle for AC/DC power transitions.
HPOWERNOTIFY ACDCNotificationHandle;
// Register for system power source change notifications.
ACDCNotificationHandle =
RegisterPowerSettingNotification(GUID_ACDC_POWER_SOURCE,
DEVICE_NOTIFY_WINDOW_HANDLE);
```

To determine the power source on a Linux platform, the application can call a database to check the state of the battery. For example, a developer can use the logic below to determine the AC/DC status of the system:

```
bool CCBatteryInfo::getUsingExternalPowerSource()
{
```

```
    bool batteryState = true;
    CCBATDBGOUT(string(__FUNCTION__) + string(" : state = DC
(battery)"));
    batteryState = false;   // DC (battery)
    break;
}

    else if(strstr(line, "state:") && strstr(line, "on-line"))
    {
    CCBATDBGOUT(string(__FUNCTION__) + string(" : state =
AC"));
    batteryState = true; // AC
    break;
            }
}

    return batteryState;
}
```

Power Plan Changes

As we mentioned earlier, Microsoft Windows provides built-in power policies: High Performance, Balanced, and Power Saver. They give the system user the option to choose between better performance and better battery life. Application software can use power polices in the following ways:

■ Adjust application behavior based on the user's current power policy

■ Change application behavior in response to a change in power policy

■ Change the power policy to suit the application behavior

Applications can register for power plan personality change notifications and use the event to change application behavior accordingly, similar to using system power-source notifications as seen in previous section.

For example, the developer may want to write application that requires maximum performance when conducting video conference calls or reduce the quality of the video streaming depending on the AC/DC state. Applications might respond in the following ways after receiving the power plan personality notification:

■ If the current power plan personality is High Performance, then the application might enable resource-intensive operations such as real-time indexing and high-resolution visualizations.

- If the current power plan personality is Power Saver, then the application might disable background updates, disable auto spell check, or reduce video quality.

- If the current power plan personality is Balanced, then the application may strive to moderate resource usage.

To register for power plan personality change notifications, developers can use the GUID_POWERSCHEME_PERSONALITY event GUID.

When setting the GUID a notification occurs immediately after registration and then whenever the power plan personality changes. This might occur when the user changes power plans by using the battery meter in the taskbar.

Background Tasks

Applications can also register for a power event notification that indicates that the system is currently active enough to support background tasks that would otherwise prevent the system from idling to a sleep state.

The background task notification is delivered to registered applications under the following conditions:

- The primary hard disk drive is on and spinning.

- The system is not on battery or DC power.

- The system is moderately idle. For example, current CPU utilization is low enough that background tasks do not impact user responsiveness and foreground applications.

- The background task notification has not been delivered in the last minute.

To register for background task notifications, the application should use the *GUID_BACKGROUND_TASK_NOTIFICATION* event GUID.

Developer Kits

To simplify access to the status of many platform components, Intel and others have built software developer kits that abstract all of the API calls into easily understood function calls. One such tool is the Intel® Mobile Platform SDK.

Summary

While power management at the operating system and platform levels has intensified, consideration for energy efficiency at the application level is still somewhat nascent. As the world moves toward green technologies and consumer demand for longer battery life in mobile devices increases, the demand for higher performance and new usage models will also continue to grow. Energy efficiency will be crucial for the computing industry in the future both to increase battery life for mobile platforms and to reduce energy expenses for desktop and server platforms. Software behavior can have a significant effect on platform power consumption and battery life. Modern processors and platforms have many energy-saving features, particularly for performance and the ability to enter low-power states when idle. Software should work in harmony with these features. To get the most benefit, developers should do the following:

■ Take advantage of performance features by emphasizing computational efficiency.

■ Be frugal with data movement to improve data efficiency.

■ Implement intelligent application behaviors by exploiting context awareness.

■ Seriously consider the impact of software at idle to improve idle efficiency.

There are many free tools from Intel and others to help you get started. Even small improvements when amplified across millions of systems can make a dramatic difference.

Chapter **6**

Idle Efficiency

They are not only idle who do nothing, but they are idle also who might be better employed.

—Socrates

Idle efficiency is absolutely critical for achieving overall platform power efficiency. Typically, platforms should be first optimized for their idle power consumption, which is the amount of power that is consumed when no user-interactive activity is occurring. Idle power consumption serves as the basis for power consumption across all other scenarios, such as DVD playback, productivity, media creation, or gaming. Therefore, reducing the idle power consumption improves the power consumption of all other system scenarios. The amount of processor activity directly correlates to processor and platform power consumption. Best-in-class systems should have total idle processor usage of less than 2 percent. However, total processor usage is not the only important metric for reducing idle power consumption. The duration of idle time between interrupts or platform break events is also important. Modern processors and chipsets achieve extremely low power consumption by transitioning into a low-power idle state during periods of idle time. However, they can enter low-power idle states only if the duration of the idle time is sufficient compared to the power and latency of entering and exiting the low-power idle state.

Idle power for mobile platforms is defined as the power a platform consumes when the system is running in the ACPI S0 state, and software applications and services may be running but are not actively executing workloads and there is minimal background activity. Usage analysis has shown that a typical mobile platform in ACPI S0 working state is typically idle for about 90–95 percent of the time as measured by the CPU C0 state residency. Figure 6.1 shows an example power profile of a mobile system over a period of time with a typical run of an office productivity benchmark.

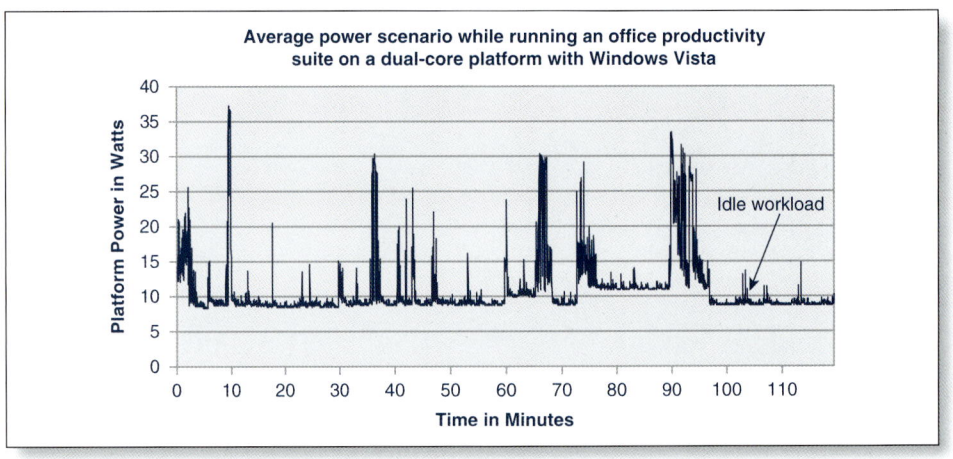

Figure 6.1 Typical Mobile Platform Power Profile in ACPI S0 State

Since a mobile platform predominantly resides in the idle state, lowering the platform idle power consumption leads to significant increase in battery life. This also benefits the average power scenarios and helps all but the most compute intensive workloads.

Improving Idle Efficiency: Deep C-State Residency

One of the key requirements for idle efficiency is to keep the platform in the deeper C-state for as long as possible. For a platform in idle state, the residency in the deepest C-state should be more than 90 percent. If the residency in C0 active state is less than 5 percent but still the deepest C-state residency is significantly lower than 95 percent, then it indicates the fact that hardware is doing automatic demotion because of extremely high C-state transitions caused by that process or module.

Also, for proper idle behavior, the residency in C0 active state should be less than 5 percent. One reason for higher C0 residency can be high activity caused by the process or drivers at idle causing the CPU to do work when the system is idle. High C0 residency may also be attributed to the bus master device making constant memory access. The CPU needs to wake up to C2 state in order to respond to these memory access requests. Figure 6.2 shows an example from a browser application exhibiting such behavior (Sabharwal, 2010).

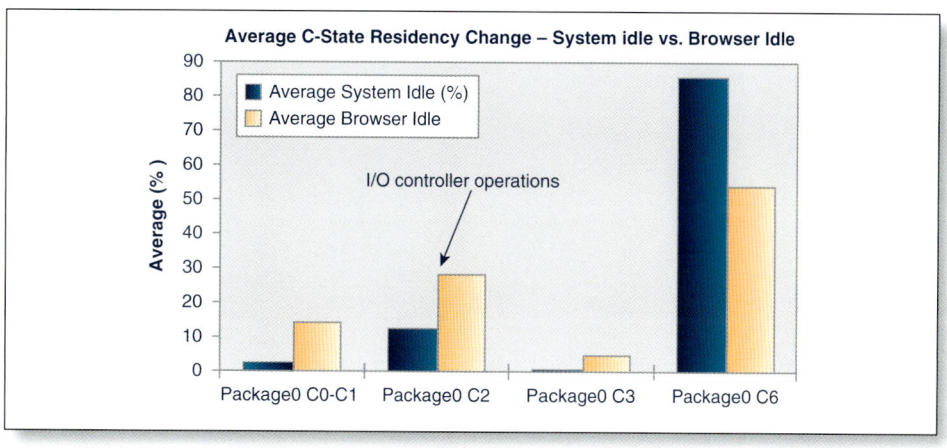

Figure 6.2 C-State Profile for Browser Application Showing High C2 Residency

The deeper power saving state comes with longer latency. So, the software workloads with tolerance to higher response time give the maximum window of platform power-down opportunity. Figure 6.3 illustrates the power consumed in different system states versus the latency for the system to come out of that state.

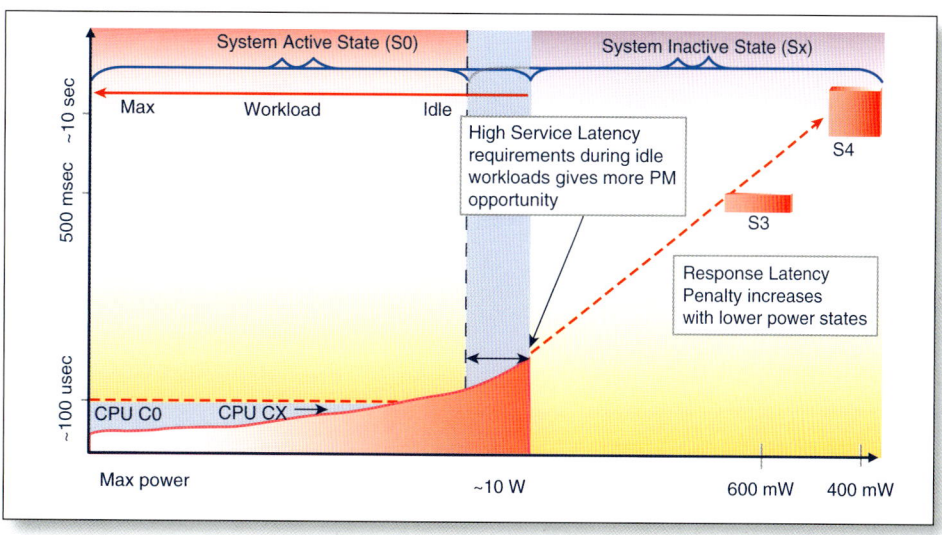

Figure 6.3 System Power Consumption versus Exit Latency

Application Software Impact to C-State Transition

Although C-state transitions are controlled by the operating system and application programs don't have any direct control over them, the behavior of application programs can have a big influence on how effectively C-states are used. Application programs primarily impact the frequency of C-state transitions. When a running thread terminates or blocks and no other thread is scheduled for the particular logical CPU, that CPU enters a lower power C-state and stays in that state until a ready thread is scheduled to execute on that CPU. There are many reasons why a running thread blocks, a common reason being the wait for external events (I/O completion, signal from other thread, and so on). Reducing the frequency of waiting for these events will help reduce C-state transitions. It is important to be aware that some OS APIs use remote procedure calls (RPCs), which block the thread. In the case of the Windows OS, Service Control APIs like QueryServiceConfig and Event Logging APIs like ReadEventLog are examples of APIs using RPCs.

The Impact of Excessive C-State Transitions: A Case Study

Software must aim to keep the number of C-state transitions as low as possible. Frequent C-state transitions from idle to active are not energy-efficient. Activity must be coalesced whenever possible to allow for higher C-state residencies.

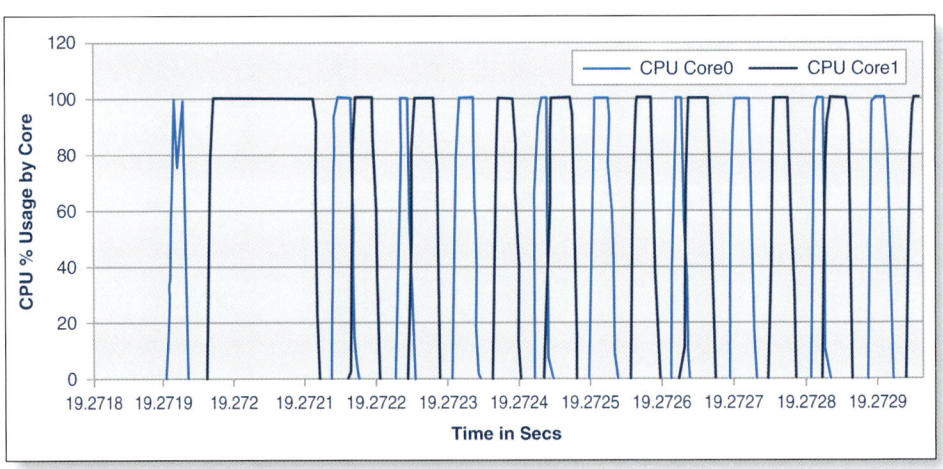

Figure 6.4   Frequent Inter-Processor Interrupt and C-State Transitions

Figure 6.4 shows a single-threaded application that has two processes that communicate frequently with each other while one process waits on the other process completion. Each process runs for a very small duration (approximately 50 µs). In a multi-core system, when these two processes are scheduled on two different cores, the communication between these two processes generates an Inter-Processor Interrupt (IPI). While one process is waiting for the other to complete, the core goes into a lower power C-state. Figure 6.5 shows the power impact of such behavior.

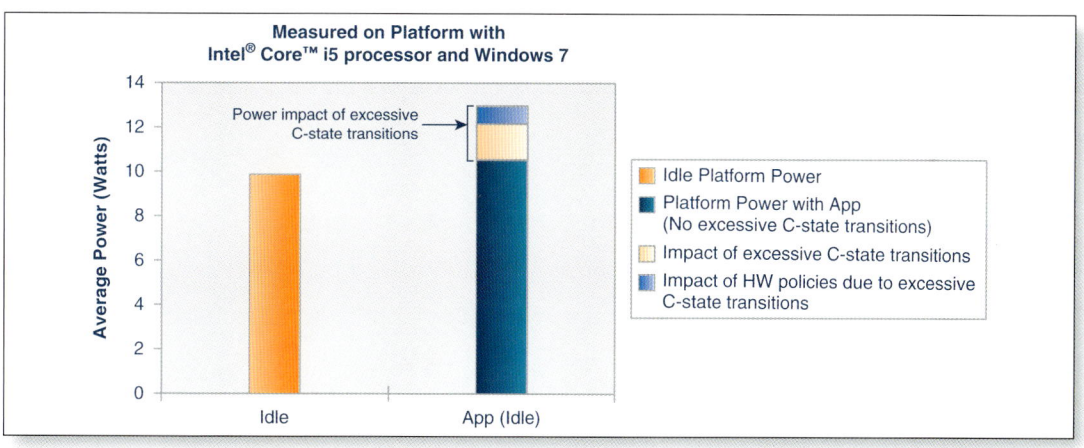

Figure 6.5   Power Impact of Excessive C-State Transitions

This sort of frequent C-state transition impacts power consumption in two ways:

■ Energy requirements to enter/exit C-state are not trivial. When the C0 (active) duration is very small, the latency to transition in and out of the C-states in comparison is appreciable and may result in net energy loss.

■ A hardware policy may demote the C-state to a lighter state based on heuristics. Even if the frequent C-state transition behavior occurs for only 2 to 3 milliseconds (ms) in a 15.6-ms window, the hardware polices may either demote the core C-state or reopen package-level cache which will impact power for the remaining 12 to 13 ms of idle period.

One way for applications and services to reduce C-state transitions is to avoid splitting a task between processes/threads unless parallel execution can occur.

If it is necessary that a task be split between processes, then coalesce work so that the number of C-state transitions can be reduced. Applications and services should also coalesce activity whenever possible to increase idle period residency.

Idle Efficiency: Hardware Considerations

This section explains the hardware level considerations, which are among the most important considerations in improving overall platform idle efficiency. These include different devices such as PCIe, USB, and so on. Frequent device activity can have a significant impact on power. Figure 6.6 shows the impact of device activity on platform power.

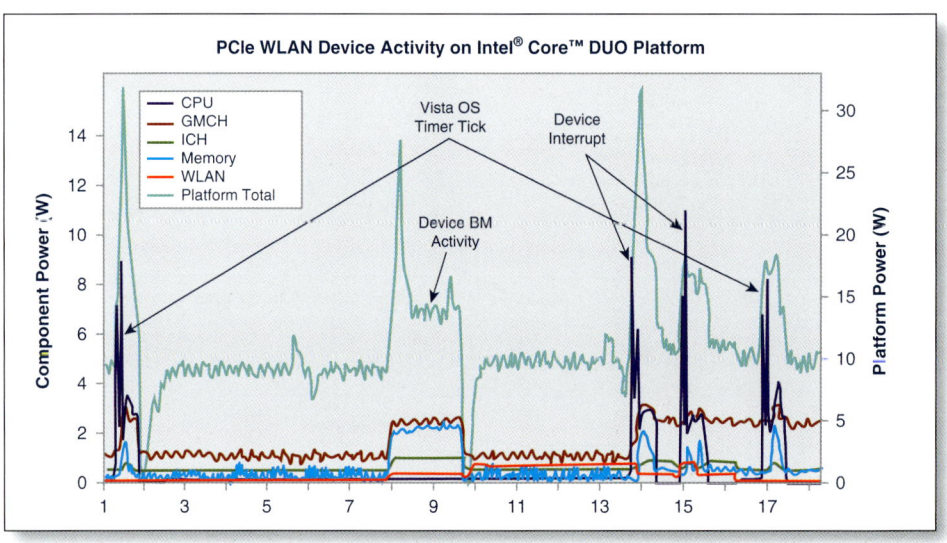

Figure 6.6   Power Spikes Caused by Device Activity

PCIe Link Power and Bus Traffic Alignment at Idle

PCI Express (PCIe) devices must support Active State Power Management (ASPM). ASPM lets the system incrementally reduce power to serial links in a PCIe fabric as the link becomes less active. The L0 link state has lower resume latency and is applicable to workloads with short intervals of idle periods whereas the L1 state has higher resume latency and is applicable for workloads with longer idle periods. Some of the common issues involving PCIe links involve the L0/L1 state not being enabled even though the hardware supports it. The other common issue is low L0s and L1 residency due to activity or device ASPM policy.

Another issue with PCIe related to power is the PCIe traffic alignment. Typically devices moving data with transaction gaps of less than 7 µs cause link and processor power state thrashing. In order to avoid thrashing, data should be buffered in the device; this will reduce host memory access. For example, in case of a 20-Mbps data rate, only 2.5 Kb of memory is needed for 1-ms buffering and this will maximize energy efficiency. To save power, it's recommended to align the bus master activity into bursts to extend idle periods on the platform. Figure 6.7 shows one example of the PCIe bus traffic alignment to increase idle periods.

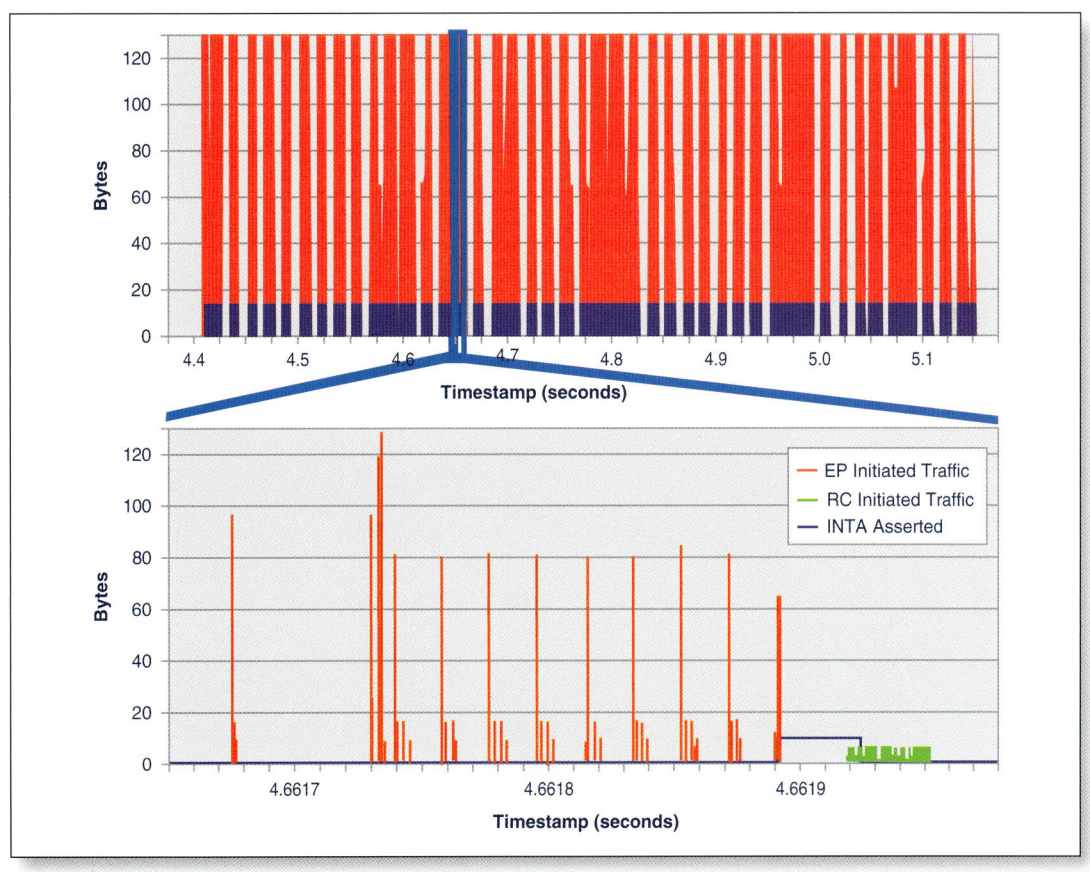

Figure 6.7   PCIe Bus Traffic Alignment (Farag, 2008)

USB Device

When a USB wireless radio is in the working state, the radio device consumes power, as does the USB controller into which it is connected. A USB device also increases the power consumption of the processor when it is active, because of frequent direct memory access (DMA) transactions by the USB host controller. However, if the device supports selective suspend functionality, the USB device can be turned off when the radio is not in use. Turning off the USB device alleviates the increased power consumption, helping to reduce overall system power consumption. When the platform is idle, the USB host controller should have 100-percent selective suspend duration. Selective suspend lets an idle device be placed into a suspend state without affecting other devices that are connected to the same hub or—in the case of a multifunction device—without affecting the other functions in the device. After all devices or functions are suspended, the entire hub or multifunction device can be powered down. The USB selective suspend callback function should synchronously power down the device, as follows:

1. If the device can wake itself, the callback arms the device for wake from S0.

2. The callback requests a D*x* IRP and sends it to the top of the stack.

3. When the parent driver receives the D*x* IRP, it powers down the device.

4. After the device has transitioned to D*x*, the USB selective suspend callback function returns.

5. After the device returns to D0, the parent driver completes the USB selective suspend request as successful.

The various modes of USB data transfers are:

■   *Bulk.* It's used to move large amounts of data

■   *Interrupt.* This mode is used to convey human perceptible data or change in status.

■   *Isochronous.* This is used to move a fixed amount of bandwidth within one negotiated constraint.

Two of the most common power issues with USB are:

1. Various transfers can create memory access as frequently as every 8 to 16 μs, preventing the platform from going to the idle state.

2. The USB link is not able to go into selective suspend state.

The Intel Battery Life Analyzer tool can be used to identify some of these issues by taking following steps:

■ Looking at the selective suspend duration of each host controller

■ Identifying the host controller with less than 100-percent selective suspend

■ Checking selective suspend duration of each device or hub under that controller

■ Identifying which device is preventing the host controller from staying in selective suspend state

■ For the device identified in the previous step, looking at the active duration of periodic and asynchronous schedules to get an idea of what kind of activity that particular device is making

Also during idle, USB 2.0 I/O buffers can be powered down. USB is a broadcast bus, hence all the connected links that are not in suspend mode receive the same data stream. Because of this, the transmit buffers may be powered down globally while any other port is receiving and similarly the receivers may be powered down selectively when a given port is not receiving. Furthermore, both transmitters and receivers may be powered down during dynamic idle conditions. This functionality saves considerable power on the high speed current sources (~50 mW per port) when idle and only delivering Start of Frame (SOF). Figure 6.8 illustrates this.

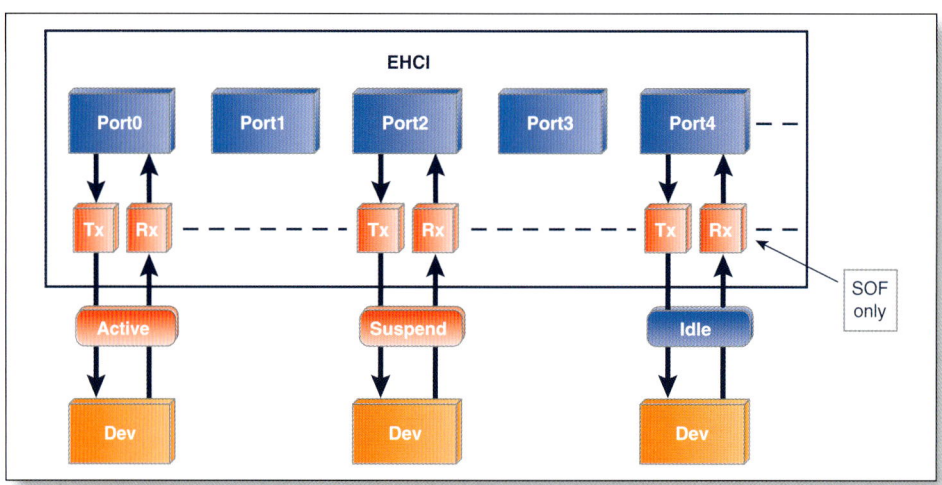

Figure 6.8   USB 2.0 I/O Buffer Power Down (Farag, 2008)

Hard Disk Spin Down

The HDD standby state is the lowest power mode where HDD dissipates the least energy controlled by OS entry. At idle, the disk should be spun down most of the time. In certain scenarios, software components can increase the power consumption of disk devices by frequently writing or reading file or registry data. Frequent intermittent accesses not only preclude the drive from going to standby (spin-down), it also precludes it from going to low power idle state. Table 6.1 shows the average power consumed by HDD in different power saving modes.

Table 6.1   HDD Power Saving Modes

State	Power	Entry	Note
Standby	~0.1 W	OS Control	Spin down
Low Power Idle	~0.6 W	Automatic after ~10 seconds	Head unloaded
Active Idle	~0.9 W	Automatic after <1 second	Servo, R/W circuit off
Performance Idle	~1.8 W	After command completion	No power saving

All disks should support idle detection and low-power states. Disk idle detection is key to achieving maximum portable computer battery life because the difference in power consumption between the spin-up and spin-down states might be 500 mW or more on portable computer form-factor disk devices. The Windows power manager uses disk activity, power policy, and system power source (AC/DC) to determine when to spin down and spin up a disk. Power policy configures the time interval between the last disk access and spin-down of the device as well as any amount of disk activity that should be ignored to be more aggressive in entering the spin-down state. For maximum power savings on portable platforms, the disk idle detection timeout should be reduced from the default value of 30 or 60 minutes. To further favor power savings, the disk burst ignore threshold should be set to a nonzero value between 15 and 60 seconds. In determining timeout values, considerations should be made that:

■ Minimum idle timeout is 30 seconds.

■ Spinning down the disk for less than 20 seconds uses more energy than keeping the drive spun up.

Periodic writes and indirect operations such as file creates, file extends, and registry writes can prevent the disk from spinning down. PerfMon supports counters that can be useful in measuring disk idle times and burst intervals.

Graphics Devices

For Graphics devices, their performance states should be tightly coupled with the Windows power policy. For idle power scenarios, the graphics device idle power can be reduced by applying techniques such as reducing the refresh rate, scaling the GPU core voltage and frequency lower etc. The white paper Mobile Battery Life Solutions for Windows 7 (Microsoft, 2009, Mobile) provides a complete description of how Windows 7 integrates display brightness into the power policy, associating different brightness-level preferences associated with different power schemes.

Idle Efficiency: System Level Considerations

This section discusses the system-level considerations, including driver and OS policies that impact idle power efficiency.

Driver Activity

It has been a common observation that the battery life on a system can change drastically with a single driver update. Drivers that use excessive system resources, such as consuming CPU time in polling loops or servicing unnecessary interrupts, can degrade overall battery life. To maximize idle efficiency, all devices and their drivers should support runtime idle detection. This means that the device automatically turns off or enters a low-power mode when it is inactive and the system is operational. Drivers generate the bulk of interrupt activity including interrupt service routines (ISRs) and deferred procedure calls (DPCs). ISRs usually happen when the CPU is idle and hence have the highest impact on platform power. DPCs are usually executed on the same logical CPU as ISRs when the CPU is already active and so they don't have as much impact on power as ISRs. At idle, ISR activity with a high number of calls/ second should be checked. Table 6.2 captures the recommended frequency of ISR activity coming from drivers at idle.

Table 6.2　Recommended Driver Activity at Idle

Driver	Interrupt Source	Typical Interrupts/Second at Idle
ACPI.sys	Motherboard	<1
dxgkrnl.sys	Graphics	<10 (depends on activity)
hal.dll	Timer Tick	64
i8042prt.sys	PS/2 KB/Mouse	0
iaStor.sys msahci.sys	SATA (HDD/DVD)	<10 (depends on activity)
ndis.sys	Network (GbE/Wi-Fi)	<40 (Wi-Fi, associated, no traffic)
USBPORT.SYS	USB (UHCI/EHCI)	0

Driver software activity can prevent the processor from entering a low-power idle state (C-state). Drivers should avoid unnecessary activity and optimize for power by using the following guidelines:

■ Implement performance optimizations, such as using fewer processor cycles to perform a specific task.

■ Avoid stalling the processor at a high interrupt request level (IRQL).

Use `KeDelayExecutionThread` wherever required to wait on the hardware to complete an operation.

■ Minimize the use of polling. If possible, use an interrupt instead.

■ If the driver must poll, consider implementing timers by using the new timer coalescing DDIs in Windows 7, which have been discussed in this chapter. Timer coalescing lets the Windows kernel align timer expiration events to improve energy efficiency.

Drivers should support runtime idle detection (also called S0 idle) so that they can transition their idle devices to a lower power state while the system is in the On (ACPI S0) state. Techniques for implementing runtime idle detection vary based on the driver model and the type of device:

■ Drivers for USB devices can use USB selective suspend regardless of the driver model.

■ Kernel-mode driver framework (KMDF) drivers for other device types can use framework mechanisms.

■ User-mode driver framework (UMDF) drivers for other device types must rely on the kernel-mode device stack to manage idle detection, power-down on idle, and wake.

■ Windows Driver Model (WDM) drivers can either rely on the Windows power manager to perform idle detection and issue device power state (Dx) I/O request packets (IRPs) to change the device power state or implement their own idle-detection code that sends Dx IRPs.

All drivers should integrate device power policy with the Windows power policy. If the device supports one or more device performance states—that is, a lower power/lower performance mode—the driver should integrate the policy for entering those states with system power policy:

■ Drivers should enable the most conservative power savings by default when they are running on DC power.

■ If possible, drivers should implement adaptive behaviors and should enable them by default for the Balanced power scheme for both AC and DC power.

Impact of OS Power Policy

Power policy refers to the OS infrastructure that helps configuration of hardware platform and devices for power savings and extended battery life. After hardware platform and device components have been selected for a system, power policy can be used to tailor that system to favor power savings at idle. Power policy includes basic system power-management settings such as the display and sleep idle timeouts. Advanced configuration options are provided for processor power management (PPM), USB selective suspend, and wireless network adapter power modes. Power policy can also contain configuration options for devices and applications that are added to the system, including vendor-specific power settings for the graphics device.

In Windows 7, power policy settings can be configured by using the PowerCfg utility (more details on this utility can be found in Chapter 7), which provides command-line access to power policy settings, power plans, and other power-management information. PowerCfg can customize settings within a specific power plan or create entirely new power plans for the system. The basic and advanced power policy settings should be customized properly for idle power efficiency. The following example uses the PowerCfg command-line tool to display the definition of the Display Idle Timeout power setting, which configures the period of inactivity before Windows automatically shuts down the system display:

```
C:\>powercfg /q SCHEME_CURRENT SUB_VIDEO
Power Scheme GUID: 381b4222-f694-41f0-9685-ff5bb260df2e
(Balanced)
  Subgroup GUID: 7516b95f-f776-4464-8c53-06167f40cc99  (Display)
    Power Setting GUID: 3c0bc021-c8a8-4e07-a973-6b14cbcb2b7e
    (Turn off display after)
      Minimum Possible Setting: 0x00000000
      Maximum Possible Setting: 0xffffffff
      Possible Settings increment: 0x00000001
      Possible Settings units: Seconds
    Current AC Power Setting Index: 0x0000012c
    Current DC Power Setting Index: 0x0000012c
```

PowerCfg defines aliases for common power-related GUIDs. In the preceding example, SCHEME_CURRENT is an alias that identifies the current active power plan, instead of specifying the full GUID of the active power plan. Similarly, SUB_VIDEO is an alias for the GUID of the video settings subgroup.

Display Idle Timeout Policy

On a modern portable computer, the attached display is the largest power consumer and requires up to 40 percent of the overall system power-consumption budget. The display idle timeout lets Windows turn off the attached display after a period of user inactivity. The display consumes very little power when it is turned off. The use of a short display idle timeout can extend the usable portable computer battery life by a significant amount. By default, Windows configures the display idle timeout to a moderately short value for portable and desktop systems, 10 minutes when connected to AC power and 5 minutes on DC. In a working paper entitled *Mobile Battery Life Solutions for Windows 7* (see Microsoft, 2009, Mobile), the authors provide the details to configure how long the computer is inactive before the display turns off using the PowerCfg alias VIDEOIDLE.

Display Brightness Policy

To reduce the idle power consumption of the attached display in a portable computer when the display is being used, the most effective way is to reduce its brightness. In LCD displays, the backlight consumes the majority of the display's power. Reducing display brightness is typically a more favorable user experience than an aggressive display idle timeout. Windows can control the brightness of the attached display in a portable computer if the display driver or system BIOS has been properly configured to support operating system control of display brightness. If the system supports brightness control within Windows, the power policy can specify:

- A default brightness setting for AC and DC power.

- A user inactivity timeout, after which Windows automatically reduces the brightness of the display.

- The brightness level when the display is dimmed due to user inactivity.

In *Mobile Battery Life Solutions for Windows 7* (Microsoft, 2009, Mobile) you will discover that the brightness level is expressed as a percentage of maximum brightness with the default being 100% on AC power and 40% when on DC. The user inactivity timeout for the brightness level defaults to 5 minutes on AC and 2 minutes on DC. Finally, the default brightness level when the display is dimmed is 30% for both AC and DC.

802.11 Wireless Power-Save Mode Policy

In modern portable computer platforms, 802.11 wireless devices are almost ubiquitous, and these devices incorporate power-management capabilities. Windows Vista and later versions provide native support for configuring the power-save mode of 802.11 wireless network adapters in power policy. By default, Windows configures the 802.11 power-save mode to Medium Power Savings for DC power and Maximum Performance for AC power. Beginning with Windows 7, Windows automatically detects whether the connected access point is compatible with the wireless multimedia (WMM) Power Save mode. If the access point is not compatible with power savings, Windows automatically configures the adapter to use Maximum Performance, regardless of the configured power savings policy. However, when Windows automatically uses Maximum Performance, the power policy is not updated in the Control Panel Power Options Advanced Settings. This configuration enables seamless connectivity by default and automatic power savings when connected to compatible access points. *Mobile Battery Life Solutions for Windows 7* (Microsoft, 2009, Mobile) provides a description of the power-save modes and related power policy settings including modes for maximum performance and low, medium, and high power save modes.

Idle Efficiency: Periodic Activity and Timer Coalescing

System power consumption and energy efficiency are heavily influenced by the amount of processor activity, including periodic activity from applications and device drivers. Modern processors can reduce their power consumption by entering into a low-power idle state during the periods of idle time between executing instructions for software activity. However, many processor power management technologies require a minimum amount of idle time to realize a net power savings. If the processor is idle for only very short periods of time, the power required to enter and exit the low-power state can be greater than the power saved. Periodic software activity and software timers heavily influence the amount of processor idle time and the duration of the idle periods. A long, uninterrupted idle period is the key for platform power efficiency. Figure 6.9 shows the impact of periodic software activity on overall platform power. A 10-percent increase in CPU utilization because of process activity results in an approximately 57-percent increase in overall platform power.

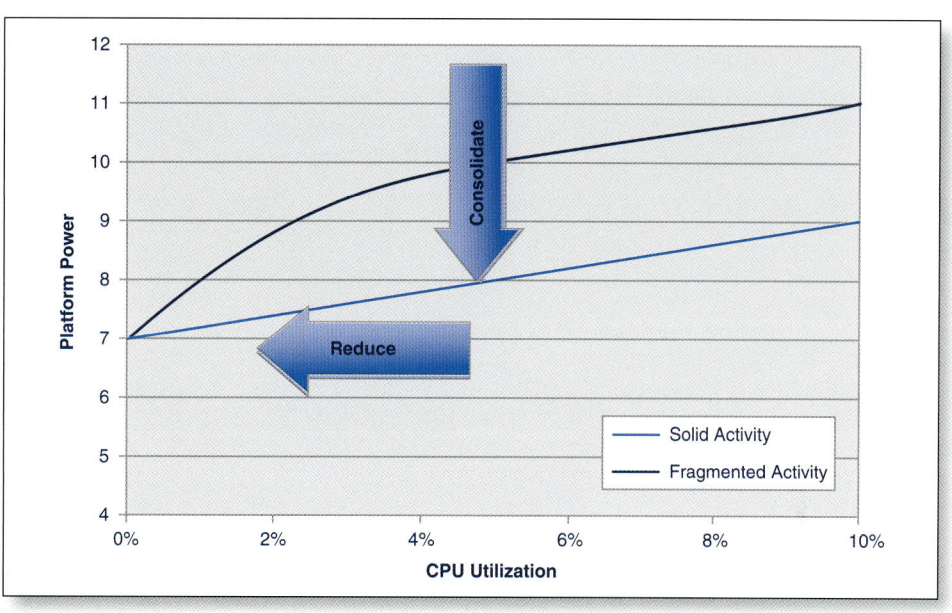

Figure 6.9   Platform Power versus CPU Utilization

Reducing Power Consumption with Timer Coalescing

Windows timer coalescing helps increase the duration of idle periods by combining different software timer expirations so that they all occur on a single timer interrupt. Software applications should minimize the generation of periodic activities. If it is possible, these periodic activities should be changed to event-driven or interrupt-based designs. However, if periodic activity is required, the code should use timer coalescing to help enable the Windows kernel to more efficiently expire the associated timer. Timer coalescing can help increase the average idle period of system processors by allowing the Windows kernel to combine periodic software timer activity to increase the average idle period.

For a thorough review of Windows timer coalescing, see Microsoft's white paper on Timers, Timer Resolution, and Development of Efficient Code (Microsoft, 2010, Timer).

Idle Efficiency: OS Timer Resolution

The default system-wide timer resolution in Windows is 15.6 ms, which means that every 15.6 ms the operating system receives a clock interrupt from the system timer hardware. When the clock interrupt fires, Windows performs two main actions: it updates the timer tick count if a full tick has elapsed, and it checks whether a scheduled timer object has expired. A timer tick is an abstract notion of elapsed time that Windows uses to consistently track the time of day and thread quantum times. By default, the clock interrupt and timer tick are the same, but Windows or an application can change the clock interrupt period.

Many applications call `timeBeginPeriod` with a value of 1 to increase the timer resolution to the maximum of 1 ms to support graphical animations, audio playback, or video playback. This not only increases the timer resolution for the application to 1 ms, but also affects the global system timer resolution, because Windows uses at least the highest resolution (that is, the lowest interval) that any application requests. Therefore, if only one application requests a timer resolution of 1 ms, the system timer sets the interval (also called the "system timer tick") to at least 1 ms. Generally, setting the timer to a value less than 10 ms can negatively affect battery life. Modern processors and chipsets, particularly in portable platforms, use the idle time between system timer intervals to reduce system power consumption. Various processor and chipset components are placed into low-power idle states between timer intervals. However, these low-power idle states are often ineffective at lowering system power consumption when the system timer interval is less than 10 ms.

If the system timer interval is decreased to less than 10 ms—including when an application calls `timeBeginPeriod` with a resolution of 1 ms—the low-power idle states are ineffective at reducing system power consumption and system battery life suffers. System battery life might be reduced as much as 25 percent, depending on the hardware platform. This is because the transitions to and from low-power states incur an energy cost. Therefore, entering and exiting low power states without spending a minimum amount of time in the low-power states may be more costly than if the system simply remained in the high-power state.

Figure 6.10 shows the impact of increasing periodic timer resolution on platform power.

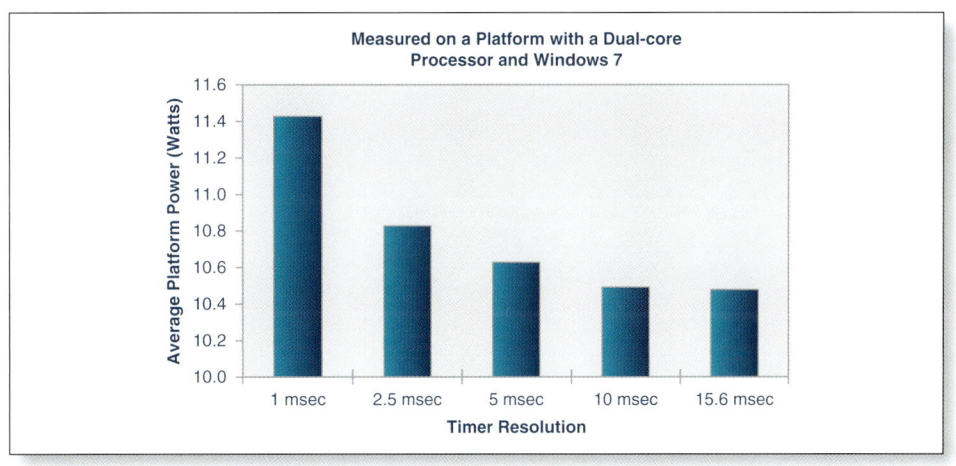

Figure 6.10 Power Impact of Increasing Periodic Timer Resolution

The PowerCfg utility with the /energy option can be used to determine whether the application increases the platform timer resolution. PowerCfg should be run while the application is running. The resulting energy report can be analyzed to see if the application changed the platform timer resolution as well as the call stack for the request. The report lists the instances of increased platform timer resolution and indicates whether the process hosting the application increased the timer resolution. More details on this can be found in Chapter 7.

It is important that application developers understand the power impact of using these high resolution timers and that they set it to the lowest resolution that meets the performance requirements of the application for the specific platform. Applications and services should use the lowest timer resolution possible that meets the performance requirements of the application. If the application requires a high-resolution periodic timer, increase the timer resolution only when the application is active. Software applications should minimize the use of APIs that shorten the timer period. In Windows, this includes, but is not limited to, timeBeginPeriod Multimedia Timer API and NtSetTimerResolution low-level API. Instead they should use the new timer coalescing API supported by the OS such as SetWaitableTimerEx (API) and

KeSetCoalescableTimer (DDI), which have been discussed extensively in the earlier sections of this chapter. Here are some further recommendations:

■ If your application must use a high-resolution periodic timer, enable the periodic timer only while the required functionality is active. For example, if the high-resolution periodic timer is required for animation, disable the periodic timer when the animation is complete.

■ If your application must use a high-resolution periodic timer, consider disabling use of the periodic timer and associated functionality when a Power Saver power plan is active or when the system is running on battery power.

Idle Efficiency: Background Activity

Frequent periodic background activity increases overall system power consumption. It impacts both the processor and chipset power. Long running infrequent events also prevents the system from idling to sleep. Background activity on the macro scale (minutes, hours) such as disk defragmentation, antivirus scans, and so on, also consume significant amounts of power. Windows 7 has introduced a unified background process manager (UBPM) to minimize the power impact from background activities. UBPM drives scheduling of services and scheduled tasks and is transparent to users, IT professionals, and existing APIs. It enables trigger start services. For instance, many background services are configured to start automatically and wait for rare events. UBPM enables the trigger-start services based on environmental changes instead. Some of the environmental change activities include device arrival/removal, IP address change, and domain join. An example of a trigger start service includes starting Bluetooth[†] services only when the Bluetooth radio is currently attached. Some of the other Windows 7 improvements to minimize frequent idle activity include:

■ Elimination of TCP DPC timer on every system timer interrupt

■ Reduction in frequency of USB driver maintenance timers

■ Intelligent timer tick distribution

■ Timer coalescing

Idle Efficiency: A Case Study

The main focus of this case study is to accurately characterize the battery life impact of applications during their "idle" state (more details in Sabharwal, 2011). Application "idle" state is defined as a state where the application is launched (login is done if needed for connected applications). For applications that require network connectivity, power measurement is done while connected to the Internet. For the experiment, we randomly selected applications in daily use by typical industry users from the following categories:

- Media playback

- Messenger/chat

- Browser

- Antivirus

To get started, we made the following setting changes to a fresh installation of Windows 7 to eliminate certain effects of overhead in the power measurements:

- Disabled screensaver to eliminate variability because of screen changes

- Disabled display dimming to avoid variability in display power usage

- Disabled system protection, auto-backup, and auto-update features to avoid these services running in the background

- Disabled scheduled disk defragmentation to avoid extraneous power usage from this source

- Stopped the Windows Search Indexer to eliminate that source of run-to-run variability

- Disabled firewall and Windows Defender to eliminate those sources of overhead

For the case study, we selected top applications in the current consumer market from different categories and measured total power above baseline using the Fluke NetDAQ instrument. Figure 6.11 shows the percentage increase of total platform power over "system idle" (total platform power with a fresh Windows install). The Y-axis shows the percentage of power increase, while the X-axis shows different application categories. For example, if system idle is 7 watts and a media application takes 30 percent of power over baseline, we can surmise that this media application consumes 2.1 watts of power at "idle." Comparing this with Figure 6.12, we can interpret that the media application decreases system battery life at "idle" by approximately 75 minutes while not "active," a clearly significant impact. From this case study, it is evident just how big an impact "idle" software can have on battery life. As discussed in earlier chapters and some of the later chapters, small changes by developers can extend the battery life of target systems.

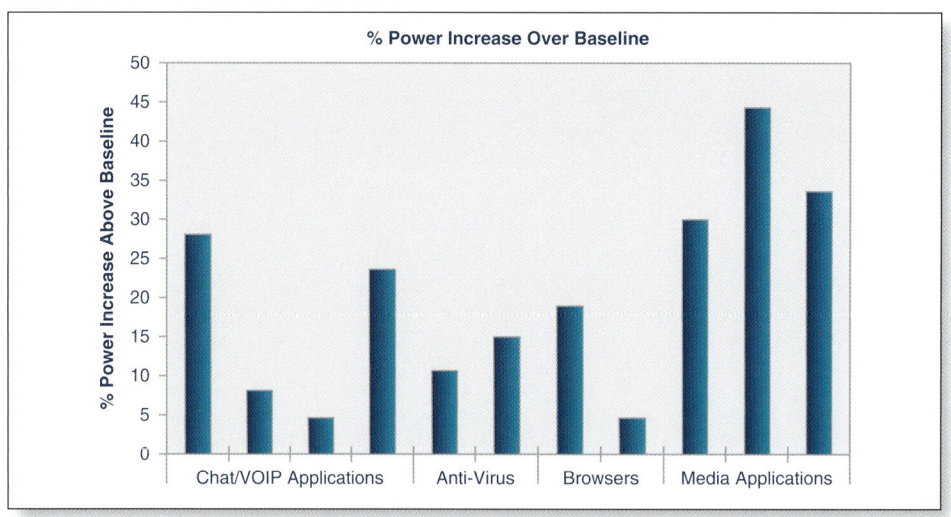

Figure 6.11 Idle Power Analysis of Consumer Client Applications

By adopting energy aware computing principles, developers code can help bring the power level of "application idle" closer to that of "platform idle."

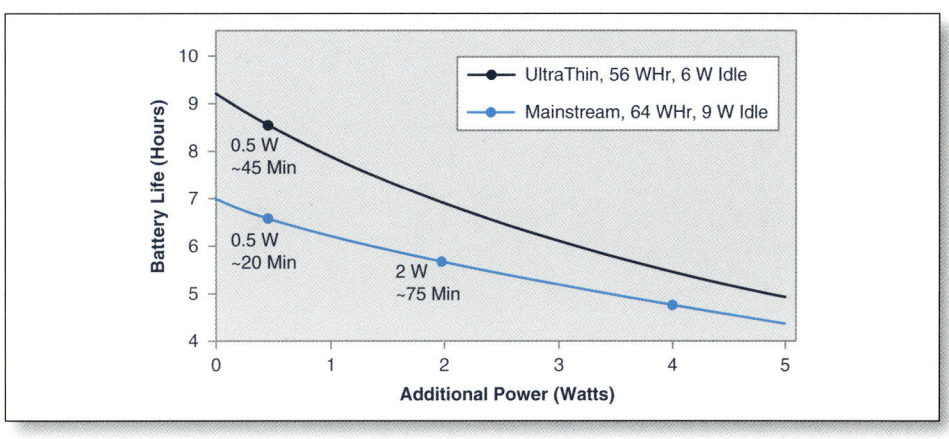

Figure 6.12 Battery Life Impact of Platform Power increase

Chapter 7

Evaluating and Measuring Software Impact to Platform Power

Measurement is the first step that leads to control and eventually to improvement. If you can't measure something, you can't understand it. If you can't understand it, you can't control it. If you can't control it, you can't improve it.

—Dr. H. James Harrington

Software plays an important role in platform energy efficiency. Platform hardware components are being aggressively designed to reduce power consumption when idle. Software must not preclude residency in low power states. Energy-efficient applications, when idle, should have minimum impact on platform power consumption. Ideally, an application at idle should consume no energy. In this chapter, a step-by-step methodology is introduced to improve software energy efficiency. In this methodology, platform power is first measured and battery lifetime is estimated. Then, power tools are used to analyze the software behavior at various angles to identify potential issues. And, finally, each issue is discussed and solved by applying the suggestions from the power tools. This metrology is designed to help people to debug power issues in order to improve software energy efficiency in a standard and convenient way.

Getting Started with Energy Measurements

To improve the energy efficiency of application software and to optimize power in mobile platforms, it is very important to know the power consumed by different hardware functional units in watts, which helps in improving processor architecture, platform technologies, and software. Various tools exist to provide a high-level estimate of the power consumed by a mobile platform. While these tools may be sufficient in understanding the high-level power consumption of particular platform, they do not provide fine-grained details of specific components. The more accurate and direct method to measure power is to use data acquisition (DAQ) tools where specific hardware components are instrumented and more granular power measurement can be logged. This method uses an instrumented platform for actual power measurement.

Fluke NetDAQ† (Networked Data Acquisition Unit)

NetDAQ is used to measure platform power consumption while transmitting data and running different applications on the system. Each NetDAQ has twenty channels that may be programmed individually to perform virtually any signal conditioning function the user requires. NetDAQ logger software for Windows† is a configuration and data management program for the NetDAQ systems.

Test Setup

The target PC has a special motherboard with built-in sense resistors. For each target component (such as a CPU) all sense resistors are wired and soldered at both ends before being connected to a module attached to the NetDAQ unit.

The NetDAQ has modules that are attached with individual wires to the target PC with which it measures the current and voltage drop across the sense resistors. The NetDAQ is connected to the host PC via a crossover network cable as shown in Figure 7.1.

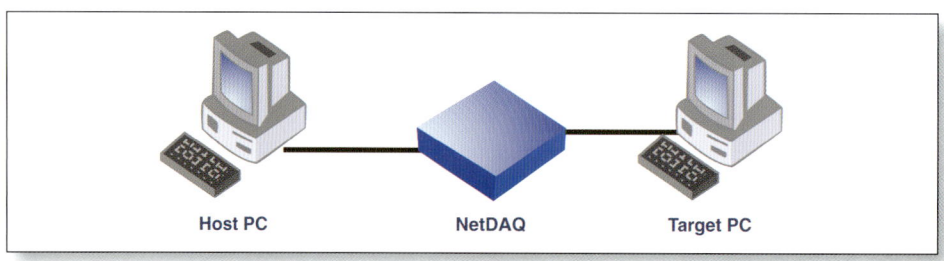

Host PC   NetDAQ   Target PC

Figure 7.1   NetDAQ Test Setup

The host PC can be any IA32 system running Windows and the NetDAQ logger. The logger collects the measured current and voltages and calculates the average power in watts (W). The sampling interval can be changed on the basis of individual analysis. This platform power measurement setup does not include the LCD.

Measuring Total System Power

The shunt resistor method is used to measure the platform power through the NetDAQ unit, as shown in Figure 7.2. We use the equation

$$P_{system} = V \times I$$

where V = voltage at input to the main system, I = Vs/Rs, and Vs = voltage drop across Rs. Therefore:

$$P_{system} = (V \times Vs)/Rs$$

$$P_{average} = \text{Average } P_{system} \text{ during testing}$$

$$\text{Estimated battery life} = \text{Battery capacity} / P_{average}$$

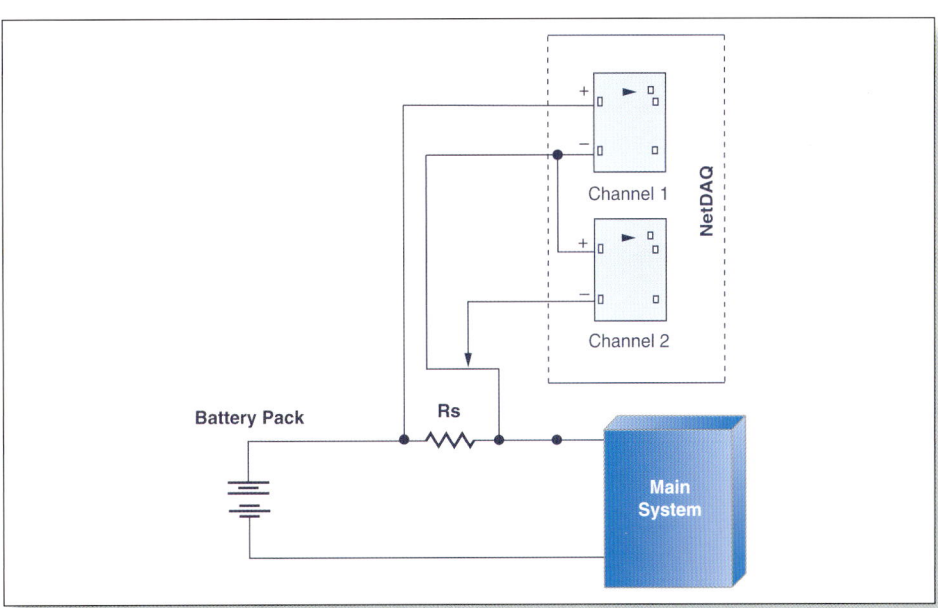

Figure 7.2   Shunt Resistor Method

Tools

Tools are a big part of any development platforms. The better your tools are, the easier it will be for more application developers to create powerful applications on top of any platform. Power tools discussed here help in diagnosing the energy problems with the applications and the system and hence provide a starting point towards creating energy-efficient applications and platforms.

Windows 7 PowerCfg

PowerCfg is a command line tool, shown in Figure 7.3, that lets users control the system's power-management settings. Users can employ PowerCfg to view or modify power plans and to detect common energy-efficiency problems when the system is idle. The command

```
powercfg /energy
```

provides an HTML report or checklist of problems based on a snapshot of the system energy consumption over a 60-second period. Users can detect power policies, sleep states that are supported in the system, USB devices that are not suspending, and applications that have increased the platform timer resolution. The data from a brief run of the tool might look like this:

```
powercfg -energy

Enabling tracing for 60 seconds…
Observing system behavior…
Analyzing trace data…
Analysis complete.

Energy efficiency problems were found.
21 Errors
17 Warnings
10 Informational
```

```
Administrator: C:\Windows\System32\cmd.exe

C:\Windows\system32>powercfg -Q
Power Scheme GUID: 381b4222-f694-41f0-9685-ff5bb260df2e  (Balanced)
  Subgroup GUID: fea3413e-7e05-4911-9a71-700331f1c294  (Settings belonging to no
 subgroup)
    Power Setting GUID: 0e796bdb-100d-47d6-a2d5-f7d2daa51f51  (Require a passwor
d on wakeup)
      Possible Setting Index: 000
      Possible Setting Friendly Name: No
      Possible Setting Index: 001
      Possible Setting Friendly Name: Yes
    Current AC Power Setting Index: 0x00000001
    Current DC Power Setting Index: 0x00000001

  Subgroup GUID: 0012ee47-9041-4b5d-9b77-535fba8b1442  (Hard disk)
    Power Setting GUID: 6738e2c4-e8a5-4a42-b16a-e040e769756e  (Turn off hard dis
k after)
      Minimum Possible Setting: 0x00000000
      Maximum Possible Setting: 0xffffffff
      Possible Settings increment: 0x00000001
      Possible Settings units: Seconds
    Current AC Power Setting Index: 0x000004b0
    Current DC Power Setting Index: 0x00000258

  Subgroup GUID: 0d7dbae2-4294-402a-ba8e-26777e8488cd  (Desktop background setti
ngs)
    Power Setting GUID: 309dce9b-bef4-4119-9921-a851fb12f0f4  (Slide show)
      Possible Setting Index: 000
      Possible Setting Friendly Name: Available
      Possible Setting Index: 001
      Possible Setting Friendly Name: Paused
    Current AC Power Setting Index: 0x00000000
    Current DC Power Setting Index: 0x00000001

  Subgroup GUID: 19cbb8fa-5279-450e-9fac-8a3d5fedd0c1  (Wireless Adapter Setting
s)
    Power Setting GUID: 12bbebe6-58d6-4636-95bb-3217ef867c1a  (Power Saving Mode
)
      Possible Setting Index: 000
      Possible Setting Friendly Name: Maximum Performance
      Possible Setting Index: 001
```

Figure 7.3   PowerCfg Command-Line Tool

Table 7.1 shows some of the issues which are detected by PowerCfg and their respective warning and error threshold levels. Using PowerCfg, typical diagnostics are generated and issues are reported regarding:

- Processor utilization: overall utilization, per-process utilization

- Power policy settings: idle timeouts, PPM configuration, Wireless Power Save mode

- Platform Timer Resolution requests

- Outstanding power requests (Display/Sleep/Away)

- Platform capabilities: sleep state availability, display dimming capability, Firmware validation problems, PCI Express ASPM status

- Battery capacity: battery static data, last full charge capacity/design capacity

- USB device selective suspend issues

Table 7.1   PowerCfg Detected Problems

Problem Area	Data Collected	Warning Threshold	Error Threshold
USB device selective suspend	Individual device suspend transitions % of time device was in suspend state	< 80% suspend time	< 50% suspend time
Power Policy settings	Idle timeouts (dim, displays, sleep) PPM configuration Power plan personality 802.11 Wireless Power Save	Idle timeouts < EnergyStar 4.0 Recommendations	Idle timeouts disabled
Processor utilization	Overall utilization Per-process utilization (any process over 0.1%) Top 3 module utilization in each process	Total utilization > 2%	Total utilization > 4%
Timer Resolution Requests	Current system timer interrupt period (example: 15.6 ms) Application with outstanding timer requests, request amount	None	Timer Interrupt period < 15.6 ms
Power Requests	Application with outstanding power requests (Display Sleep, Away Mode)	None	Each outstanding power request
Platform Capabilities	Sleep state availability Display dimming capacity Firmware validation problems PCI Express ASPM status	None	If any capability is disabled or missing
Battery Capacity	Battery static data (make, model, serial number, manufacture date) Last full charge capacity/design capacity	(Last Full Charge Capacity/Designed Capacity) < 50%	(last Full Charge Capacity/Designed Capacity) < 40%

Xperf

The xperf command-line tool is a part of the Windows Performance Toolkit and it is important for developers working on systemwide performance analysis. Xperf is capable of monitoring systemwide events in kernel for a period of time and generates reports for graphical review and for analysis. Specifically, xperf can be used to collect events and use them to correlate with system status, such as idle, video/audio playback, surfing, and so on, to diagnose performance issues.

Xperf tool provides the following features:

◼ ETW trace control

◼ ETW trace merging and enhancements by including other events

◼ Executable image and symbol identification

- Trace dump capabilities

- Support for post-processing by using actions

Xperf gives information of system events such as:

- Sampled profile

- Context switches

- DPCs and ISRs

- Disk I/O

- Registry/file accesses

- System configuration

Xperf generates a trace file that contains a wide range of OS performance analyses.

- All processes/threads

- User and kernel mode

- DPSs and ISRs

- Scheduling

- Disk and file I/O

- Memory

- Network

Xperf can identify system performance issues like responsiveness, high CPU usage, high Disk usage, and battery life issues.

This tool manages the end-to-end operations that are needed to generate a trace file for analysis. An overview of xperf is shown in Figure 7.4.

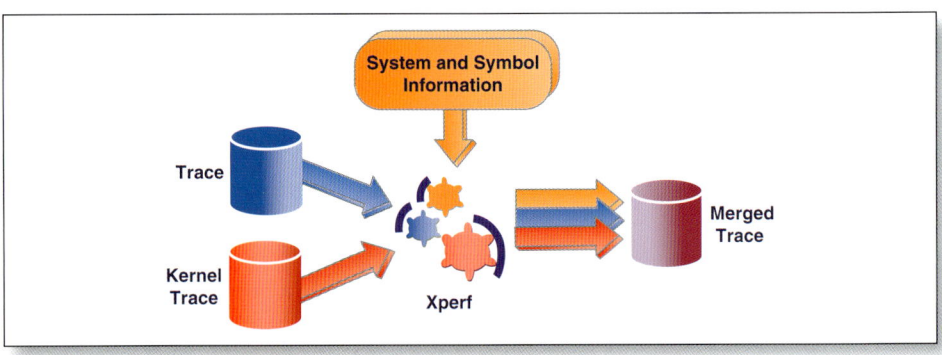

Figure 7.4　Xperf Tool Overview (Newton, 2008)

Xperf MSI files in the SDK installation can be located at:

```
SDKROOT\<path-goes-here>\xperf
```

To install the tools, users need to double-click the MSI file that corresponds to the target computer system's processor architecture. The installer adds the xperf installation path to the target system's global PATH environment variable. This makes the xperf command available from any command prompt window. Installation of the tools can be automated by using the built-in Windows command msiexec as follows:

```
msiexec /i xperf_x86.msi /quiet /l* i.txt INSTALLDIR=c:\xperf
```

Figure 7.5 shows a simple Xperf trace. To install Xperf and Xperfview, use these steps:

1. Install the tools from the appropriate MSI file for the target system's processor architecture x86 (32-bit), x64, or Itanium®-based. Default installation path can be used or an alternate path can be selected such

as, for example, `C:\xperf`. The installer will add the Performance Analyzer installation path to the system's PATH environment variable.

2. Open an elevated command prompt window.

   1. Click Start, click All Programs, and then click Accessories.

   2. Right-click Command Prompt, and click Run as administrator.

3. In the command prompt window, type the following command to turn on the Windows kernel event provider and send data to the default file `\kernel.etl`:

```
xperf -on DiagEasy
```

4. Compile a program or browse some Web pages.

5. Use the following command to stop the kernel logger, and then merge and save the trace data to a `Trace.etl`:

```
xperf -d trace.etl
```

6. View the trace file and also to launch Performance Analyzer by using this command:

```
xperf trace.etl
```

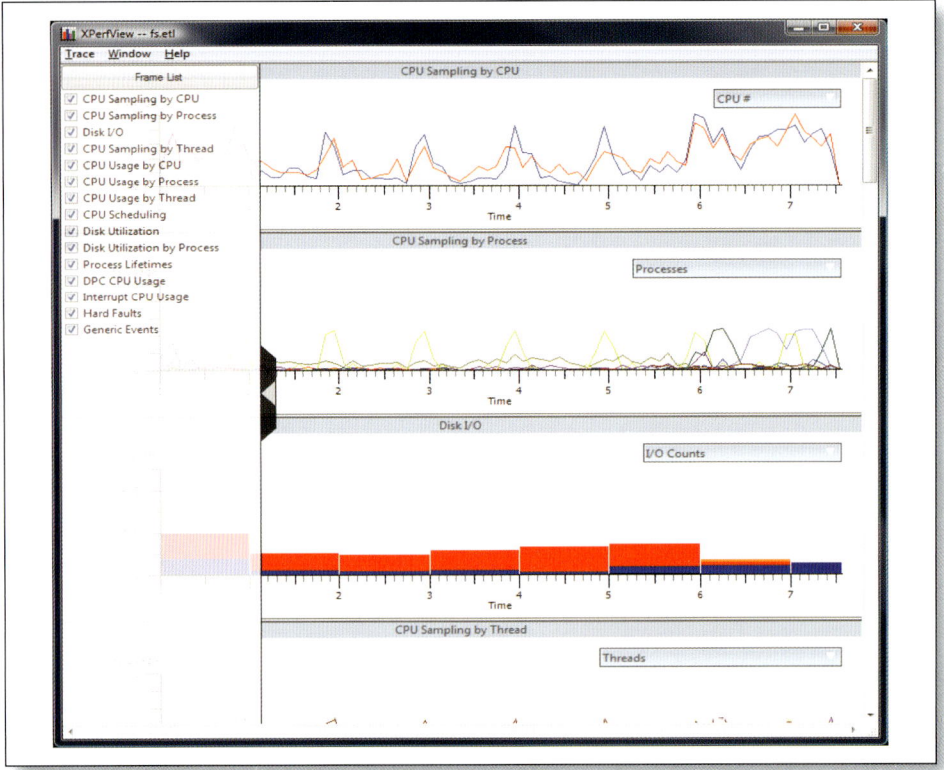

Figure 7.5 Sample Xperf Trace

PwrTest

The power management test tool (PwrTest) shown in Figure 7.6 enables developers, testers, and system integrators to exercise and record power management information from the system. PwrTest can be used to automate sleep and resume transitions and to record processor power management and battery information from the system over a period of time. PwrTest is included as a part of the Windows Driver Kit and it features robust logging and a command-line interface.

```
C:\Program Files\Microsoft PwrTest>pwrtest /info:ppm
PROCESSOR_POWER_INFORMATION
          CPU Number              = 0
          MaxMhz                  = 1833
          CurrentMhz              = 1833
          MhzLimit                = 1833
          MaxIdleState            = 3
          CurrentIdleState        = 3

InstanceName: ACPI\GenuineIntel_-_x86_Family_6_Model_14\_0_0

Processor Performance States
  PerfStates:
    Max Transition Latency:   10 us
    Number of States:         11

    State  Speed (Mhz)      Type
    -----  -----------      ----
      0     1833 (100%)    Performance
      1     1333 ( 72%)    Performance
      2     1000 ( 54%)    Performance
      3     1000 ( 54%)    Throttle
      4      880 ( 48%)    Throttle
      5      750 ( 40%)    Throttle
      6      630 ( 34%)    Throttle
      7      500 ( 27%)    Throttle
      8      380 ( 20%)    Throttle
      9      250 ( 13%)    Throttle
     10      130 (  7%)    Throttle
```

Figure 7.6 Summary of the Processor Power Management (PPM) states

The usage of PwrTest is as follows:

```
pwrtest /scenario [/options]
```

Possible scenarios are:

- sleep for sleep/resume transition testing
- ppm for processor power management testing
- battery for battery information testing
- info for system capabilities information

- ■ `es` for thread execution state changes

- ■ `idle` for power idle statistics

- ■ `disk` for disk idle statistics

- ■ `device` for device idle statistics

PwrTest may also be used to review and log processor power state transitions. It supports two basic modes of operation for these tests:

- ■ A sampling mode that summarizes usage over the sampling period.

- ■ An event driven mode that logs transitions as they are initiated by the kernel power manager.

Figure 7.7 is an example usage of PwrTest in sampling Processor Power Management States (PPM) mode. In this mode, PwrTest provides several command-line options that can be used to tailor the sampling rate and information logged.

```
C:\Program Files\Microsoft PwrTest>pwrtest /ppm
        Elapsed  Idle   C1   C2   C3    P.     Freq   Freq      Perf/
Cpu       [ms]   [%]   [%]  [%]  [%]   State   [%]   [MHz]    Throttle
---     -------  ----  ---  ---  ---   -----   ----  -----    --------
  0       5007    98    0   73   26      2      54   1000        p
  1       5007    99    0   93    6      2      54   1000        p
  0      10014    97    0   72   27      2      54   1000        p
  1      10014    97    0   91    8      2      54   1000        p
  0      15021    88    1    0    0      2      54   1000        p
  1      15021    89    1    0    0      2      54   1000        p
  0      20028    99    0    0  100      2      54   1000        p
  1      20028    98    0    0  100      2      54   1000        p
  0      25035    98    0    0  100      2      54   1000        p
  1      25035    98    0    0  100      2      54   1000        p
  0      30042    98    0    0  100      2      54   1000        p
  1      30042   100    0    0  100      2      54   1000        p
  0      35049    98    0    0  100      2      54   1000        p
  1      35049    98    0    0  100      2      54   1000        p
  0      40056    99    0    0  100      2      54   1000        p
  1      40056    97    0    0  100      2      54   1000        p
```

Figure 7.7 Sampling Processor Power Management States

PwrTest also enables testing of suspend and resume transitions. Figure 7.8 shows the PwrTest output of S3 resume testing.

```
C:\Tools\pwrtest>pwrtest /sleep /s:3 /c:2

NO.0 Transition--TargetState:S3
  TargetState : S3
  EffectiveState : S3
  SleepTimeMs : 00004870
  ResumeTimeMs : 00001098
  DriverWakeTimeMs : 00001075
  HiberWriteTimeMs : 00000000
  HiberReadTimeMs : 00000000
  BiosInitTimeMs : 00000149
  Transition StartTime: 01/20/2006 17:14:57::915
  Transition EndTime:   01/20/2006 17:15:57::619

NO.1 Transition--TargetState:S3
  TargetState : S3
  EffectiveState : S3
  SleepTimeMs : 00004227
  ResumeTimeMs : 00001116
  DriverWakeTimeMs : 00001068
  HiberWriteTimeMs : 00000000
  HiberReadTimeMs : 00000000
  BiosInitTimeMs : 00000149
  Transition StartTime: 01/20/2006 17:17:33::199
  Transition EndTime:   01/20/2006 17:18:33::149
```

Figure 7.8 S3 Resume Testing

To acquire S3 resume information, PwrTest first registers with ETW to enable the kernel power manager's ETW events and record them to a trace file. Then PwrTest processes the ETW trace file after the system has resumed, to display the system's total resume times as well as the times that are required for each phase of the resume process.

PowerTop

PowerTop is a Linux tool that helps find those programs that are having power issues while the computer is idle. PowerTop combines various sources of information from the kernel into one convenient screen so that the user can see how good of a job the system is doing at saving power and which components are the biggest problems.

Requirements

For PowerTOP to work best, use a Linux kernel with the tickless idle (NO_HZ) feature enabled (version 2.6.21 or later). Currently, only 32-bit kernels have support for tickless idle; 64-bit kernels are expected to gain this feature in version 2.6.23.

PowerTOP works best on a notebook or at least a computer with an Intel mobile processor (certain small non-laptop devices also contain a mobile processor). Figure 7.9 shows a sample screen-shot of output from PowerTOP tool followed by an explanation of the various terms as seen in the sample output.

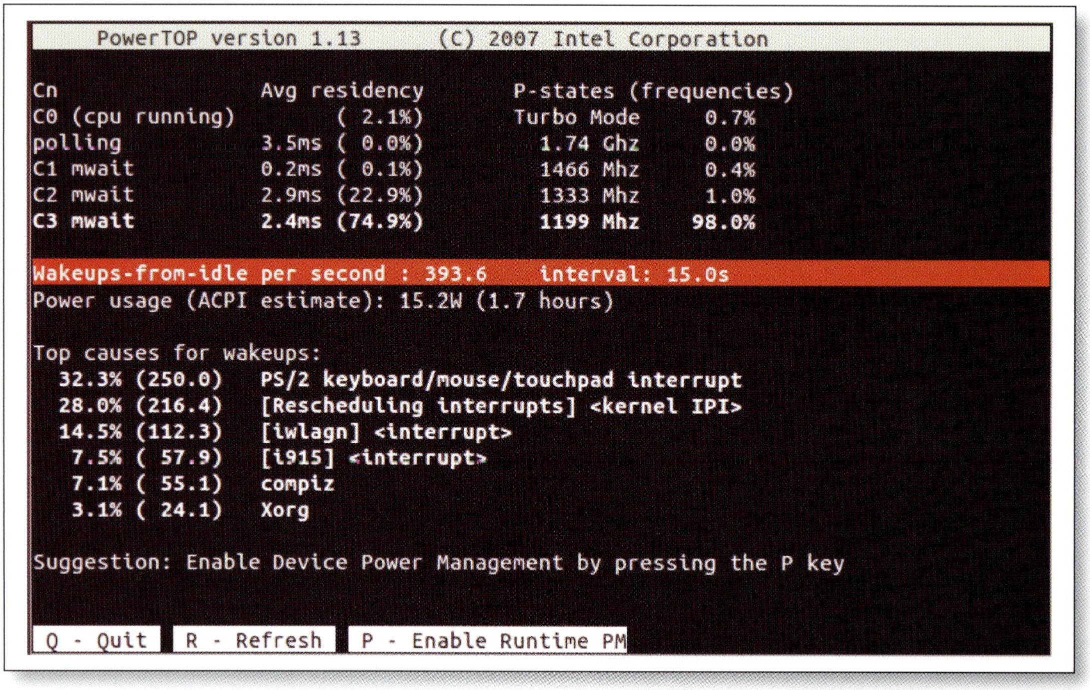

```
        PowerTOP version 1.13       (C) 2007 Intel Corporation

Cn                      Avg residency        P-states (frequencies)
C0 (cpu running)            ( 2.1%)          Turbo Mode     0.7%
polling             3.5ms ( 0.0%)            1.74 Ghz       0.0%
C1 mwait            0.2ms ( 0.1%)            1466 Mhz       0.4%
C2 mwait            2.9ms (22.9%)            1333 Mhz       1.0%
C3 mwait            2.4ms (74.9%)            1199 Mhz      98.0%

Wakeups-from-idle per second : 393.6      interval: 15.0s
Power usage (ACPI estimate): 15.2W (1.7 hours)

Top causes for wakeups:
  32.3% (250.0)    PS/2 keyboard/mouse/touchpad interrupt
  28.0% (216.4)    [Rescheduling interrupts] <kernel IPI>
  14.5% (112.3)    [iwlagn] <interrupt>
   7.5% ( 57.9)    [i915] <interrupt>
   7.1% ( 55.1)    compiz
   3.1% ( 24.1)    Xorg

Suggestion: Enable Device Power Management by pressing the P key


 Q - Quit    R - Refresh    P - Enable Runtime PM
```

Figure 7.9   Power TOP Running on a Laptop (PowerTop, 2007)

Wakeups per Second indicates how often CPU is woken up to work and prevents it from sleep mode to save power. We would like to see zero or a low number of wakeups per seconds when the system is at idle. PowerTop uses ACPI to collect power usage data and estimates how much battery lifetime is left. PowerTop gathers the 10 processes that most frequently wake the CPU up. PowerTop gives suggestions for the user to improve energy efficiency for the system based on the information it has obtained.

PowerInformer

PowerInformer, shown in Figure 7.10, is a tool developed to provide basic power relevant statistics to a developer. They can use these statistics to optimize their applications such that they match battery life constraints while also meeting performance requirements. Some of the main features include calculating the average residency and the percentage time of the C1, C2, and C3 states of all logical processors.

PowerInformer features include:

- Battery and power status indicators

- Processor (physical, core, and logical) detection

- Percentage time of C1, C2, and C3 states of the system and of all logical processors

- Average residency of C1, C2, and C3 states of the system and of all logical processors

- Percentage time of the system and of all logical processors

- Percentage time of the P-states of the system

- System calls per second

- Interrupt rate of the system

- Disk I/O operation (access, read, and write) rates

- File I/O operation (control, read, and write) rates

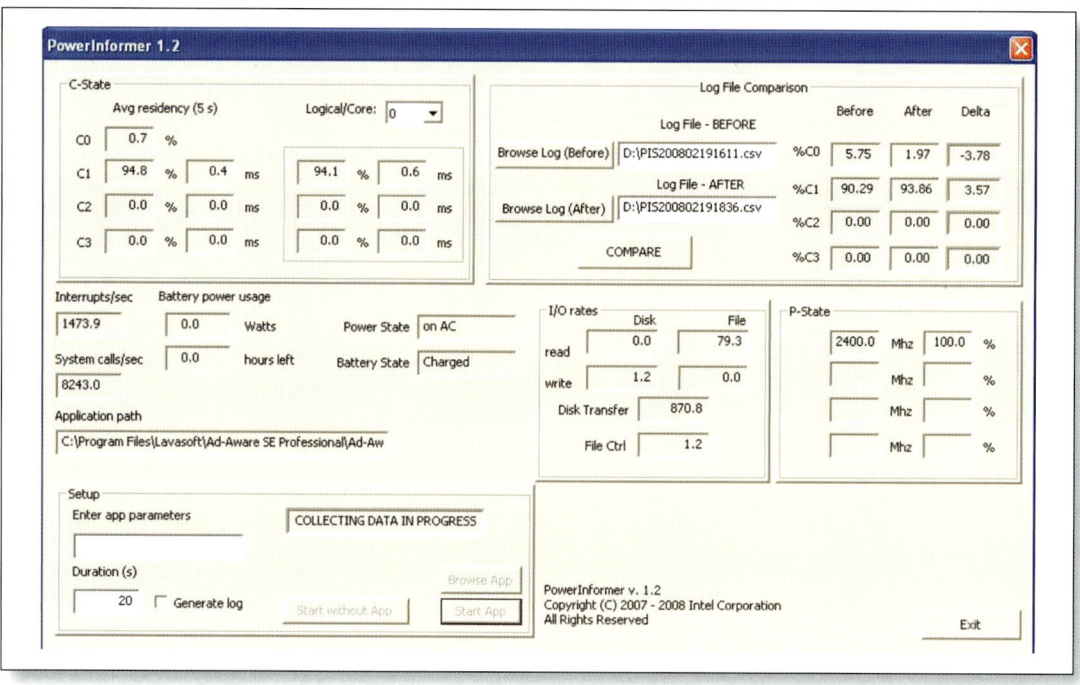

Figure 7.10 Power Informer Tool

Perfmon and CStResMon

Perfmon allows monitoring of performance counters available in Windows. The counters relevant for power include %C-state residencies, %P-state residencies, and interrupt rate.

Windows Perfmon offers a way to measure C-state information. While using perfmon, ACPI C-states are mapped to various hardware C-states as shown in Figure 7.11. For example, the CPU hardware C6/C7 residency information is accumulated, and represents as OS C3 states in Perfmon.

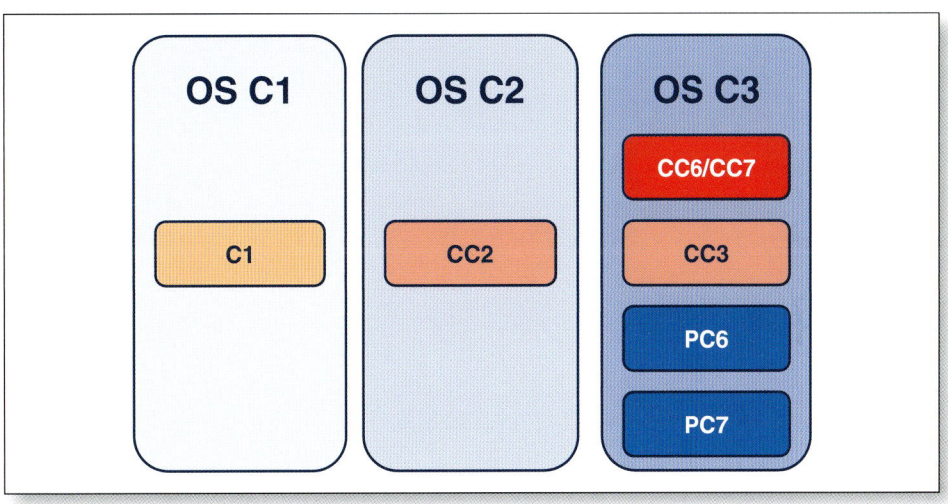

Figure 7.11 OS C-states mapping

The Intel CStResMon Utility, shown in Figure 7.12, is a performance extension DLL that plugs in to the Perfmon application in Windows. CStResMon monitors the C3, C5, C6, and C7 states (if supported by the processor) occurring in the system processor. This utility reads the C3, C5, C6, and C7 Residency Timers to report the respective C-state of the processor as a percentage of time.

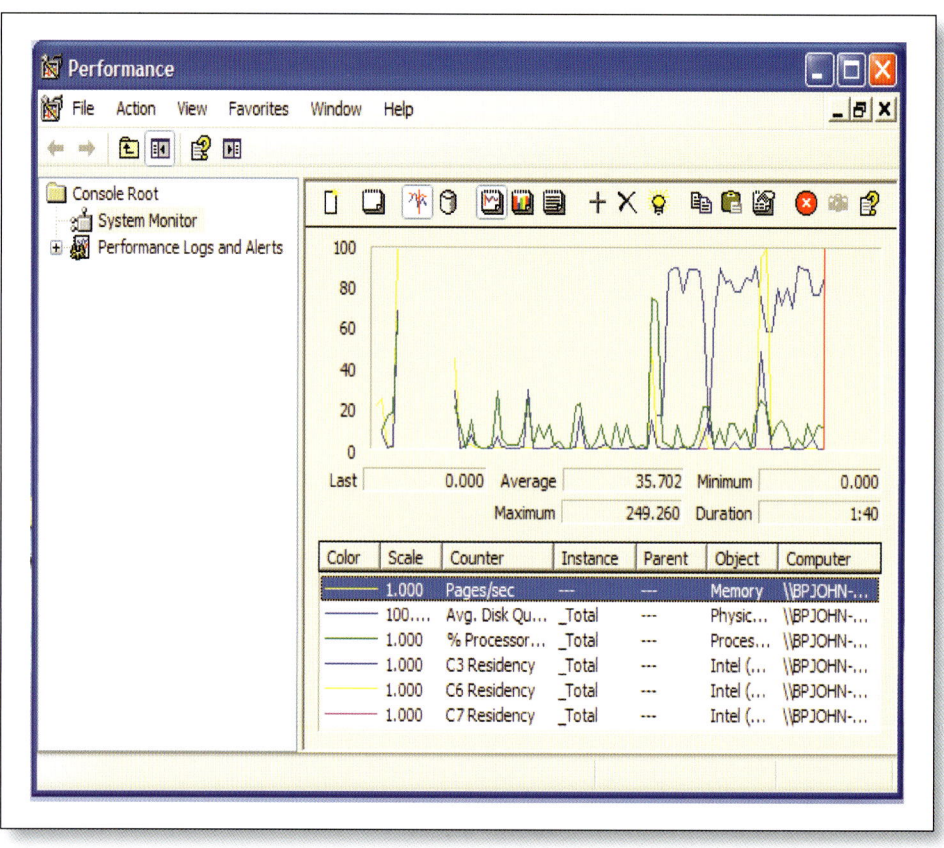

Figure 7.12 The Intel CStResMon Utility

Battery Information Monitoring Tools

In addition to using Perfmon to collect battery status, other tools can be used to extract the battery information.

BatteryMan

BatteryMan, shown in Figure 7.13, is a battery-information tool that is integrated into the WinTestCPUID utility. To run BatteryMan, click Start → All Programs → WinCPUID → WinTestCPUID, and then click BatteryMan.

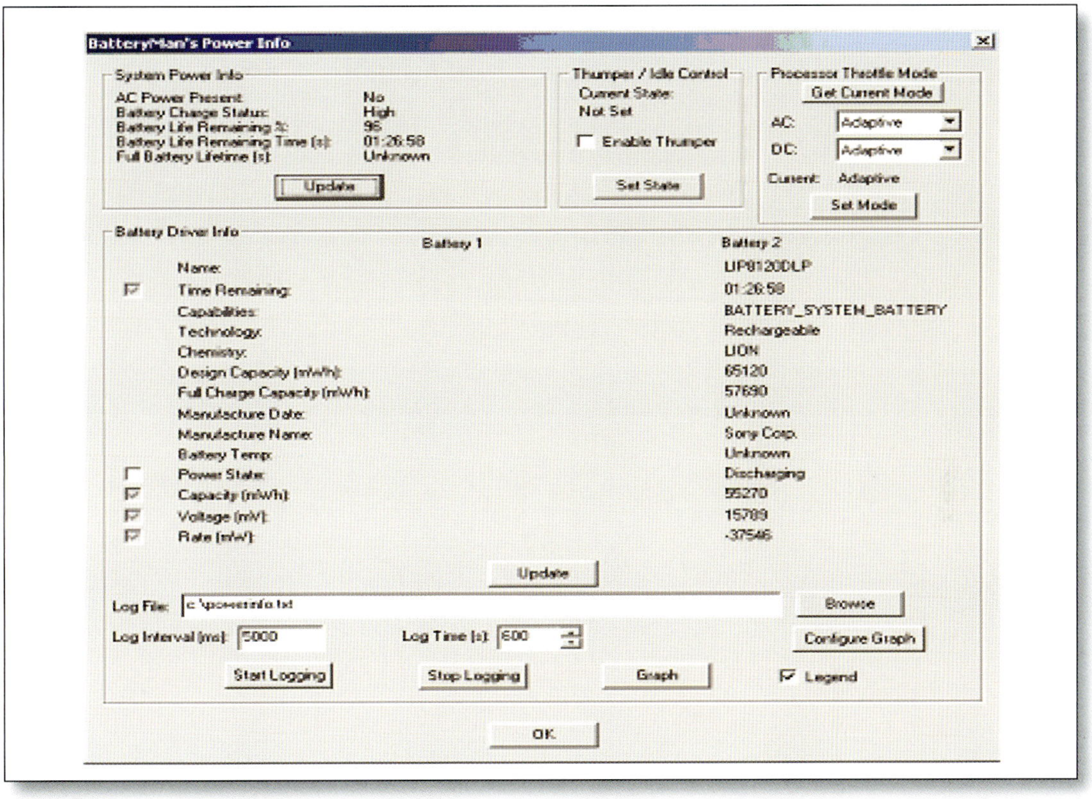

Figure 7.13 BatteryMan

It displays the detailed battery-driver information for up to two batteries. This information is retrieved using the IOCTL method and the display is updated in the same manner as the System Power Info. If the system has multiple battery bays, the information will appear in the slot corresponding to the manufacturer's numbering of the bay containing the battery.

Intel Performance Power Monitor

Intel Performance Power Monitor, shown in Figure 7.14 monitors CPU utilization, CPU frequency, percent memory, battery charge rate, battery drain rate, percent capacity of the battery, as well as the time remaining on the battery.

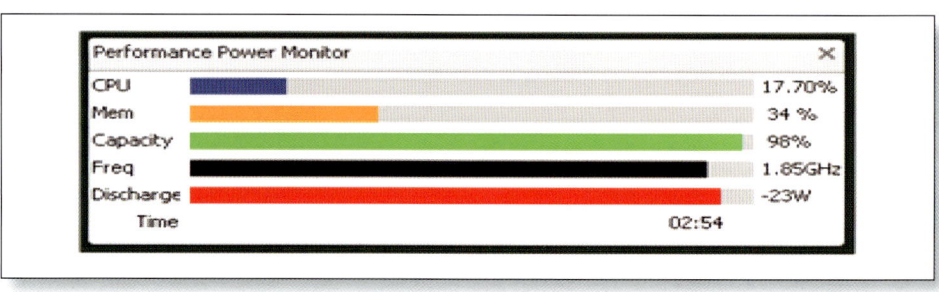

Figure 7.14 Intel Performance Power Monitor

Intel Battery Life Analyzer (BLA)

Intel Battery Life Analyzer (BLA) Tool is a software tool that analyzes hardware and software platform components and identifies their impact on battery life. It is designed as a solution to analyze and summarize data typically provided by several resources. BLA points out misbehaving drivers, processes, and hardware that prevent the platform from entering low power states. Figure 7.15 shows a sample snapshot of the BLA tool.

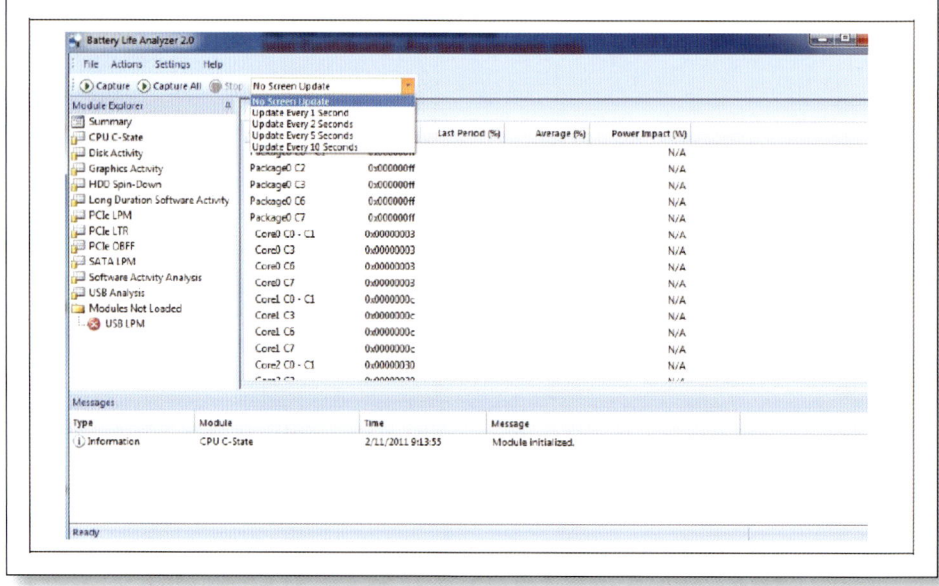

Figure 7.15 Sample Screenshot of BLA tool

Intel Energy Checker

Intel Energy Checker, as shown in Figure 7.16, determines how energy-efficient a system is by using the metric of *how much useful work is done by the system* versus *how much energy is consumed by the system during the work*. It is aimed to provide a standard for software energy efficiency to help ISVs on making their software products energy-aware.

Energy Efficiency (EE) = useful work / Energy

Intel Energy Checker APIs provide developers with application instrumentation to collect particular counters, and then other applications can later read those counters to analyze the trend over time. Intel Energy Checker is a tool that interfaces with applications through custom APIs to deliver:

■ A report of the productivity of a system

■ The application's energy profile

■ The ability to report in runtime

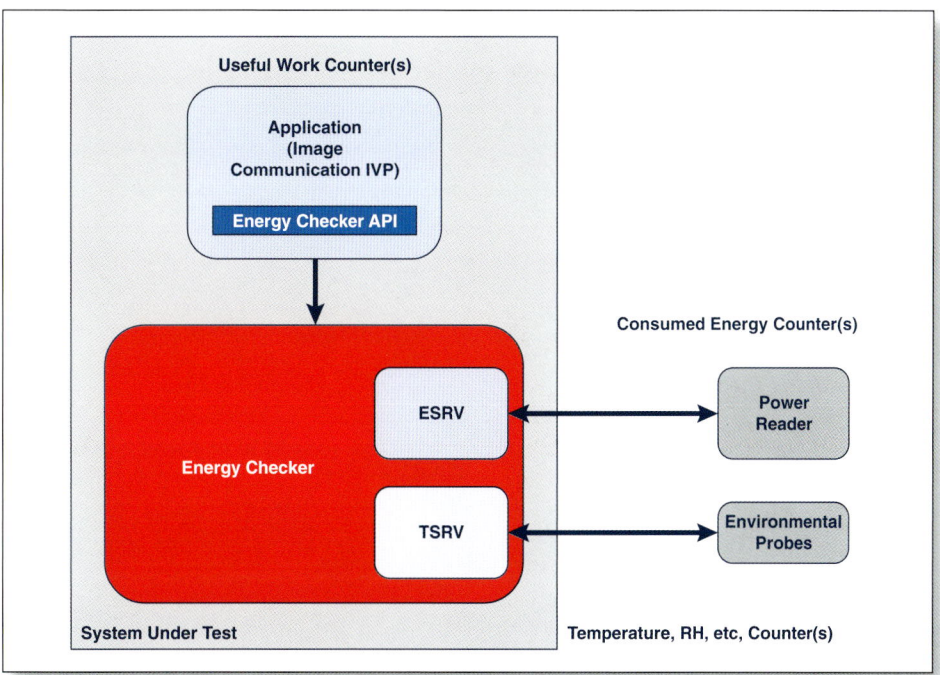

Figure 7.16 Intel Energy Checker Overview

Minimal steps are required to explore potential hot spots:

1. ISV defines the useful work done by the software

2. Instruments the software to expose it

After software is analyzed, to make the software energy-aware:

1. Use SDK tools to get energy consumption

2. Compute software EE metric(s)

3. Take action(s) based on software EE

Intel Energy Checker SDK comes with one code file and one header. Five APIs are provided. Figure 7.17 shows how to use these APIs in the code:

- int pl_open(char *, unsigned int, char *, uuid_t *);

- int pl_attach(char *);

- int pl_read(int, void *, unsigned int);

- int pl_write(int, void *, unsigned int);

- int pl_close(int);

At minimum:
  Call `pl_open` at startup
  For each work unit(s) {
    Call `pl_write` to export
      Work done
      SW phase (if applicable)
  }
  Call `pl_close` at end

In an energy-aware SW:
  Call `pl_open` at startup
  Call `pl_attach`[1] **at startup**
  For each work unit(s) {
    Call `pl_read` **to import**
      Energy
    Call `pl_write` to export
      Work done
      EE metric(s)
      SW phase (if applicable)
  }
  Call `pl_close` at end

Figure 7.17 APIs for Intel Energy Checker

Figure 7.18 shows the screen shot from a sample run of Energy Checker.

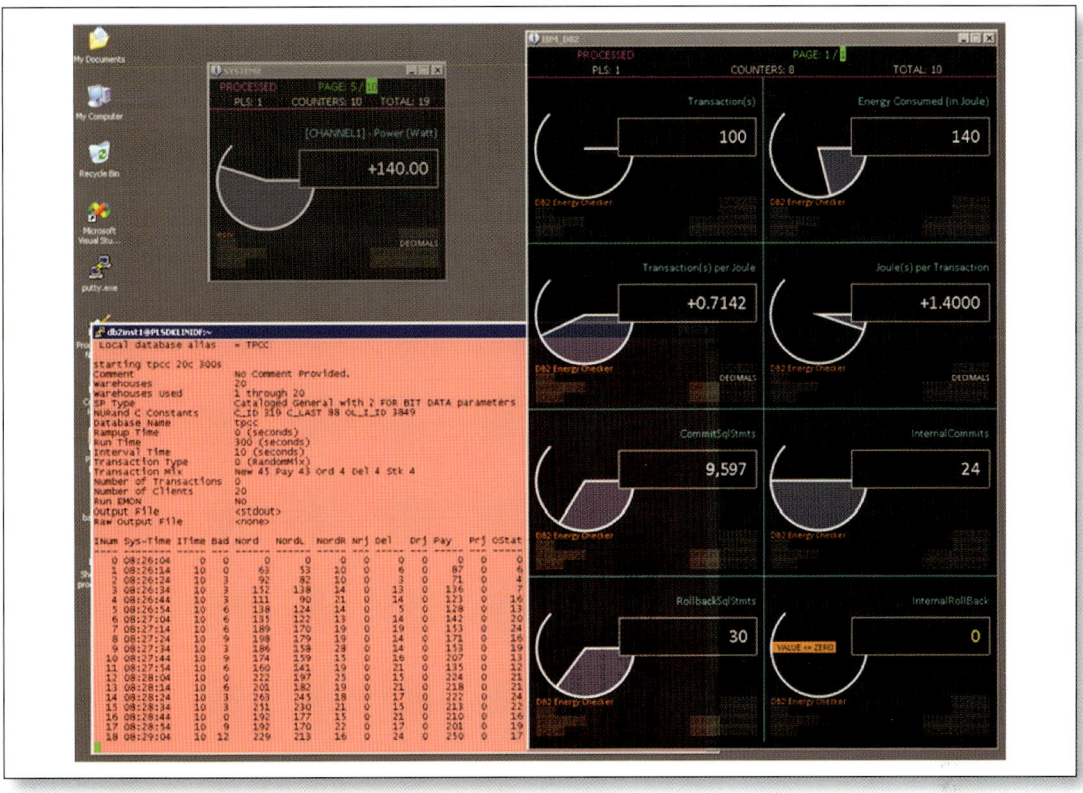

Figure 7.18 Example Run of Intel Energy Checker

Tools Usage: Identify Power Issues

This section will go through the debugging process of power issues on Intel® Architecture mobile platforms using the following tools:

■ Intel Battery Life Analyzer

■ PowerCfg Windows 7 built-in command

■ Microsoft Windows Performance Toolkit (xperf)

■ Sysinternals Process Monitor

To make the description as specific as possible, examples shown in this chapter are captured on Intel® Core™ i3/5/7 mobile processor based platforms with the Windows 7 operating system unless otherwise noted. Results may be slightly different with other environments (Jeyaseelan, 2011).

Debug Strategy

It is very difficult to debug multiple issues at one time and separate the impact of one piece of software from the others. So, in debugging the issue of particular software, it is highly recommended to install the software to a clean setup ("plain vanilla" OS and minimum drivers, without value-add software for the add-on devices) and compare the system behavior before and after installing the software.

CPU/Chipset Power Issues

This section will cover how to debug the various power issues related to CPU and chipsets.

CPU C-State Residency

It is recommended to start debugging by measuring CPU C-state (package and core) residency. From CPU C-state residency numbers, the following information can be determined:

■ How optimal CPU and chipset are power managed

■ The type of the issue that is increasing platform power consumption

Use CPU C-State Analysis of Battery Life Analyzer (shown in Figure 7.19) to measure CPU C-state residency. A well power-managed system should show high (greater than 98 percent for core C-state, greater than 95 percent for package C-state) residency in the deepest C-state supported by the platform.

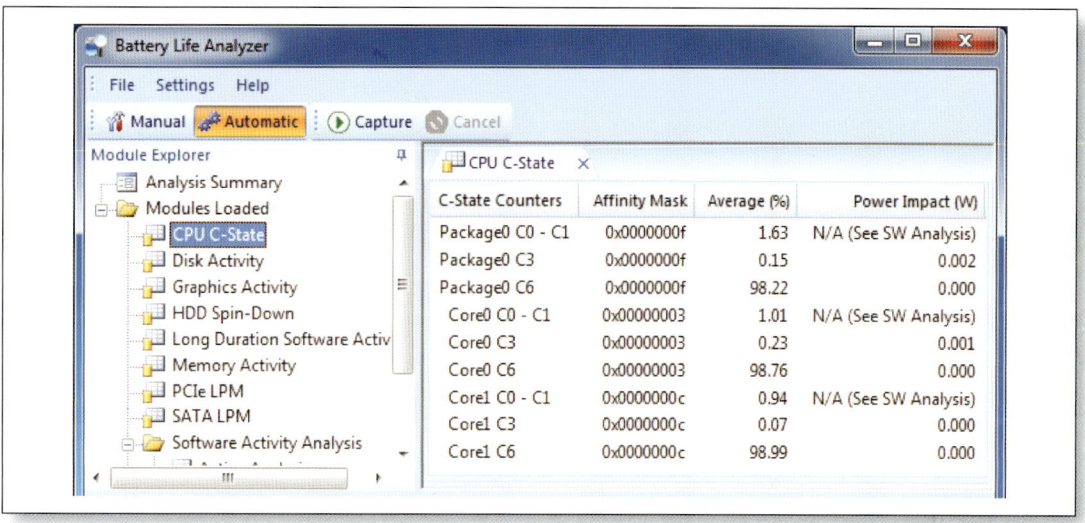

Figure 7.19 C-State Residency Numbers from Clean Idle System

If high C-state residency is not seen in the deepest C-states, the following are some common causes for the issue:

1. If Core C0 state residency is high (greater than 1.5 percent)

   ■ Process or driver's activity is consuming CPU cycles
     Proceed to the section "CPU Utilization Issues" to determine which software component is consuming CPU cycles.

   ■ Timer resolution increased by application
     Proceed to the section "Timer Resolution Issue" to determine which software component changed timer resolution.

   ■ Excessive driver activity
     Proceed to the section "I/O Issues" to determine which driver is consuming CPU cycles.

2. If Core C3 state residency is high (greater than 1.5 percent)

   ■ Frequent C-state transition caused by device interrupt
     Proceed to the section "I/O Issues" to determine which device driver is causing frequent activities

■ Frequent C-state transition caused by software activity

Proceed to the section "CPU Activity Frequency Issues" to determine which software component is causing frequent activities.

3. If Package C0-1 state residency (for Huron River platform, package C2 state residency) is significantly higher than all core's C0 residency.

■ CPU package C state pops up to C1 (or C2, in case of Huron River platform) state to respond to snoop cycles generated by bus master devices

Proceed to the section "Frequent Snoop Cycle Issues" section to determine which device is causing the issue.

CPU Utilization Issues

There are many tools for CPU utilization measurement, but most of them don't reflect the real impact of software activity because of the following reasons.

Most tools measure CPU utilization with a *sampling-based* method. They are built on OS accounting APIs, which is sampling-based information. Here, sampling-based means CPU utilization is observed at every timer tick interrupt, which usually happens every 15.6 ms. As illustrated in Figure 7.20, software activities that start at the timer tick interrupt and end before the next timer tick are not observed by these tools at all. This type of software behavior is common among many background applications and media (isochronous) applications.

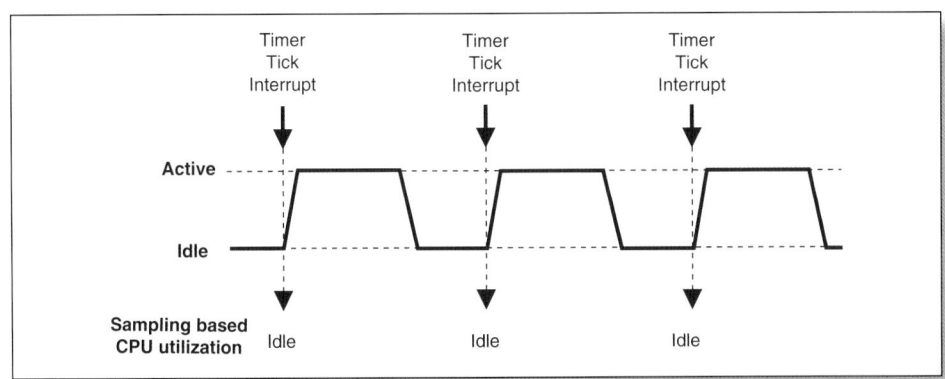

Figure 7.20 Typical CPU Activity Pattern of Background Process and Sampling-based CPU Utilization

For multi-core CPUs, power consumption is determined by the total of the duration each core is active, and the duration the package is active (the duration at least one core in the package is active). The mathematical average of all logical CPU utilization, which is measured by most tools, only reflects the first part of the power. To address these issues, Battery Life Analyzer uses fine-grain process information (microsecond-resolution time stamp for activity start and stop) and shows the total active duration of both package and logical CPU. It is highly recommended to use Battery Life Analyzer instead of traditional CPU utilization tools to get the better picture of the software impact to the platform power.

In addition, Battery Life Analyzer shows CPU utilization with two numbers. One (logical) is the total each logical CPU's utilization. This is a good representation of the power consumed by the CPU core. The other one (platform) is the duration at least one logical CPU is active. This is a good representation of the power consumed by the package (except for cores). As illustrated in Figure 7.21, platform CPU utilization can vary for the same logical CPU utilization (for the same amount of instruction execution) depending on how much overlap is happening between logical CPUs. It is recommended, especially for the workloads with higher CPU utilization, to lower the platform CPU utilization for the same logical CPU utilization.

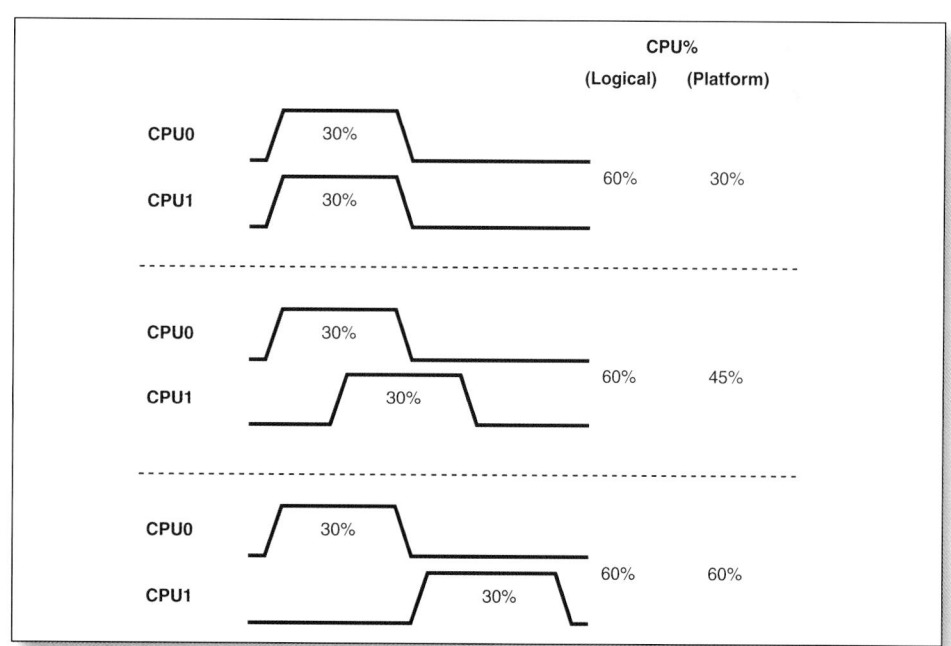

Figure 7.21 Battery Life Analyzer CPU Utilization Metrics: Logical and Platform

Identify Software Components with High CPU Utilization

Figure 7.22 shows an example of the background process activity on the system. The user is not explicitly running any application program, but background tasks are consuming CPU cycles. Battery Life Analyzer highlights software components causing high CPU utilization. In this example, two components are showing very high CPU utilization (for idle).

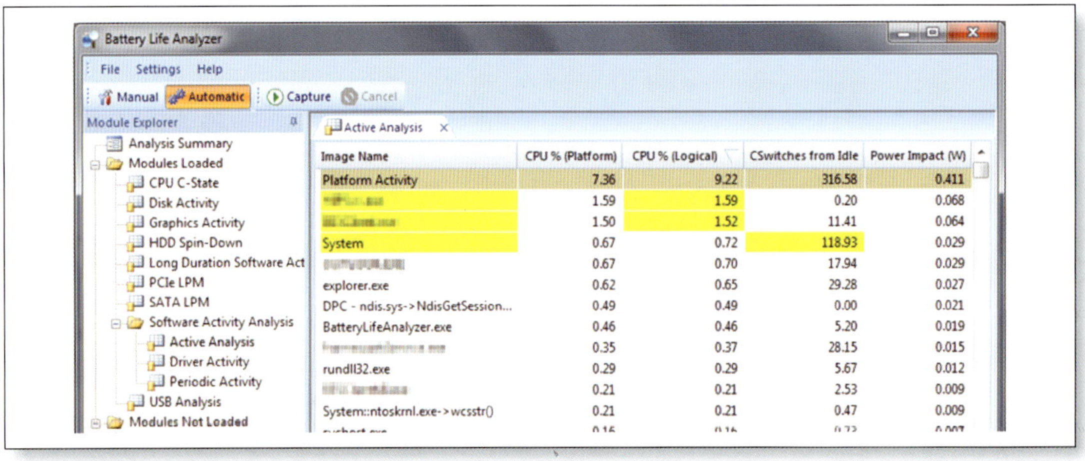

Figure 7.22 Battery Life Analyzer: Active Analysis

To measure the impact of particular software, just reading the numbers for that component is not enough because one component can affect the behavior of other components. For example, if the process of interest is communicating with server processes through the COM interface, the activity increase is also seen in the server process. The best practice of measuring the impact of particular software is, as described in the "Debug Strategy" section, to compare clean setup with and without the particular software and see the difference in the Platform Activity row.

Understand Why CPU Utilization Is High

Once the component with high CPU utilization is identified, the next step is to understand why CPU cycles are spent by the component. For the owner of the software, it may not be so difficult to determine problems. Otherwise, the following methods will help explain the behavior of the processes:

■ Hotspot analysis (with Intel® VTune™, Microsoft Windows Performance Analyzer) will show where the most CPU cycles are spent.

■ File, registry, and network I/O analysis (with Sysinternals ProcMon tool) will give some understanding about what kind of activity is happening. See the section "I/O Issues" for more details.

■ Based on the nature of the activity, it can be determined if those activities are really necessary or not.

Timer Resolution Issue

The Windows OS default timer resolution is 15.6 ms and if a shorter period is shown, it means some software program requested a shorter period. To determine which process requested timer resolution change, run the `PowerCfg` command with the `/energy` command line option. (PowerCfg is a Windows 7 built-in command, and has to be executed with Administrator privilege). This program observes software activities for about a minute and dumps the result in a file named `energy-report.html`. The process that requested the timer tick period change can be found in the Information section near the end, as shown in Figure 7.23.

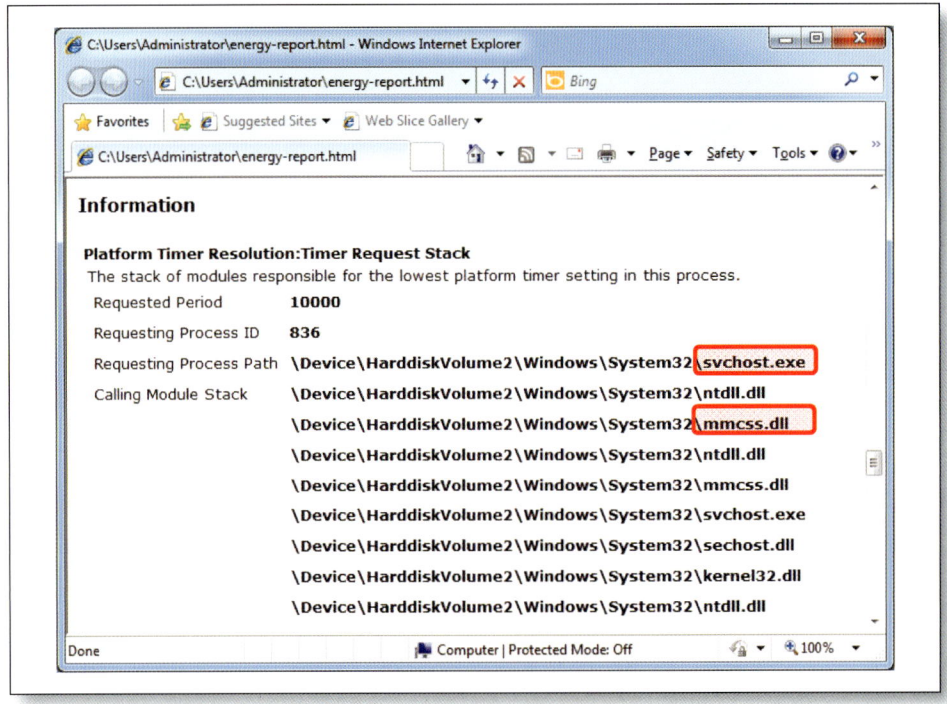

Figure 7.23 PowerCfg: Timer Resolution Change Request

If the process name is `svchost.exe` and the calling module stack includes `mmcss.dll`, this request was made by the Multimedia Class Scheduler service (MMCSS OS component); this case can be safely ignored if this happens while a multimedia application is running.

CPU Activity Frequency Issues

This section covers how to debug the frequent CPU activities which leads to higher power.

Identify Software Components Causing Frequent Transition

Frequent CPU state transition between active state and idle state consumes more energy. Battery Life Analyzer provides two methods to identify the process that is causing frequent transition. The first method is to count the context switch from idle thread to the active thread. The "CSwitches from Idle" column in the Active Analysis shows how many C-state transitions were caused by each component, including processes and drivers. After running Software Activity Analysis, the data is sorted by CPU utilization by default. Click the column header for "CSwitches from Idle" to find out which component caused the most C-state transitions.

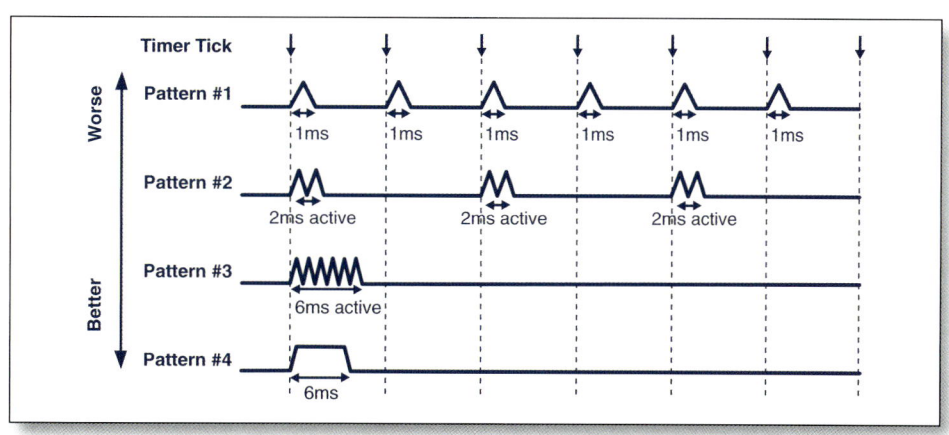

Figure 7.24 Battery Life Analyzer: Number of C-State Transitions Caused by Each Component

In the example shown in Figure 7.24, System, csrss (Win32 subsystem), and dwm (Desktop Window Manager) are OS components and high activities made by these components are usually caused by other processes' activity.

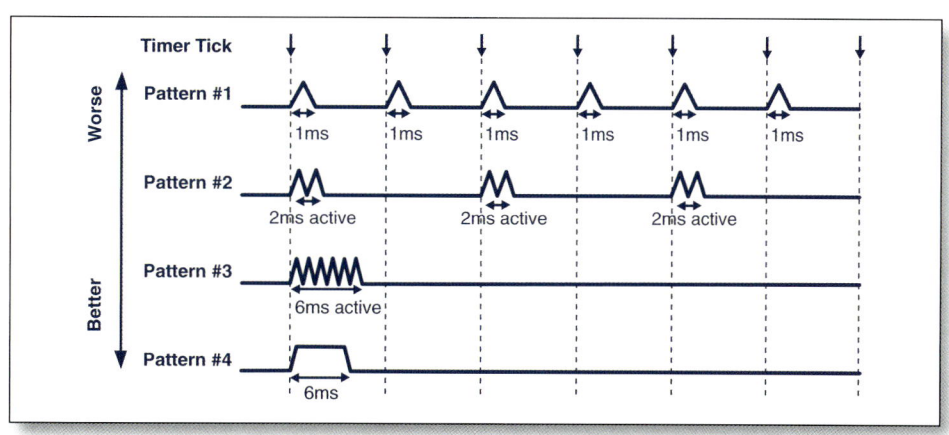

Figure 7.25 Different CPU Activity Patterns with Same CPU Utilization

Although "CSwitches from Idle" numbers can tell the difference between Pattern 4 and Patterns 1–3, it cannot tell the difference between Patterns 1–3. To distinguish the difference between these patterns, use Periodic Activity Analysis of the Battery Life Analyzer.

Periodic Activity Analysis summarizes software component's activity by timer tick period and displays the histogram by the amount of activity that has happened during each period. For the activity patterns shown in Figure 7.25, the histogram values in Table 7.2 will be shown as the result of analysis.

Table 7.2   Battery Life Analyzer: Periodic Activity Analysis with Various CPU Activity patterns

	0 μs	. . .	≤1 ms	≤2 ms	≤5 ms	>5 ms
Pattern #1	0% (=0/6)		100% (=6/6)			
Pattern #2	50% (=3/6)			50% (=3/6)		
Pattern #3	83.3% (=5/6)					16.7% (=1/6)
Pattern #4	83.3% (=5/6)					16.7% (=1/6)

Figure 7.26 shows an example from an idle system with many background processes making small activities.

With Periodic Activity Analysis, the following can be determined:

1. How frequent each component is making activity

    0μs column shows the percentage of the timer tick period without any activity by each component. So, 100 percent in this column means that the software component didn't make any activity during data collection (desired behavior for idle scenario). On the other hand, 0 percent means this component made some activity at every timer tick period. Such components tend to have more impact to the platform power consumption for the same total CPU utilization.

2. How many activities are happening at each tick period

    If there are more than few hundreds of μs (the exact threshold is dependent on the CPU architecture) activities per timer tick period, the CPU will start to demote the C-state to a shallower one. By looking at the top row (Platform Activity: the total activity of all components), how often long (less than 200 µs) activity is happening, and which component is contributing most for that can be determined.

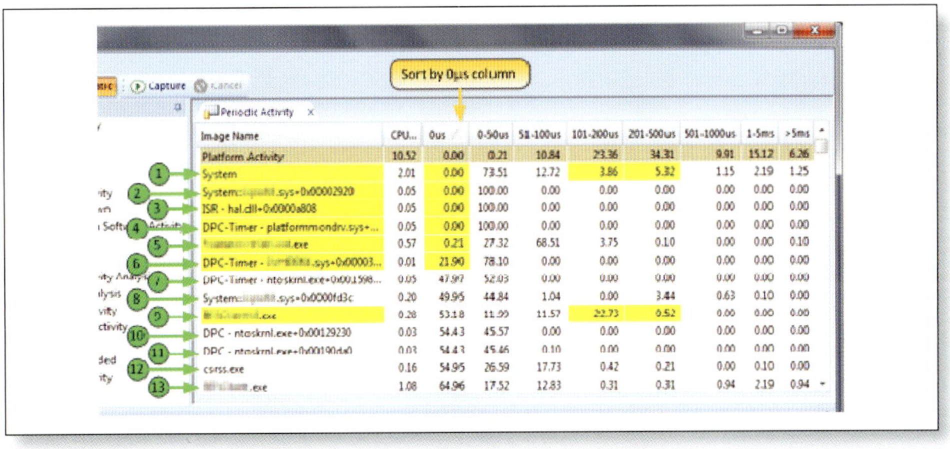

Figure 7.26 Battery Life Analyzer: Periodic Activity Analysis

In Figure 7.26, notice the following:

- #3 (`ISR - hal.dll`) is the OS timer tick itself, and it's normal for this component to make activity every timer tick. This can safely be ignored.

- #4 (`DPC - Timer - platformmondrv.sys`) is the activity of Battery Life Analyzer. This can safely be ignored, too.

- #2 (`System::****.sys`) is the activity of a third-party driver (kernel mode thread). Although the duration of activity is always very short (less than 50 µs), it is making activity every timer tick (0µs column is 0) and it is not desired behavior.

- #5, #6, #8, #9 are all third-party components making frequent activity. In particular, #9 is making relatively long activity frequently (22.73 percent in the 100–200 µs range) and potentially causing C-state demotion.

Understand Why Frequent C-State Transition Is Happening

Once the software that is causing frequent C-state transition is identified, the next step is to determine why and which part of the code is causing the issue.

The exact procedure varies from case to case, but this section explains two common cases: one is the case where excessive use is made of the short duration timer, and the other case is where multiple threads are becoming alternatively active.

As the main focus of Battery Life Analyzer is to identify the bad behaving component in the platform and not meant to do the deep analysis, Microsoft Windows Performance Analyzer (xperf) can be used as a primary tool for the detailed analysis. The following sections demonstrate how to identify and debug two common cause of the frequent C-state transition.

Debugging Excessive Use of Short Duration Timer Issue

Below are the sequence of steps which explains the analysis steps using Xperf.

1. Install Microsoft Windows Performance Analyzer (xperf) to the target system.

2. (Optional) If the target system is x64 platform, it is recommended to create DWORD registry key DisablePagingExecutive with value 1 under `HKLM\System\CurrentControlSet\Control\Session Manager\Memory Management`, and reboot the system. This registry setting ensures complete kernel stack dump.

3. Open command prompt as Administrator

4. Start data collection:

   ```
   xperf -on DiagEasy -stackwalk CSwitch
   ```

5. Leave the system idle for few minutes.

6. Stop data collection:

   ```
   xperf -d output.etl
   ```

   This will create the log file (`output.etl`) in the current directory.

7. Open the log file with viewer:

   ```
   xperfview output.etl
   ```

8. Enable symbol decoding with Trace → Load Symbols.

9. Scroll down to the CPU Scheduling graph.

10. Right-click the graph and select Summary Table in the popup menu.

11. Arrange the columns in the following order (left to right) by dragging column headers:

    ■ NewProcess

    ■ NewThreadId

    ■ NewThreadStack

    ■ Separation (orange) bar

    ■ Count

    ■ Sum:TimeSinceLast (μs)

12. Look for the process that was identified as a cause of the frequent C-state transition by Battery Life Analyzer. In this example, notice the process #5 in Figure 7.26.

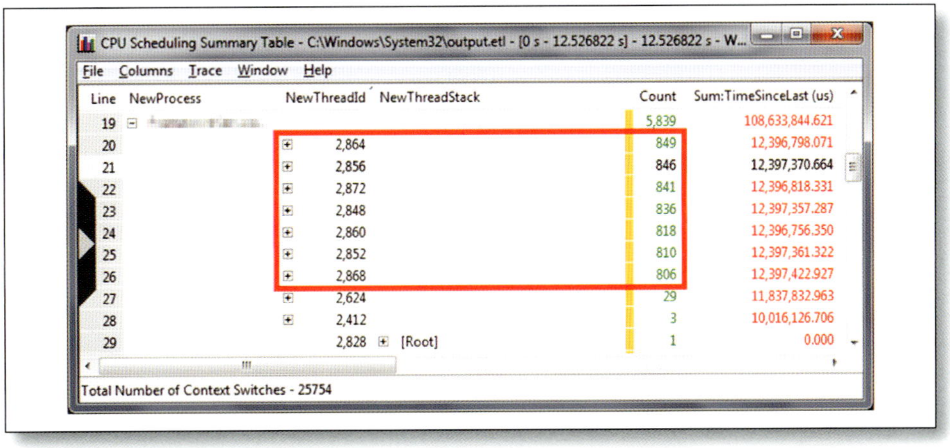

Line	NewProcess	NewThreadId	NewThreadStack	Count	Sum:TimeSinceLast (us)
19	⊟ ▓▓▓▓▓▓▓			5,839	108,633,844.621
20		⊞ 2,864		849	12,396,798.071
21		⊞ 2,856		846	12,397,370.664
22		⊞ 2,872		841	12,396,818.331
23		⊞ 2,848		836	12,397,357.287
24		⊞ 2,860		818	12,396,756.350
25		⊞ 2,852		810	12,397,361.322
26		⊞ 2,868		806	12,397,422.927
27		⊞ 2,624		29	11,837,832.963
28		⊞ 2,412		3	10,016,126.706
29		2,828 ⊞ [Root]		1	0.000

Total Number of Context Switches - 25754

Figure 7.27 Windows Performance Analyzer: Thread List

Notice the list of the threads. In this example, seven threads (thread id:2864, 2856, 2872, 2848, 2860, 2852, and 2868) are showing high context switch numbers in the Count column, as shown in Figure 7.27.

By expanding one of the threads, note each context switch per line as shown in Figure 7.28. The column Sum: TimeSinceLast (μs) shows these context switches are happening approximately 15–16 ms apart. This means each thread is making activity every timer tick period (15.6 ms).

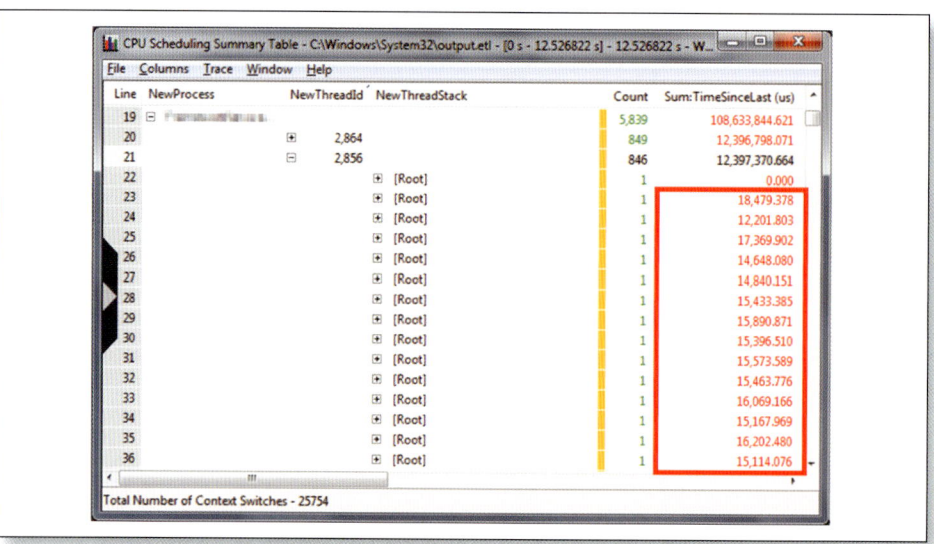

Figure 7.28 Windows Performance Analyzer: Thread Activity

Furthermore, by examining the stack dump, shown in Figure 7.29, at each context switch, it can be seen that this is caused by the repeated call of Sleep() API.

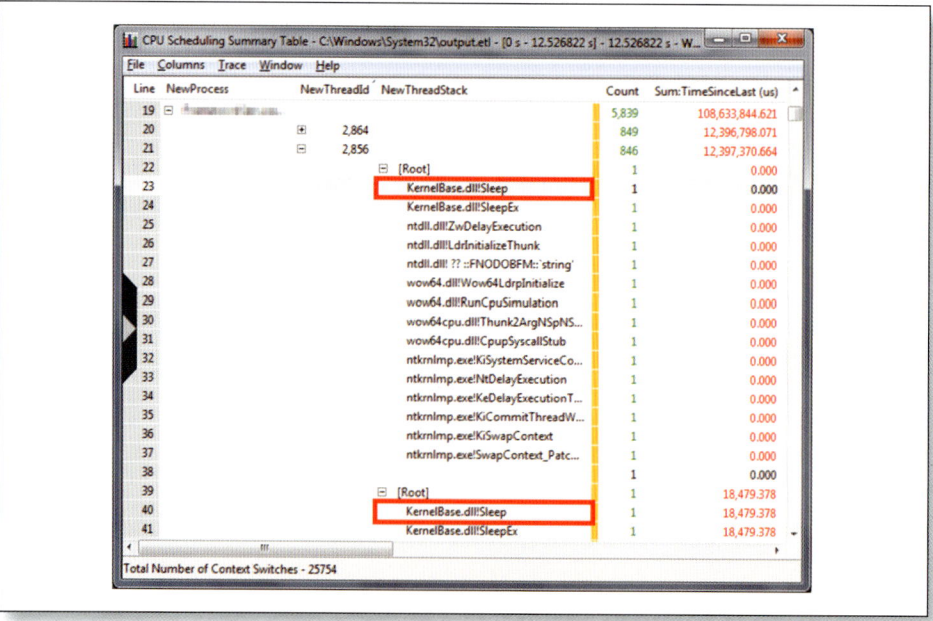

Figure 7.29 Windows Performance Analyzer: Stack Dump

From these information, it is evident that this process creates multiple threads and each thread is looping with Sleep() API.

Debugging an Occasional High C-State Transition Issue

In the previous example, the problem is happening all the time. However, some types of programs cause frequent C-state transitions for a limited time (but repeat it). For such types of program, the period where high C-state transition is happening needs to be identified first. This section uses process #13 in Figure 7.26 as an example.

Follow steps 1 through 8 of the previous section.

1. Display *Stack Counts by Type* and *CPU Usage by CPU* graphs (the first two graphs).

2. Right-click the 0.5 to 1.0 second range in one of these graphs and select Zoom to Selection.

3. Scroll horizontally through all of the data and look for the section with a high number in the *Stack Counts by Type* graph (this means high context switch), and high (20 to 80 percent, but not 100%) CPU utilization on multiple CPUs like the example shown in Figure 7.30.

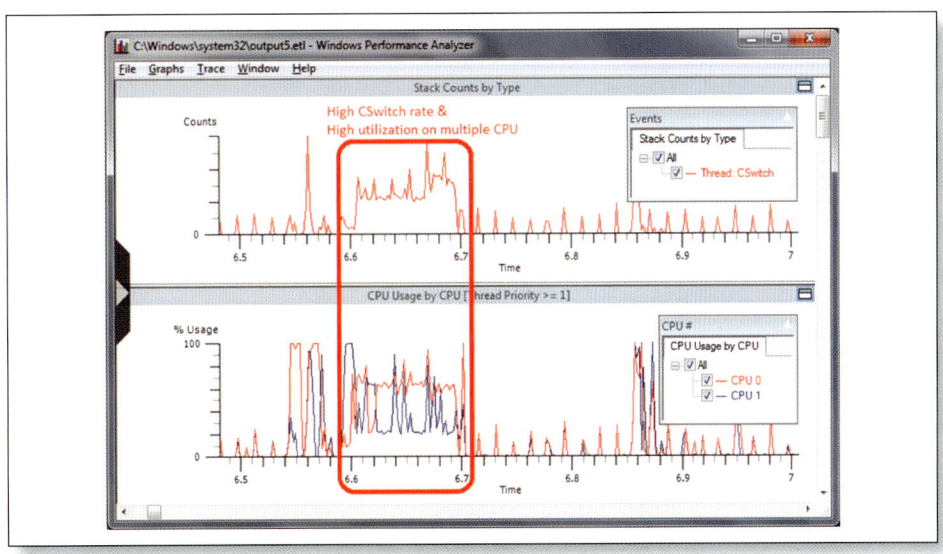

Figure 7.30 Xperf: Occasional High CPU C-State Transition

4. Zoom in the *CPU Usage by CPU* graph until each C-state transition can be seen separately (in other words, until CPU utilization for each CPU toggles between 0 percent and 100 percent), as shown in the example in Figure 7.31.

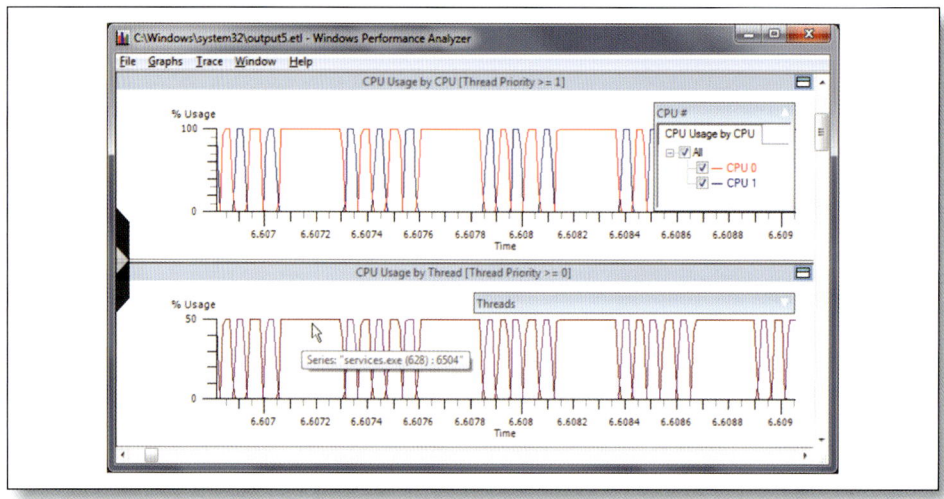

Figure 7.31 Xperf: IPI Storm Example

By comparing the *CPU Usage by CPU* and *CPU Usage by Thread* graphs, you can find each CPU's activity is completely synchronized with a thread's activity. Which process is causing this problem can easily be determined by hovering the mouse cursor over each thread's line. In this case, one of the threads belongs to `services.exe` (shown by a brown line), and the other thread belongs to a third party application that was shown as process #13 in Figure 7.26 (shown by a purple line).

5. The next step is to determine what kind of code sequence is causing the C-state transition. To do so, scroll down to the *CPU Scheduling* graph, select several cycles of the transitions, right-click the graph, and select Summary table.

6. Arrange the columns in the following order (left to right):

    ■ SwitchInTime (s)

    ■ Cpu

- ■ NewProcess

- ■ NewThreadId

- ■ NewThreadStack

7. Click the SwitchInTimes (s) column and sort the entries in ascending order.

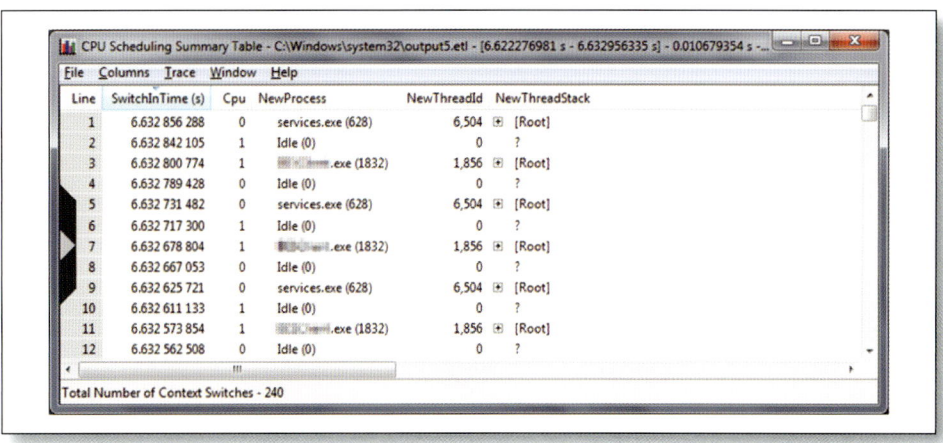

Figure 7.32 Xperf – IPI Storm Detail

In this example, shown in Figure 7.32, `services.exe` (Process ID: 628, Thread ID: 6504) and the other thread (Process ID: 1832, Thread ID: 1856) are running alternately running on CPU0 and CPU1 respectively.

8. Expand NewThreadStack at each context switch to the active thread and find out which API call caused the thread to enter wait state.

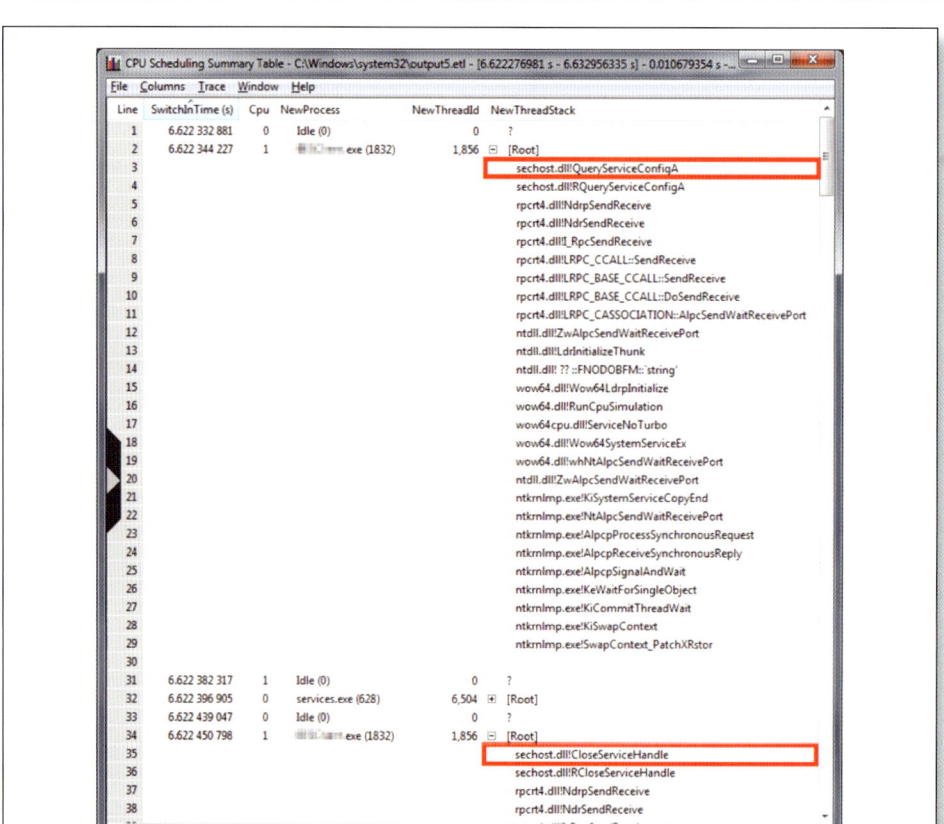

Figure 7.33 Xperf: IPI Storm Stack Dump

In the example shown in Figure 7.33, Thread ID 1856 was blocked when the application called `QueryServiceConfig()` and `CloseServiceHandle()`. When these Win32 APIs are called from the application, they communicate internally with `services.exe` through a remote procedure call (RPC), and while it's waiting for the response from `services.exe`, CPU1 enters the C-state. When `services.exe` is ready with the result, it sends IPI (Inter Processor Interrupt) back to CPU0 and brings the thread back to active state. In return, `services.exe` finishes with the RPC and enters C-state until the next RPC comes in.

Apparently, this application program enumerates all services in the system and repeats `OpenServiceHandle()` (not shown in the figure), `QueryServiceConfig()`, and `CloseServiceHandle()` API calls for each service. This causes thousands of C-state transitions on CPU0 and CPU1.

I/O Issues

Even if the software consumes very small CPU cycles and few C-state transitions, software still can make large impact to the battery life of the entire system by increasing I/O subsystem power consumption. This section discusses how to identify I/O activities for each device class.

Disk I/O Issues

Process Monitor (ProcMon) from Sysinternals is a useful tool for disk I/O analysis. Please see the References section for the availability of this tool.

When analyzing file/registry access, the following aspects of file system activities and registry activities need to be checked:

1. Activity type

   Most disk I/O activities are caused by an application program's file access or registry access. Generally speaking, repeated read access to the same file or registry entry doesn't cause much impact because they're cached. However, if different files or registry entries are accessed (like scanning all files in the file system) or write access happens, they will increase the activity of disk drive and the link to the disk drive.

2. Activity timing

   As shown in Table 7.1, HDD has multiple power saving states, but they take certain duration inactivity before those states are enabled. So, the same rule illustrated in Figure 7.36 applies to disk access. Time stamp of file/registry access that potentially causes disk access (as described above) has to be checked. For example, if read access to different files are happening once every second, it will most likely keep the drive in active idle or performance idle state and loose the opportunities for HDD to enter Low Power Idle or Standby (spin-down) state.

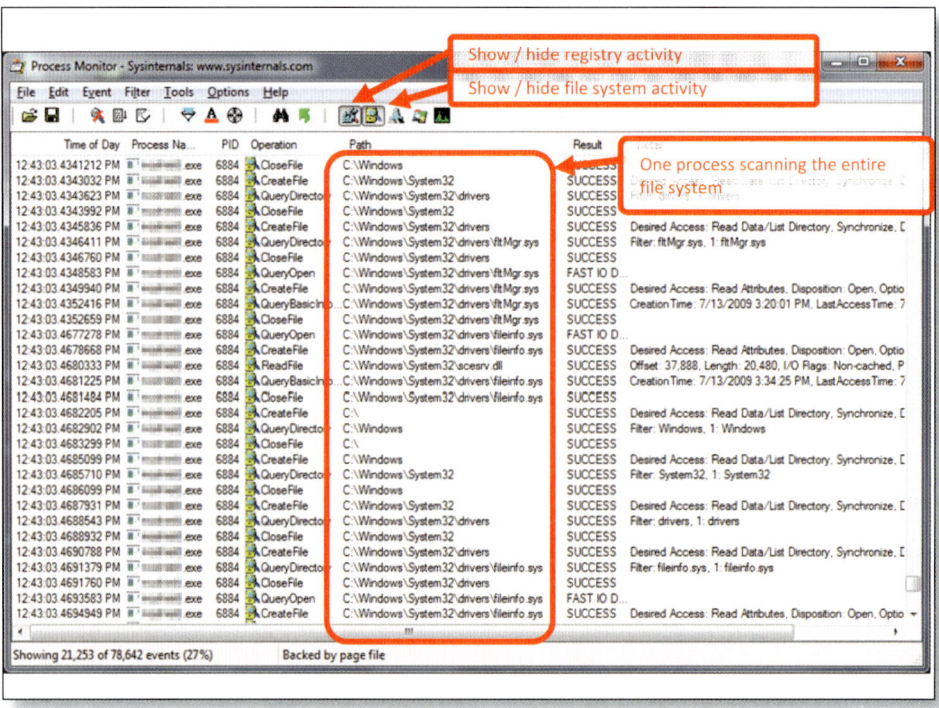

Figure 7.34 ProcMon: File System and Registry Activity

Network I/O Issues

Network I/O activities can also be monitored with Process Monitor, as shown in Figure 7.35. Which process is sending/receiving packets and the destination/source of those packets can be determined from the output of the program. Using this information, it can be determined whether these activities are necessary or not.

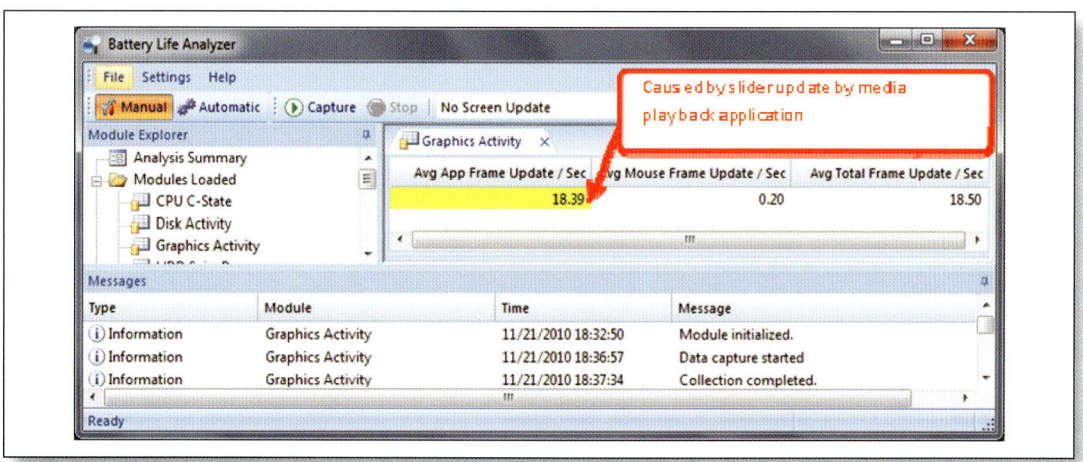

Figure 7.35 ProcMon: Network activity

Graphics I/O Issues

By default, Windows (after Vista SP1) suppresses vertical blank interrupt (VBI) generation of the graphics adapter after 10 VBI cycles with no graphics activity. To take advantage of this power-saving feature, the number of frames updated—even if the number of pixels updated are very small—should be minimized. Battery Life Analyzer shows the number of frames updated.

Figure 7.36 Battery Life Analyzer: Graphics Activity Analysis

Please note that graphics activity happens every time the application program tries to overwrite the screen with same image. In Figure 7.36, a media playback program is calling an API to update a slide (which shows current playback position) very frequently. However, only few of them actually make the image change. Other calls only overwrite the same slide image.

USB I/O Issues

USB (up to USB 2.0) is a polling-based interface and even when there is no meaningful data transfer to/from a device, the host controller has to poll the devices constantly and that activity keeps a large portion of the platform active. To minimize the power impact of a USB subsystem, well behaved devices implement Selective Suspend state. Devices enter Selective Suspend state when they are not used or they are in long idle state. Once all downstream devices are in the Selective Suspend state, the USB hub can enter Selective Suspend. Similarly, the host controller can enter Selective Suspend after all downstream device enters Selective Suspend and the USB subsystem becomes quiescent. For more details about Selective Suspend state implementation, please refer to the Microsoft whitepaper on the topic. A link to the whitepaper can be found in the References section.

If software accesses USB devices frequently (once per minute or more), it will significantly reduce the opportunity for the USB host controller to enter Selective Suspend state.

Battery Life Analyzer's USB analysis feature measures the duration of Selective Suspend for each host controller, hub, and devices. To verify USB devices are in the Selective Suspend state, start looking at the host controller. If the host controller's selective suspend duration is high enough (greater than 90 percent), there is no problem with the devices under that host controller. Otherwise, find the device showing low selective suspend duration under that host controller.

Frequent Snoop Cycle Issues

Modern devices, including all devices discussed above, transfer data to memory using a bus master transfer. This can happen at any time and if the CPU is in idle state but the cache memory is still active (that is, CPU package C-state is in C3 or C6), it causes the CPU package to wake up (to CPU package C1 or C2 state) to snoop the cache memory, and this can cause a significant platform power increase if this situation happens frequently. As discussed in the "CPU C-State Residency" section, this can be observed as high CPU package C1 or C2 state residency.

If high CPU package C1 or C2 state residency is seen, the next step is to determine which device is causing the problem. The easiest way is to remove each potential device one by one and see if it affects the package C-state residency. If it is not possible to remove a device physically, the next best thing is to disable it in the device manager.

Chapter **8**

Embedded Applications

To raise new questions, new possibilities, to regard old problems from a new angle, requires creative imagination and marks real advance in science.

— Albert Einstein

Embedded applications run the gamut of specialized computing needs. Ranging from telecommunications to medical equipment, embedded systems tend to have one thing in common; they are good at doing one specific function. Unlike their more general computing counterpart, the PC, embedded systems often operate in extreme conditions. These conditions could be extreme temperature conditions ranging from -40 to $+85°$ C, to "always on, always available" mission-critical computing applications such as military/aerospace. In this chapter, we discuss several embedded applications, their thermal environments, and some of their unique power management considerations.

Telecommunications Market

The telecommunications market consists of service providers, datacenters, base stations (transmitters/receivers), and cell phones. For the purpose of this chapter, we will omit discussions on cell phone devices as they are considered mobile consumer devices versus traditional embedded systems. The role of telecommunications has never been more important than today. Sending and receiving information is growing exponentially each year. From business transactions to social networking and from packet processing to cell phone short

173

message services (SMS), demands on telecommunications service providers is on the rise. Hardware and software will have to scale out to take on additional data flow demand while keeping an eye on overall power consumption. Power management will play a key role in the ability of the telecommunications market's ability to grow affordably. Typical telecommunications embedded systems, such as the one shown in Figure 8.1, require low power processing, high reliability and availability, and higher ambient operating temperatures. Certain guaranteed throughputs must be maintained per service level agreements (SLAs) between carriers and service providers. As such, system designers must use care in implementing embedded system power management features to limit unresponsive behavior or dropped packets of data.

Figure 8.1   ATCA Board with DP Intel® Xeon® Processors

Thermal Considerations

A majority of telecommunications embedded systems within the United States adhere to Network Equipment Building Systems (NEBS) environmental conditions guidelines. NEBS is a multilevel set of specifications that address acoustics, fire hazard, thermal margins, airflow, and failure/backup protocol. Though not a telecommunications mandate, NEBS-compliant systems allow for standardized equipment and overall lower development costs due to hardware compatibility from vendor to vendor and generation to generation. Thermal environmental specifications within NEBS (GR-63-CORE and GR-1089-CORE†) allow for the inlet airflow temperature to reach 55° C, which is much warmer than traditional computing ambient temperatures (typical office PC ambient temperature is between approximately 25 and 30° C). Because of this higher ambient inlet temperature, thermal solution design must comprehend a more efficient thermal resistance requirement. The properties of the system are governed by the following equation:

```
Theta_ca = (T_case − T_amb)/TDP
Where Theta_ca = thermal resistance from case to ambient
And T_case (or T_c) = case temperature of the microprocessor,
    T_amb = local ambient temperature near microprocessor,
And finally, TDP = Thermal Design Power specification
```

Ideally, designers should aim to for low-powered components that allow for a higher thermal resistance requirement (Theta_ca). As you can see by the above equation, one method to achieve a higher thermal resistance (higher equals easier to cool, lower equals more difficult to design), is to use microprocessors with a lower the TDP.

State Management

Intel processors and chipsets utilize various states to lower overall power consumption when demand is low, and "wake" on command to accommodate spontaneous computational needs. As described in Chapter 3, these states include C-states, P-states, and S-states.

One special variation of a P-state (P0), also known as Turbo, allows a processor to operate above a specified frequency if thermal conditions exist to do so. This added turbo boost increases frequency and voltage, and thereby throughput for an unspecified amount of time depending on the available thermal margin and duration. Each lower or deeper level of a state can put the processor and/or system into lower power consumption. On the flipside however, the deeper the state, the longer it takes for the system to come back to full functionality. These latency times range from microseconds to milliseconds, and may be unacceptable for some embedded applications. Power management algorithms can be written to balance the tradeoffs between power conservation and system response time. The states described above conform to the open standard Advanced Configuration and Power Interface (ACPI) specification for power management. Figure 8.1 shows a typical telecommunications blade in an ATCA form factor (Advanced Telecommunications Computer Architecture).

Military, Aerospace, and Government (MAG) Markets

MAG markets differ from telecommunications in several ways. More emphasis is focused on reliability and quick boot-up time. Failsafe mechanisms must be added to ensure the embedded systems will operate flawlessly despite perhaps being put into a "deep sleep" a majority of the time. Examples of MAG embedded systems include various types of mobile military communications equipment designed to be portable and rugged for in-field use under extreme environmental conditions, such as the one shown in Figure 8.2. These devices often need to withstand extreme temperatures and harsh dust and moisture climates. Low power microprocessors are often selected for these markets due to their higher T_{case} specifications and lower TDPs.

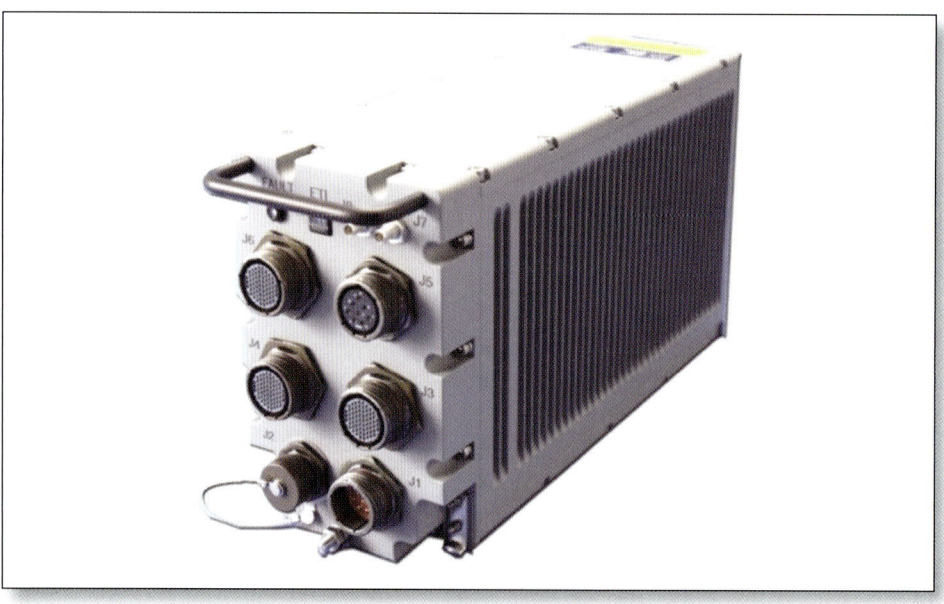

Figure 8.2   Ruggedized 6U System, 5-Slot, Passive Convection from Kontron

Note: A microprocessor with an integrated heat spreader (IHS) specifies a T_{case}, and one with a bare die (no IHS) specifies a $T_{junction}$.

Another military trend in computing is wearable computers whereby soldiers wear very low power embedded computing systems that can communicate, enhance visibility, and dictate operations in the field of battle. These systems typically run on batteries and/or have solar charging technology to power them, making power management a key factor. Intel provides US Department of Defense (DoD) developers and system integrators with a comprehensive selection of ruggedized, interoperable commercial off-the-shelf (COTS) solutions at multiple levels of integration, with a clear upgrade path and long-term road maps of products. For more information on military embedded applications, see (Intel, 2011, MAG). Figure 8.2 shows a ruggedized military embedded system.

Aerospace applications, on the other hand, need to operate at extreme altitudes and pressures and also require high reliability and failsafe operation. Examples of aerospace usages include avionic control systems, in-flight infotainment, and other real-time control systems.

Power Management Challenges for MAG

Military and aerospace applications must strike a fine balance between power consumption, battery life, and system response time (which is arguably more critical than telecommunications). Specifically, the instant availability for, say, a defense installation to be wakened from deep sleep in the middle of a frigid cold region to be alerted and possibly deployed within seconds requires the highest level of robustness from both the hardware and software systems. In these critical applications, performance is the top priority, while power savings may be a distant second. Turbo mode may also be a good application to utilize in a HUGI (Hurry Up and Get Idle) fashion.

In-Vehicle Infotainment (IVI)

In-vehicle infotainment, as shown in Figure 8.3, has been around for a long time. From AM/FM radios with CDs, cassettes, and yes, even 8-track players, to today's standalone navigation units and personal video game players, automobile passengers prefer to be entertained and kept aware of their surroundings. Fast-forward to today with the Internet, ever-present via Wi-Fi[†], WiMax[†], 3G/4G, Google Maps[†], and demands for intelligent IVI solutions are exploding. Intel has been working with automakers and their original design manufacturers (ODMs) to come up with safe in-vehicle computing that offers entertainment, Web access, navigation, real-time traffic reporting, and communication between home, office, and car.

Figure 8.3   In-Vehicle Infotainment System

Thermal Challenges for IVI

Automotive devices are typically designed for temperatures ranging from −40 C to +85° C. This extreme ambient temperature range requires a system to be available at subzero conditions where crystal formations alone could render a rotational platter on a hard drive to malfunction. Just imagine what it would do to a liquid crystal display! On the other end, 85° C (a mere 185° F!) is no joyride either. Designing an embedded computing system to operate within this wide range of environmental conditions requires components that can withstand the temperatures and also utilize as little power as possible. While most of the current IVI systems in the market make use of a system fan to help remove warm air from the internal electronics, a fan may not always be an option. Other methods for heat removal may be employed including natural convection, conduction to the chassis, or remote exchange cooling (removing the head via a heat pipe or other device to another area where it can then be cooled by other sources of airflow). The majority of IVI solutions are located behind the dashboard in a 1-DIN or 2-DIN form factor. They usually include an integrated touchscreen display, computer, and GPS system. Intuitively, you might think a hot summer's day in the middle of the Death Valley would be the most extreme heat scenario. Surprisingly, this may not be the case. It very well could be in the middle of winter with the heater full-on cooking your IVI system from behind the dashboard.

Power Management for IVI

Unlike the PC or Mac[†] in your home, an IVI system must operate at a very low power consumption level. Because drawing too much power from the 12V car battery would eventually prohibit your vehicle from starting, power management becomes a top priority. The family of Intel® Atom® processors is designed to meet power levels below 5 watts and employ power management states such as sleep and deep sleep. Putting a microprocessor into a sleep state such as S3 will allow an IVI unit to use almost no power.

Home Energy Management Systems (HEMS)

A new emerging market that is quickly growing is home energy management. As the market name implies, the primary goal of this embedded application is to monitor your home's usage of utilities such as electricity, gas, and water. Gathering a home's energy/utility demands and intelligently reporting your usage trends allows for endless customization of these systems from a central, connected location. Examples include alerting a person that they are washing clothes during peak electrical rates, while waiting one hour would save on the overall electrical bill. Another example is an alert on your smart phone that you left your lights on in the kitchen, even allowing you the ability to adjust climate remotely. Intel has developed a reference design based on the Intel Atom processor for HEMS that enables an ODM to accelerate their time to market.

Thermal Challenges for a HEMS System

While no standard form factor has been settled upon by industry leaders, some things are certain: the HEMS device should look like a consumer electronic device, comfortable in any room, and should not utilize a lot of power itself while monitoring your power (obviously). Intel's home energy reference design, codenamed Dashboard (Figure 8.4), measures approximately 7" wide × 12" tall × 1" deep, is designed to mounted on a central wall location, and operates without a fan. The device can act as a hanging clock display, or power down graphics entirely when not in use, has wireless connectivity, and can control various utilities within a smart home. The microprocessor power consumption should be less than 5 watts TDP to allow for fanless designs. Environmental conditions should account for venting, though exposure to some elements such as sunlight and moisture must be considered. Skin temperature is also a factor. A homeowner should not expect to reach for a touchpad and feel a hot surface; therefore, a rear conduction and/or natural convection thermal solution should be designed. Typical home ambient temperatures range from 20 to 30° C.

Figure 8.4   Intel® Home Energy Dashboard Proof of Concept

Power Management Challenges for HEMS

How do you save energy while consuming energy? How does a computing device become part of the solution and not part of the problem? If a home energy management system can save an average home ~2.5 kWHr per day, then it would more than pay for the 30–50 WHr it sips. What's more, as tomorrow's smart home gets "smarter," creating energy through alternate sources such as solar, geothermal, and other methods, energy could actually be sold back to the grid (also known as utility providers' infrastructure). Predictive energy usage patterns could be tracked and programmed so as to minimize utilization during peak rates while maximizing energy efficiency: all of which help save the climate and perform our fair share. The ideal HEMS embedded device should have some sort of sensor (for example: a motion sensor) that, when approached, would wake the system from a power-down state to allow for energy monitoring, programming, or other embedded applications. What's more, this device could also be "wakened" via the Internet to allow for full remote control. If this all seems like something out of the Jetsons, get used to it because embedded devices and ubiquitous connectivity are here to stay!

Retail Market

Of all the embedded applications discussed so far, perhaps no market can benefit more from power management than the retail market. From point-of-sale (POS) terminals to ATM banking machines, from hospitality booths to walk-up kiosks, retail embedded applications really need to go on a power diet. Specifically, these devices need to power down during nonoperational hours or off-peak times. Why have ten cash registers "ON" all day everyday if only one or two checkout lanes are required? Why not stay in sleep mode until a system update from corporate comes down the wire via Intel® Active Management Technology (Intel, 2011, AMT)? Initial studies have shown potential power consumption savings of up to 70 percent over non–power-managed systems. Multiply that times the number of retails stores in a chain and it adds up quickly.

Form factors such as the futuristic one shown in Figure 8.5 on Intel's Retail Proof of Concept (POC) are somewhat typical of standard desktop computing guidelines. ATX or mini-ITX motherboard specifications, along with processor and system fans, are often allowed. However, in some applications, such as a banking ATM sitting outside a building or storefront, special thermal requirements must be considered. Specifically, anyone designing for a computing chassis within a larger cabinet, which then sits in high external ambient temperatures, must comprehend sufficient airflow design and non-susceptibility to environmental conditions (dust, rain, security breach, and so on).

Figure 8.5   Intel® Retail Proof of Concept

Digital Signage

Today's digital signage has come a long way from the old store posters once seen in malls across the country. Rich multimedia content running on large displays (think 55" LCDs!) now highlight products and advertisements while intelligently capturing audience interest, gender, age, and other characteristics through advanced anonymous video analytics. Report gathering, such as the number of targeted audience views, can be directly correlated to a specific ad to gauge the impact or success of the ad campaign. This is all done analytically through hardware and software developed specifically for the digital signage industry.

Intel is developing new digital signage form factor Proof of Concepts (see Figure 8.6) aimed to show retailers what is possible. The compute portion of the digital signage system resembles a standard ATX or mini-ITX motherboard; however the chassis must be placed inconspicuously within the display such that maximum viewing is achieved with little to no noise and/or heat coming from the rear of the unit. Some newly developed digital signage displays include pluggable compute modules in the rear of the display that can be upgraded as technology advances. In the example in Figure 8.6, two embedded PCs are located within the bamboo base at the bottom of two very large displays. The displays themselves are actually being projected from a distance behind and onto the glass allowing potential customers to see products "through" the screen into a virtual store.

Figure 8.6 Intel® Digital Signage Proof of Concept

Power Management Considerations

Power management considerations include custom sleep states that allow for a static image to remain visible while putting the rest of the system into a low power down mode. Upon motion or sound detection (simulating an approaching customer), the display would wake to full functionality and could begin video analytics and engage the prospective consumer.

Industrial Control Systems

Industrial Control Systems (INDU) covers a wide variety of human machine interface (HMI) applications ranging from factory control of manufacturing robotics (Figure 8.7) to remote control management of utilities such as oil and water drilling. In typical industrial control systems, data is gathered from a field device and reported back to a centralized location where they get supervisory controlled by an operator. These field devices along with the supervisory controlled systems must be flexible and scalable for developers to create programmable logic control (PLC) software applications to meet various industrial I/O requirements. Example form factors are mini-ITX and nano-ITX motherboard specifications, with chassis design usually thin yet sturdy to survive factory conditions. Ambient temperatures are higher than traditional computing environments (~40° C), with processor TDPs ranging from 3–40 watts depending on specific applications. In systems under 10 watts, it is possible to design for a passive heat sink and fanless solution. Above 10 watts usually requires forced air convection. Industrial settings also require unique shock and vibration capabilities that must be considered as well.

Figure 8.7   Industrial Control Robotic Assembly System

Power Management Challenges for Industrial Control

Due to ruggedized factory conditions, which often call for $24 \times 7 \times 365$ operation, implementation of power management features within an embedded computing system becomes more challenging. Putting a system in a light "sleep state" between control operations while not losing response time due to wakening latency requires detailed workflow information. Intel processors can go into advanced sleep states hundreds of times per second. In fact, intermittent power savings opportunities exist in the time during keystrokes while running an industrial control application. The Intel Atom family of processors are specifically designed to utilize very low power while operating at high efficiencies.

Medical Segment

Medical-grade computing systems also fall under embedded applications. Specific examples of embedded medical devices include point-of-care terminals, patient monitoring systems, tiny handheld and portable diagnostic devices. Very high-end medical imaging systems (Figure 8.8) need lots of computing and graphics horsepower to calculate and render critical anatomical information to doctors in an expedient way. When not in use, these high-end systems must go into power savings modes to avoid contributing to rising room temperatures and overall facility cooling costs.

Thermal Challenges and Boundary Conditions

Thermal challenges and boundary conditions unique to medical involve the need for sterilization of computing hand held devices, bio-compatibility, and resistance to shock/vibration. Low power processing is essential for optimal weight and portability of some devices, while graphics computation is critical for imaging applications. Fans may or may not be allowed in medical systems depending on individual device size restrictions. Example: it is not practical to have an operating fan on an ultrasonic device that must be subject to cleaning requirements and potentially create the hazard of electrical shock. Device skin temperature is also a factor to avoid patient/care giver burning or irritation.

Figure 8.8   Technician on MRI Workstation

Power Management Challenges

Power management challenges for medical applications consist primarily around excelling in graphical display of patient imaging combined with power savings when not in use. Medical imaging applications specifically can take advantage of Intel Turbo states when thermal margin exists and accelerate computation while the processor is below its maximum case temperature. If intelligently designed, this scenario could exist indefinitely. In the case of handheld devices, particularly those based on batteries, power management becomes more meaningful. The ability to use a device such as a portable ultrasound machine for 4–8 hours on use/standby becomes an advantage for the health providers and their daily operation.

Embedded Gaming Industry

Embedded gaming consists of computer-based slot machines, lottery terminals, and arcade gaming consoles, to name a few. Demand for high-end graphics on these devices is growing as the sophistication of modern-day game versions have become digital. High-resolution displays with full HD video on larger and larger touch screens are becoming the new norm, all in an effort to capture one's attention.

Typical form factors for these embedded gaming devices resemble those of thin clients (ATX or mini-ATX style), however due to the extremely high security requirements of gaming systems and dealing with money, these chassis are embedded within the overall cabinet (Figure 8.9). This creates higher local ambient temperatures for the computing system and generally a need for a system fan within the gaming cabinet for proper ventilation.

Figure 8.9   Intel Embedded Gaming POC

Power Management Challenges for Embedded Gaming

One key challenge for gaming establishments is how to save power on rooms of these digital slot machines while still creating the visual attraction, as shown in Figure 8.9. In other words, put the system to sleep, but leave appealing graphics on the screen. As we described in the chapter on *Idle Efficiency*, this involves putting the systems into low power modes whereby voltage and frequency can be scaled down and unused components within the processor can be turned off without impacting the user experience. In addition, with Intel® AMT, these systems can be serviced/updated remotely even when powered down thereby removing the need to access and service each machine individually and potentially compromising the security of the cabinet assembly.

Table 8.1 provides a summary of embedded market segments along with their representative form factors, thermal boundary conditions, and applications.

Table 8.1   Various Embedded Applications

Market Segment	Form Factor(s)	Thermal Boundary Conditions	Applications/ Usage Conditions
Telecommunications	ATCA Blades, AMC Cards, Custom FFs	0–55° C	Routers, switches, Cellular base stations
Military, Aerospace, Government (MAG)	ATX, cPCI, custom blade FFs		Security, aviation
In-Vehicle Infotainment	2-DIN, Dash mount	−40 to 85° C	Automotive, entertainment, navigation
Home Energy Management Systems (HEMS)	Thin Form Factor, Tablet-like, mini-ITX	5–40° C	Residential, commercial, energy management
Retail Environment	ATX, mini-ITX	5–40° C	Point of sales, cash registers, shopping
Digital Signage	ATX, mini-ITX, pluggable module	0–55° C	Advertisement, entertainment, kiosks
Industrial Control Applications	Mini-ITX, nano-ITX, CommExpress	0–55° C	Factory automation, machine-to-machine,
Medical	ATX, mini-ITX,	5–40° C	Imaging, health monitoring
Embedded Gaming	ATX, mini-ITX	5–40° C	Video gaming devices, lottery

Chapter 9

Computing on the Go—Smart Phones, Tablets, and Netbooks

It's the little details that are vital. Little things make big things happen.

—John Wooden

In recent years, there has been a tremendous shift in the market for personal computing. Users are in the midst of a mass transition from stationary desktop computers to a mix of mobile architectures: PDAs, smart phones, tablets, portable media players, and netbooks. Portable music players are now ubiquitous and mobile phones have been adopted faster than any other technology in history. Netbooks, tablets, and smart phones are projected to follow a similar trend in the coming years. Although mobile architectures provide the convenience of portable computation, entertainment, and communication, their utility is severely constrained by their battery life. Power is one of the most critical factors on small form factor devices such as tablets and handheld devices as battery life directly affects the user experience on these devices. Also, operation at lower temperatures leads to prolonged system life. As the demand for mobile architectures continues to grow, it will become increasingly important to focus on understanding and optimizing the power consumption of these energy-constrained architectures.

Software development for battery-powered mobile devices is a tricky business because they are constrained platforms. One excellent example of this is Apple's iOS 5. Released in late 2011 with the iPhone 4s, some users who installed it on their iPhone 4 models experienced noticeably lower battery life. Apple responded quickly with an updated version (5.0.1) that fixed the bugs affecting battery life.

Applications intended for mobile devices are typically developed using development kits and emulators and later tested on a real device. Generally, developers are mainly concerned about correct application behavior. Software designed without considering its energy use can easily impact the standby and active use time of mobile phones. Admittedly, detailed power consumption profiling often requires a costly and cumbersome measurement setup.

The exploding number of features on today's smart phones or tablets is rapidly adding to the amount of processing power and related hardware needed for their implementation. Consumers desire more performance, more impressive multimedia, faster data connections, and better usability. As a result, devices are getting more power-hungry, to the point where power consumption and thermal issues become seriously limiting factors.

Power management is required because smart phones are battery-operated devices and run on a limited power supply. Additionally these phones are becoming smaller in physical size, which can make excessive power consumption heat them up more easily. Battery technology improves at a steady rate, but is not able to keep pace with the continuous upscaling of processing performance and resource usage. Current battery technology cannot offer the energy densities required to make the power consumption problem disappear. Given that battery technology does not seem to provide the necessary improvements regarding energy and power management, the next solution is to try improving the phone platforms so that the desired features can be implemented at a much lower cost in energy consumption.

This chapter explores what distinguishes these small form factor devices from traditional computing devices and presents a couple of specialized tools and methodologies for analyzing power. Finally a set of case studies are presented. Note that some methodologies for software energy efficiency described in earlier chapters such as computational efficiency, data efficiency, and context awareness also apply for small form factor devices. However, special considerations must be taken into account when designing and implementing software for these devices.

What Makes These Types of Devices Different?

These types of devices belong to an innovative segment of the industry where changes are happening very rapidly compared to the traditional computing arena. New device types and extended hardware/software capabilities (such specialized sensors) are introduced all the time.

Before we move further analyzing the energy-efficiency implications, first let's define what devices we consider to be part of this category, also referred to as small form factor devices.

- ■ Netbooks

- ■ Smart phones

- ■ Tablets

- ■ Mobile Internet devices (MIDs)

- ■ Portable media players

The list goes on, but what is specific with these types of devices is that they are highly integrated, often system-on-a-chip (SoC) designs that enhance the ability of the hardware to use power more efficiently, but also introduce complexity for developers aspiring to develop energy-efficient software.

Tradeoffs and Specialized Hardware

Since low power is essential for this category of devices, many hardware and software tradeoffs have been made, all impacting the overall device performance and potentially limiting the ability to support certain use cases. The following tradeoffs are commonly made:

- ■ Reduced processor performance to minimize heat dissipation, allowing fanless designs and longer up time

- ■ Simpler CPU architecture: ARM/Intel® Atom™ versus Intel® Core™— shorter pipeline, smaller cache, in-order, reduced instruction set, and so on

- ■ Reduced memory to minimize power usage (refresh) and size footprint

- Reduced storage capabilities: solid state drives (SSD) and flash memory storage are common; hard drives are increasingly uncommon

- Latency tradeoffs due to "pushing down the idle floor," shutting down power islands); devices frequently go to a low power state standby mode

- Elimination of "real" multitasking (iPhone[†])

- Removing unnecessary functionality or reducing media quality; a simplified UI will likely go hand in hand with this effort

In essence it is important to favor simplicity over performance to support the features and energy efficiency requirements central to the specific device type or customer segment.

Furthermore, compared to traditional computing platforms, it is common that devices in this category have additional specialized hardware components to accelerate frequently used functions and save energy when performing compute-heavy tasks, such as:

- Media acceleration
  - Video decode/encode
  - Audio decode

- Sensors/capabilities
  - GPS
  - Accelerometers
  - Proximity sensors
  - Compass
  - Communications: cellular (3G and so on), WiMax[†], Bluetooth[†]

Figure 9.1 shows an overview of a typical mobile platform architecture.

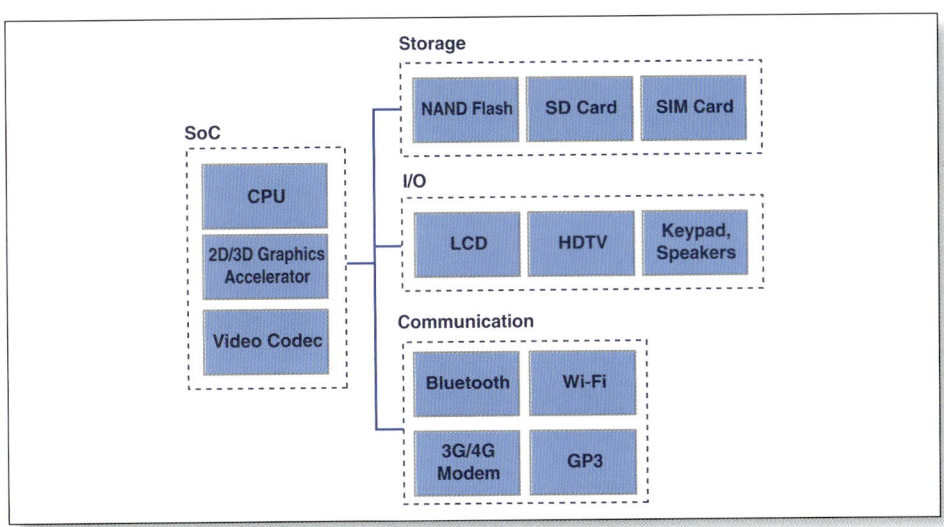

Figure 9.1   A Typical Mobile Platform Architecture

Hardware and Software Ecosystem

Supporting the multitude of specialized hardware and software components adds complexity when it comes to overall power management. The OS and applications needs to be aware of the dependencies and to adjust state depending on the active usage profile.

Compared to the traditional desktop and notebook ecosystem, the ecosystem of a small form factor device is highly fragmented both from a hardware and a software perspective. This manifests itself in the use of a few different processor architectures, many different operating systems and application runtimes, and a set of chipset manufactures using similar IP blocks.

Hardware/OS Power Management

A central part of the hardware and software stack for energy-efficient small form factor devices is a power management subsystem (OSPM). Normally this is a collaboration between hardware and software components allowing fine-grained power control over the device depending on use case. Devices are commonly built with a highly integrated SoC including a power management integrated circuit (PMIC), which has the ability to turn power on/off to a set of components (power islands). The PMIC is controlled by the OS power management software subsystem, which controls the power state of the device components based on profile and well-defined use cases.

An OSPM allows definition of use case profiles where, depending on use case, the minimum number of components required for the functionality is powered on. For instance:

■ Video playback (ON: hardware decode, hardware audio, display; OFF:)

■ Audio playback (ON: hardware audio; OFF: display)

■ Reader (ON: display; OFF: network, hardware audio/video)

■ Idle (OFF: everything but the bare essentials [if phone: 3G access…])

It's important to understand that the available system power states of a typical small form factor device are quite different from a traditional computation device. For instance, unless a specific interactional use case is enabled, a smart phone will go into standby idle state by default after a short period of time. In this state the device consumes very little energy and does not respond to user input (except for specially defined hardware interrupts). A key design aspect is also the ability to very quickly get out of the standby state into a fully operational active state.

Power Measurement on Handheld Devices

The power measurement methodology involves measuring the battery lifetime and measuring the isolated component power consumptions inside the handheld devices by putting a sense resistor across the target components. This is similar to the NetDAQ setup as described in Chapter 7, "Evaluating and

Measuring Software Impact to Platform Power." Figure 9.2 shows a typical lab setup for measurement of power on these small form factor devices.

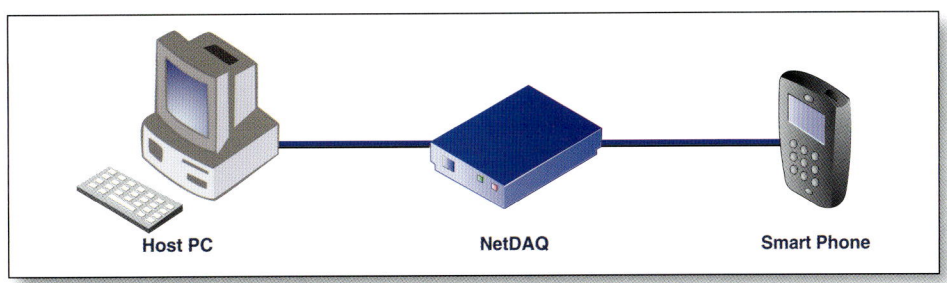

Figure 9.2   NetDAQ Test Setup

Measure Battery Lifetime Using Battery Drain Rate

In the handheld devices, set the power options to shut down the system at the lowest possible battery level (such as, for example, 3 percent), and then charge the battery back to 100 percent. A software tool should be used to log current time periodically, for example at one minute intervals, and a workload scenario should be chosen depending on the test purpose to run on the device. The experiment is set by unplugging the system, recording the start time of the battery life test, waiting until system shutdown (because of the need to run out the battery and to recharge and reboot the system) and checking the last log time. The data is collected by repeating the test four times (the first run is for battery conditioning: discard the result) and, finally, calculate the average of three runs (the second, third, and fourth runs).

$$\text{Battery life} = \text{end time} - \text{start time}$$

$$P_{average} = \text{battery capacity/battery life}$$

Fluke NetDAQ (Networked Data Acquisition Unit)

The NetDAQ unit is used to measure system/component power consumption while transmitting data, running different applications on the system. Each NetDAQ has 20 channels that may be programmed individually to perform virtually any signal conditioning function the user requires. NetDAQ logger software for Windows is a configuration and data management program for the NetDAQ systems.

■ The Target PC (shown in Figure 9.2) has a special motherboard with built-in sense resistors. For each target component (such as the CPU) all sense resistors are wired and soldered at both ends before being connected to a module attached to the NetDAQ unit.

■ The NetDAQ has modules that are attached with individual wires to the handheld device and measures the current and voltage drop across the sense resistors. The NetDAQ is connected to the Host PC via a crossover network cable as shown in Figure 9.2.

Measure the System/Component Power

The shut resistor method as illustrated in Figure 9.3 is used to measure the system/component power through the NetDAQ unit. We use equation

$$P = V \times I$$

where

$$V = \text{Voltage at input to the main system}$$
$$I = Vs/Rs, \text{ and } Vs = \text{Voltage drop across Rs}$$

Therefore,

$$P = (V \times Vs)/Rs$$
$$P_{average} = \text{Average P during testing}$$
$$\text{Estimated battery life} = \text{Battery capacity}/P_{average}$$

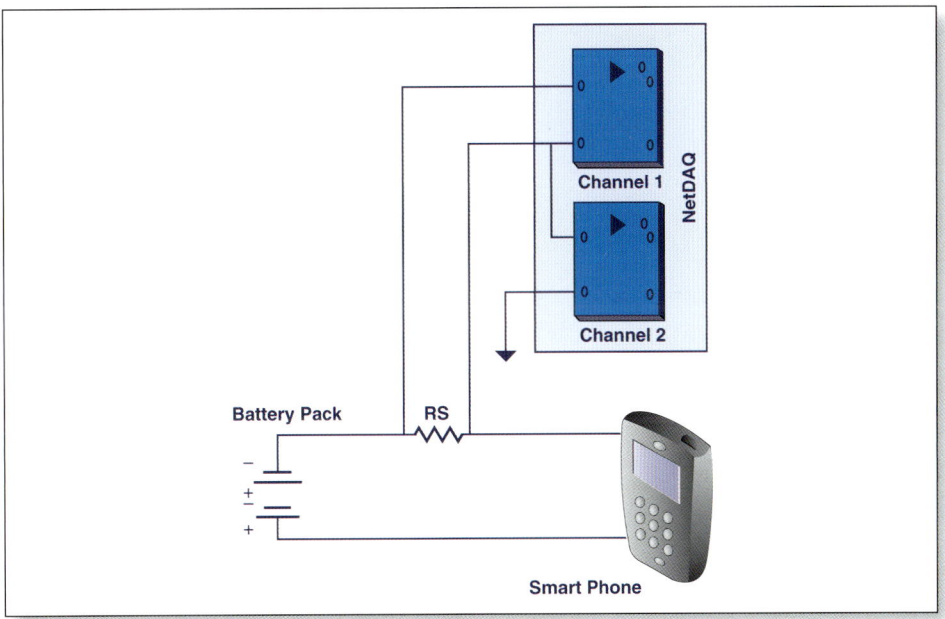

Figure 9.3   Shunt Resistor Method

The component-wise energy breakdown in smart phones helps in understanding which components draw most of the energy from the battery. Here is an example of power consumption profile for videoconferencing usage on a smart phone, which application processor contributes 0.6 W, wireless modem needs 1.2 W, and display backlight requires 0.4 W out of 3 W of total smart phone power. We can see a bulk of the power is consumed in the wireless modem; hence the power optimization effort should be concentrated on reducing the power in wireless TX/RX. The Energy Profiler tool discussed in the next section can be used to gauge the wireless power levels as well as the signal strengths during different time instances of the conferencing.

The major power consumers on these handheld devices are (in decreasing order): wireless modems (WLAN, 3G, GSM/EDGE), application processor, and display backlight. An important share of the total power is consumed by a mix of components with marginal power consumption by themselves, such as the radio modem control processor and different integrated circuits. Knowing that three components may account for roughly 65 percent of the total energy consumption, it becomes clear that reducing the load on those components will have a noticeable effect on the overall energy consumption. In practice, taking energy considerations into account will result in a more responsible use of the available resources. For example, since radio interfaces tend to be rather power-hungry, they should be disabled whenever possible.

Android

Android is a set of open-source software stacks, including operating system, middleware, and applications, for mobile devices. (Android Open Source Project, 2011) Android software was initially developed by Android Inc., which was purchased by Google Inc., in 2005. Google published the entire Android source code in 2008 under an Apache License. The Android Open Source Project is currently the official site that maintains the Android source code and development cycle (Heger, 2011).

The Android mobile operating system is developed based on a modified Linux 2.6 kernel. The difference between a modified and standard Linux kernel is that some of the libraries and drivers are either modified or completely rewritten to maximize the efficiency on running on mobile systems that with limited resources. Another reason for developing new libraries stemmed from licensing issues so the Android community decided to implement its own C library (Bionic C) and Java virtual machine (Dalvik Virtual Machine: DVM). However, since the Bionic library does not support the full set of the GNU library and Android is outside the typical Linux development cycle, this makes it difficult to port existing GNU/Linux applications and libraries to Android. (Android OS, 2011 and Maker, 2009).

Standard Linux Power Management

Power management (PM) is crucial in modern computer systems. PM helps to conserve power consumption by shutting down components as the system is at idle for some time. A Linux-based system has its own power management as a component in the kernel. The Linux PM manages power consumption via either Advanced Power Management (APM) or Advanced Configuration and Power Interface (ACPI) (see TLDP, 2011). In APM mode, the BIOS controls the system's power management without operating system involvement. ACPI is the successor to APM, which allows the operating system to directly control the system component's power states. In ACPI mode, the operating system plays a key role and is responsible for managing power consumption of the system (Vaddagiri, 2004).

Android Power Management

Apart from standard Linux, Android supports its own power management aiming to consume no power when the CPU is at idle. Android implements, on top of Standard Linux Power Management, a more aggressive, energy-saving–oriented power management policy (see PowerManager in Figure 9.4). Applications and services must request CPU resources with "wake locks" through the Android application framework and native Linux libraries in order to keep the CPU power on. If Android detects no wake lock, the system will soon be put into deep sleep to save energy (Android Power, 2011).

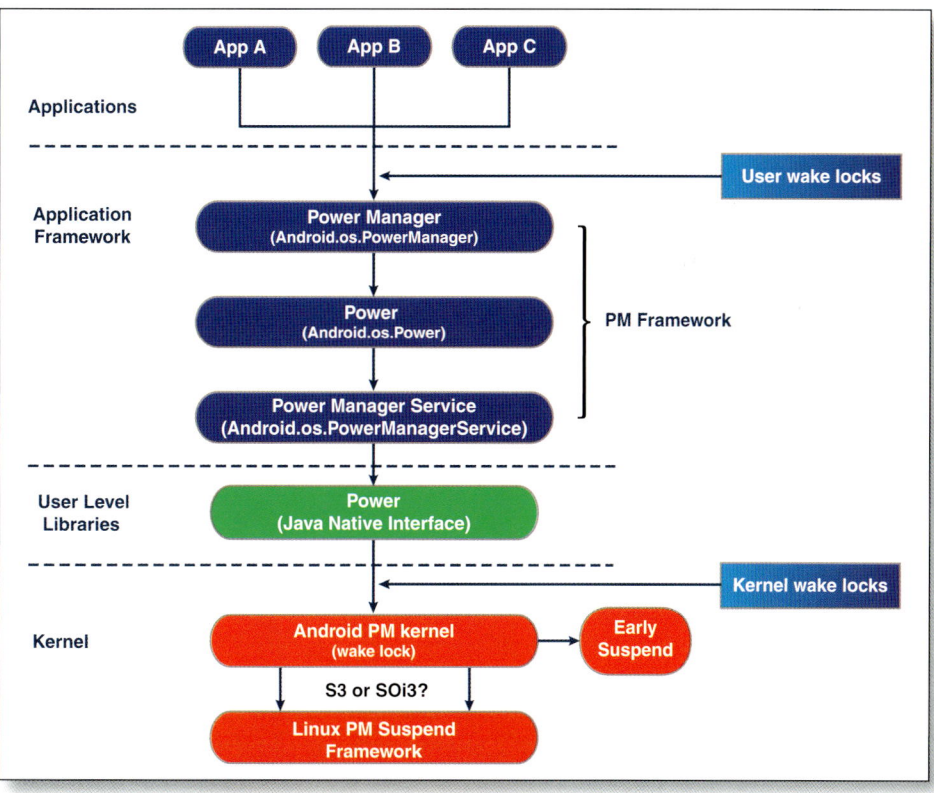

Figure 9.4　Android Power Management Architecture and Wake Locks

The wake locks are used to power on/off CPU, screen, and keyboard hardware components by requests from applications based on their nature of behaviors. Typically, all power management calls to generate wake locks follow these five steps:

1. Request a handle to the PowerManager service.

2. Create a wake lock and specify the power management flags for screen, timeout, and so on.

3. Acquire wake lock.

4. Perform an operation (play MP3, open HTML page, and so on).

5. Release wake lock.

Android Power States

The Standard Linux kernel has Suspend and Resume states. Upon entering into Suspend state, the system first freezes all processes, then it puts all the drivers into suspend mode, and suspends the CPU and hardware components. In Resume state, the system is awakened by interrupt and it will then enable IRQ, resume the CPU, wake up hardware components, restore processes, and notify Linux Power Management that the system has left the Suspend state (Zhang, 2010).

The Android-patched Linux kernel adds two additional power states, Early Suspend state and Late Resume state, as shown in Figure 9.5, to improve the efficiency of saving power in transitioning from Normal state to Suspend state. Early Suspend is the state between Suspend state and point at which the screen is turned off: hardware components like LCD backlight, sensors, and touchscreen will stop for battery life. Late Resume executes after the system resume is complete, and it resumes the hardware components suspended during early suspend.

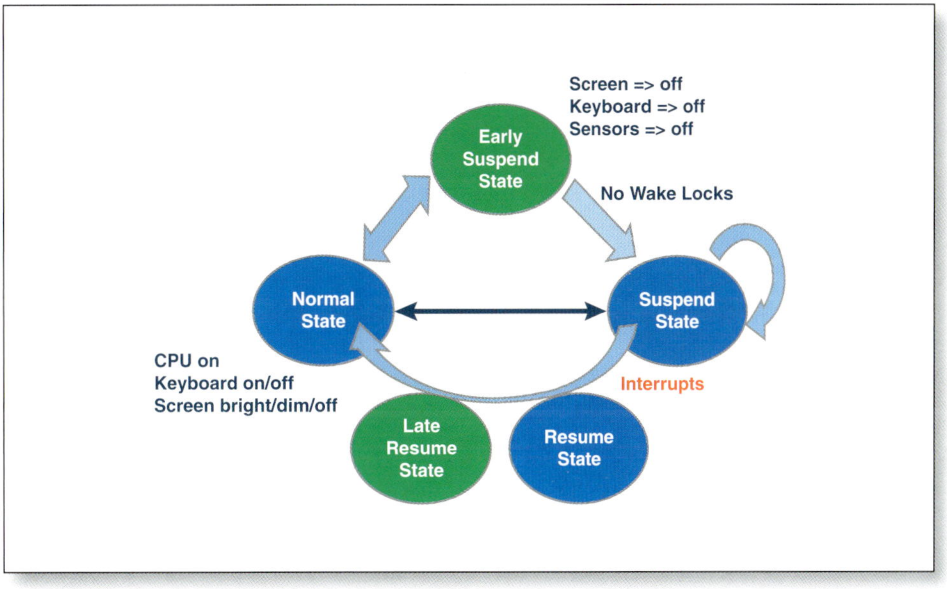

Figure 9.5   Android Power States

TOP

The Top program (Top, 2011) gives us an overview of the system states by providing real-time CPU, memory, and I/O usages of the system as shown in Figure 9.6. It also shows all the current tasks serviced by kernel on the system and lists them from top to bottom by CPU utilization. With such system and task states on hand, it is easy to determine the rough system status and which tasks occupy most CPU times and system memories.

The system states and task list are updated every five seconds by default, and the task list is configurable. In the task list, each task is shown its Process ID (PID), CPU utilization, number of threads (#THR), running User ID (UID), command line being executed (Name), Virtual Set Size (VSS), and Resident Set Size (RSS). The VSS indicates the size of virtual memory that is associated to the task whereas RSS tells the amount of physical pages allocated to the task.

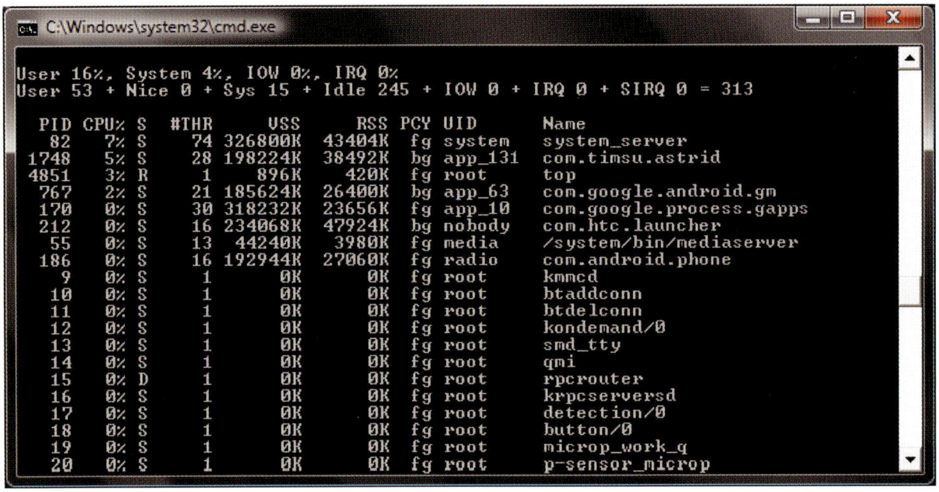

```
 C:\Windows\system32\cmd.exe

User 16%, System 4%, IOW 0%, IRQ 0%
User 53 + Nice 0 + Sys 15 + Idle 245 + IOW 0 + IRQ 0 + SIRQ 0 = 313

  PID CPU% S  #THR     USS     RSS PCY UID      Name
   82   7% S   74 326800K  43404K  fg system   system_server
 1748   5% S   28 198224K  38492K  bg app_131  com.timsu.astrid
 4851   3% R    1    896K    420K  fg root     top
  767   2% S   21 185624K  26400K  bg app_63   com.google.android.gm
  170   0% S   30 318232K  23656K  fg app_10   com.google.process.gapps
  212   0% S   16 234068K  47924K  bg nobody   com.htc.launcher
   55   0% S   13  44240K   3980K  fg media    /system/bin/mediaserver
  186   0% S   16 192944K  27060K  fg radio    com.android.phone
    9   0% S    1      0K      0K  fg root     kmmcd
   10   0% S    1      0K      0K  fg root     btaddconn
   11   0% S    1      0K      0K  fg root     btdelconn
   12   0% S    1      0K      0K  fg root     kondemand/0
   13   0% S    1      0K      0K  fg root     smd_tty
   14   0% S    1      0K      0K  fg root     qmi
   15   0% D    1      0K      0K  fg root     rpcrouter
   16   0% S    1      0K      0K  fg root     krpcserversd
   17   0% S    1      0K      0K  fg root     detection/0
   18   0% S    1      0K      0K  fg root     button/0
   19   0% S    1      0K      0K  fg root     microp_work_q
   20   0% S    1      0K      0K  fg root     p-sensor_microp
```

Figure 9.6 Top Example Run

PROCRANK

The Procrank program (Android Memory, 2011) provides more detailed memory usage per process with Vss, Rss, Pss, and Uss while the Top program only gives us Vss and Rss. In the Android system, Pss and Uss memory utilizations are more meaningful than Vss and Rss:

- Vss: Virtual set size

- Rss: Resident set size

- Pss: Proportional set size

- Uss: Unique set size

Uss indicates the set of pages that are allocated uniquely to this process. It also indicates the amount of memory will be freed after this process is stopped. Pss refers to the amount of memory shared with other processes in the way that memory is divided evenly among the processes. Memory owned by multiple processes will not be freed unless all processes that share this memory are terminated. Pss indicates the amount of memory this process is contributing.

The Procrank program also shows the process ID (PID) of the processes and the command line of how each process is launched. A snapshot of Procrank is shown in Figure 9.7.

```
# /data/local/procrank1
/data/local/procrank1
  PID      Vss      Rss      Pss      Uss  cmdline
 2490  115068K   85680K   55509K   48876K  system_server
 2603   44984K   44980K   21790K   19448K  com.sec.android.app.twlauncher
 5581   43104K   43100K   18176K   13876K  com.google.android.youtube
 2589   40168K   40164K   17195K   14708K  com.swype.android.inputmethod
 2666   33604K   33584K   11792K   10288K  com.google.process.gapps
 3065   33000K   32996K   11224K    9176K  com.google.android.apps.reader
 2594   31024K   31020K    9422K    7356K  com.android.phone
 3350   31292K   31288K    8891K    5616K  com.google.android.apps.maps
 3892   30652K   30644K    8775K    7156K  com.google.android.gm
 2391   29936K   29932K    6573K    4268K  zygote
 2667   26284K   26280K    6315K    5376K  android.process.acore
 2395    8804K    8796K    4669K    4032K  /system/bin/mediaserver
 4383   25492K   25488K    4560K    2680K  com.weather.Weather
 4805   24672K   24668K    4256K    2996K  com.cooliris.media
 2596   24072K   24068K    4214K    3260K  android.process.media
 4835   24276K   24272K    4028K    2688K  com.fsp.android.h
 5748   23620K   23616K    3766K    2456K  com.ebay.mobile:remote
 5703   22960K   22956K    3453K    2024K  com.android.settings
 2750   22984K   22980K    3443K    2536K  com.sec.android.app.sns
 4818   23152K   23148K    3384K    2472K  com.android.providers.calendar
 3879   22952K   22948K    3207K    2164K  com.sdgt1.mediahub.pl.tmo
 3053   22536K   22532K    2890K    1936K  com.google.android.apps.uploader
 3885   22560K   22556K    2880K    2004K  com.sec.android.providers.downloads
 4906   22356K   22352K    2731K    1840K  com.osp.app.signin
 4844   21452K   21448K    2364K    1504K  com.sec.android.providers.drm
```

Figure 9.7   Procrank Snapshot

Dalvik Debug Monitor Server (DDMS)

The Dalvik Debug Monitor Server (DDMS) is a debugging tool that comes with the Android SDK (Android Debugging, 2011 and Android Developers, 2011). It is integrated into the Eclipse development tool. All DDMS features can be accessed through the Eclipse IDE. DDMS offers features such as Threads, Heaps, and an Allocation Tracker to track detailed memory usages within a process. These features are valuable for tracking memory usage that may impact application performance.

To access memory tracking features, users can use the tab in DDMS Perspective from within the Eclipse IDE. The Threads feature in DDMS shows the active threads within a VM. The Heaps feature shows how much heap memory the process is using at runtime. The heap usage information can be retrieved at any time during the execution of the application. Also, through the Allocation Tracker tab, DDMS lets users to track the memory allocation of objects. Therefore, users are able to track the objects that are being allocated to memory and see which classes and threads are creating the objects. The Allocation Tracer feature allows users to see how objects are being created in real time when certain actions are performed on the application.

OProfile

Shown in Figure 9.8, OProfile is a system-wide performance profiler for Linux-based systems. It is designed to profile all the running code on the system at low overhead. OProfile consists of several tools, including a kernel driver, a daemon to collect data, and post-processing tools to transform the trace log into human readable information (OProfile, 2011). It supports hardware performance counters of microprocessors, such as ARM and Intel Atom, which are commonly used on the Android platform. All running code on the system is profiled; this includes hardware, and software interrupt handlers, the kernel, kernel modules, shared libraries, and applications.

```
$   opreport
CPU: CPU with timer interrupt, speed 0 MHz (estimated)
Profiling through timer interrupt
          TIMER: 0|
  samples|        %|
    64451   99.5628   vmlinux
       93    0.1437   opreport
       67    0.1035   libc-2.3.5.so
       44    0.0680   libstdc++.so.6.0.4
       25    0.0386   bash
       21    0.0324   oprofiled
        9    0.0139   Id-2.3.5.so
        5    0.0077   ext3
        4    0.0062   libcrypto.so.0.9.7f
        3    0.0046   jbd
        2    0.0031   libproc-3.2.5.so
        1    0.0015   grep
        1    0.0015   dm_mod
        1    0.0015   ip_conntrack
        1    0.0015   ip_tables
        1    0.0015   libpthread-2.3.5.so
        1    0.0015   oprofile
        1    0.0015   dirname
        1    0.0015   libdns.so.20.0.2
        1    0.0015   cfenvd
        1    0.0015   sshd
```

Figure 9.8   Sample Oprofile Output

OProfile is an optional component during kernel build. Android may or may not enable OProfile features by default. We can determine whether OProfile is enabled by checking the <mydroid_folder>/kernel/.config file (CONFIG_OPROFILE = y, CONFIG_HAVE_OPROFILE = y). For Android without OProfile enabled, we need to manually rebuild the kernel and to have OProfile component included. (Android Debugging, 2011).

PowerTutor

PowerTutor (Gordon, 2010) is a power monitoring application that allows users to track whether their applications on mobile devices are properly used and allows developers to improve their code to consume lower power by monitoring the power usages of the devices within smart phones (Figure 9.9). PowerTutor is originally from the Empathic System Project sponsored by the University of Michigan, Northwestern University, and Google. PowerTutor currently supports HTC G1, HTC G2, and Nexus One mobile devices for best accuracy.

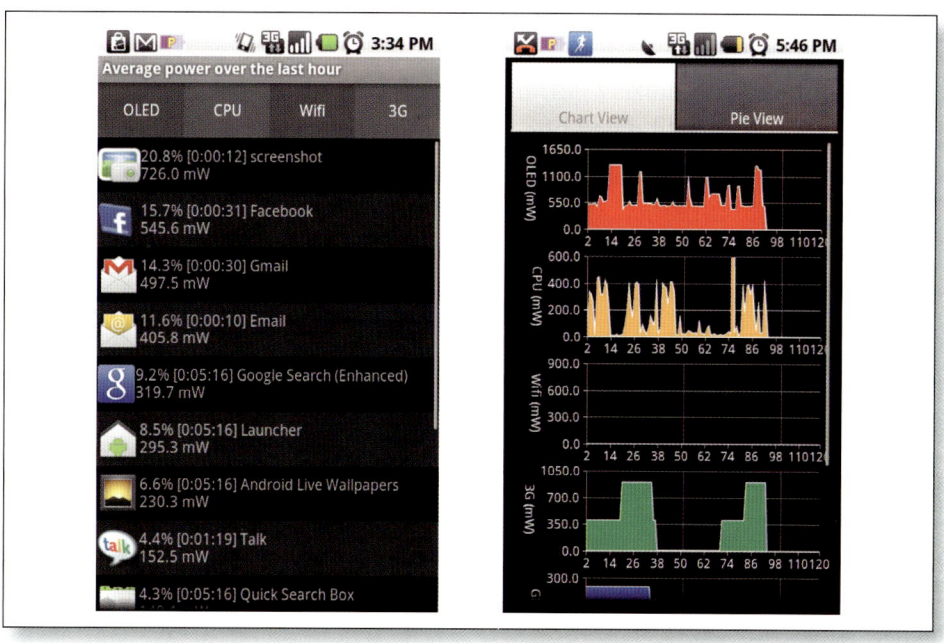

Figure 9.9 PowerTutor on Android Smart Phone (Gordon, 2010)

PowerTutor provides component-level online power estimation for smart phones. It offers timed series of power predictions for smart-phone components. PowerTutor is capable of estimating power consumptions in real time for CPU, LCD panel, GPS, Wi-Fi module, and audio components.

PowerTutor predicts component-level power usage through pre-trained models for each component. The model for each component takes inputs of voltage reading and state of discharge from battery, and the component activity, and then outputs estimated target component's power. The models used for online prediction must be trained for different hardware platforms.

TraceView

TraceView (Android Debugging using DDMS, 2011 and Bray, 2010) is a graphical tool for visualizing the application's trace log generated by either DDMS or by using the Debug Class in the code. It can aid in analyzing an application's bottlenecks and improve the application's performance. DDMS provides a convenient way, using start/stop buttons, to generate trace logs and automatically launch TraceView for a graphical view of the log. TraceView through DDMS is not as fine-grained as using Debug Class to insert code into the application, but this method is still useful.

Using Debug Class (Android Developers - Profiling with Traceview and dmtracedump) in the code to generate a finer granularity trace, we first insert the code `Debug.startMethodTracing()` to turn on the trace before the profile code region, and insert the code `Debug.stopMethodTracing()` to turn off the trace after the profile region of interest. After the application is executed, the trace log will be generated and stored in a target location.

When the trace log is generated, we can launch TraceView for a graphical view of the profiled application. TraceView renders graphical representations of application activities into two panels: Timeline and Profile. The Timeline panel describes methods called of each thread during the profile duration. The Profile panel indicates the summary of what was happening inside each method. Expanding each method in the Profile panel presents more useful information on the percentage of time used, parent/children calls, and average time per call.

Dmtracedump

Dmtracedump (Android Developers - Profiling with Traceview and dmtracedump) is another graphical tool for Android, aiming to visualize call-stack diagrams from trace log files. The tool relies on the Graphviz Dot utility for making graphic output so Graphviz has to be installed before using Dmtracedump. Dmtracedump loads a trace log file and displays the call-stack diagram in a tree that shows the call flow from parent nodes to child nodes.

Nokia Symbian

Symbian is an embedded operating system for smart phones currently maintained by Nokia. It's originally developed by Symbian Ltd for ARM-based architectures.

Nokia† Energy Profiler

Nokia Energy Profiler (Nokia Energy Profiler, 2009 and Nokia Energy Profiler quick start) is a standalone test and measurement application for power. The tool enables testing and monitoring of an application's energy usage in real time on target devices. Its main objective is to graphically show the total power consumption of the device on which it is executing. To see sample images of various system views, reference the Nokia Energy Profiler quick start web site while reading this section. The Nokia Energy Profiler supports the following views:

- Power

- Current

- Processor

- RAM Memory

- Network Speed

- WLAN

- Signal Levels

- Energy

- Voltage

Power View

Power view shows power consumption over a measurement period. The basic unit is a watt (W). The view can be switched between average and instant power. The average bar displays the mean power value for the active measurement region that is delimited by vertical grey markers. Time-selection mode enables examination of a particular section of the graph. Battery time is the estimated time that will elapse before the battery is fully discharged. This estimate is based on the average power measured over the entire region of the graph.

Current View

Current view displays current consumption, which is the measured current draw from the battery. As the battery discharges, voltage drops and current increases so that power consumption stays roughly constant. Current consumption for the same use case varies according to battery-charge level.

Processor View

Processor view shows the CPU load over a measurement period as a percentage of the total available CPU-processing capability. Values are between 0 percent and 100 percent, where 0 percent is no processing and 100 percent is maximum processing.

RAM Memory View

RAM Memory view displays the RAM memory usage over the period. The unit is megabytes. The view has a line that represents the allocated memory, and a line that shows the total RAM available. The RAM available to software differs from the total amount of physical DRAM in a device, because memory may be reserved for exclusive use. A delta symbol indicates the difference between maximum and minimum memory usage over the region. This difference in the amount of memory used is the overall operating system usage, not just that of the application. The delta symbol value illustrates the memory dynamics of the application during the measurement. The memory may have been allocated not only by the application but also by the operating system components it depends on. For this reason, a difference in initial and final memory-usage values does not necessarily mean a memory leak. It is wise to check applications running in the background if memory consumption slowly rises over days, which eventually causes a memory-full error.

Network View

The network view presents the downlink (download) and uplink (upload) speeds through the IP stack. The unit is kilobytes per second. Downlink and uplink speeds are shown simultaneously on the screen in green and orange, respectively. The average and instant bars are for either downlink or uplink data, depending on the selected input.

WLAN View

WLAN view shows received-signal strength when the device is connected to a WLAN base station. In the active standby screen, the WLAN icon is visible in the top-right corner. The received-signal strength is measured in decibels referred to 1 milliwatt (dBm), and values typically are in the range of -40 to -90 dBm. Values closer to -40 indicate very good signal conditions.

Signal Levels View

The Signal Levels view shows the cellular signal levels as RX and TX levels. The RX level corresponds to the power of the received cellular signal. The TX level refers to the transmission power from the cellular radio. Both measures are in dBm. TX levels show up only during active transmission periods (voice or data). RX levels are available whenever the device is connected to a cellular network. This means there is no RX level in the Offline phone profile.

Energy View

Energy view shows the cumulative energy consumed over the measurement period. The unit used is milliampere-hour (mAh). Although this is not the unit for energy, it is commonly used to rate the capacity of rechargeable batteries. Energy view is not available during recording because it is computed in real time.

Voltage View

Voltage view shows the battery-voltage levels. As the battery discharges, its voltage level decreases from roughly 4.2 V to 3 V until the phone switches itself off. Shutdown actually happens before the battery is totally exhausted, and thus the Battery Time estimate and true operating time are slightly different.

Apple iOS[†]

Apple first developed iOS for iPhone devices and later extended it to Apple's other products such as iPod Touch and iPad. Apple's iOS is renown for this user interface because it offers intuitive multi-touch features that enable users to directly control the elements on the smart-phone panel.

Apple Energy Diagnostics

Apple provides an instruments application to collect data about a process over time. Each instrument collects and displays a different type of information, such as file access, memory use, and so forth. The energy diagnostic instruments provide diagnostics regarding energy usage in iOS devices. They also measure the on-off state of major device components. The data collected can later be analyzed to see how much of the device's battery life each function consumes. It will tell the developer how long each of the devices various components is used and which devices were turned on and for how long. On small form factor devices, GPS in particular is a resource hog and consumes much of the device's battery life. Turning off location services once a location is obtained is ideal. The Energy Diagnostics instrument will help identify optimum use of the device's resources.

The behavior of iOS based devices depends on the mode of operation (AC or DC). The differences characteristic of being on AC or DC can cause changes in the instruments data and in particular for the Energy instruments. The Energy Usage instrument measures energy usage since startup and provides a macro measurement of a substantial workflow. The numeric scale is useful for comparison of different runs. Power source events (flags) can be added programatically. The Apple Instruments User Guide (Apple Instruments, 2011) provides much more detail on the typical energy instrument workflow and on the energy usage information that is collected.

Launching Instruments

Apple's Xcode Tools installation package includes Instruments. The Apple Instruments User Guide (Apple Instruments, 2011) provides more information on different ways to launch instruments. Among these are:

- Launch an instrument by double-clicking the Instruments application icon in the Finder. The <Xcode>/Applications directory has the Instruments application (<Xcode> is the root directory of the Xcode installation).

- Launch Instruments by double-clicking an Instruments template or trace document.

■ Launch Instruments from Xcode and target an executable in the project. An Instruments template can be chosen from the Run > Start with Performance Tool menu in Xcode.

Creating a Trace Document

Once Instruments is launched, the application automatically creates a new trace document. One can also create a new document by choosing File > New. For each new document created, Instruments prompts to select a starting template, which define the initial set of instruments that can be used in the trace document. More information regarding the trace documents is available in the Apple Instruments User Guide (Apple Instruments, 2011).

Small Form Factor Devices: Software Considerations

Software considerations for handheld devices should take into account the special power saving modes that are offered by these devices. For example, applications might use a buffering mechanism to minimize the frequent use of the network infrastructure. Another approach is to avoid unnecessary network traffic and allow networking devices go to a low power state for longer periods.

Some of the guidelines to develop energy-efficient software for handheld devices include:

1. *Design Energy Efficient User Interfaces*: Display power is the biggest consumer of total platform power. Fancy, active user interfaces keep the display alive and consuming significant power. A large chunk of time keeping the display alive is spent simply waiting for the input by the user. Techniques for creating a power-optimized user interface include:

    (i) Using touch inputs wherever possible instead of using large text based inputs

    (ii) Providing quick access to frequently-used functions

    (iii) Avoiding unnecessary animations or progress indicators on the user interface

    (iv) Using text auto-completion wherever possible

2. *Exploit Hardware Acceleration Blocks*: Most of the hand held devices these days have specific hardware blocks such as media decoders, image processing blocks, etc. Software should take advantage of these hardware acceleration blocks and offload as much computation as possible in order to save energy.

3. *Optimize the processing done in Cloud*: Many applications today take advantage of connectivity and processing data in the cloud infrastructure. While the cloud processing typically delivers better performance, the tradeoff is considerable data transfers which consumes more energy. Since specific protocols are used to connect to cloud infrastructures, optimizations may be obtainable in the traffic pattern or data could be compressed with a lightweight process on the handheld device.

4. *Perform batch processing*: Applications should try to perform tasks in a batch run instead of scheduling them periodically over time. This will help lengthen the idle periods and keep the system low power states for longer durations.

Chapter 10

Writing Energy-Efficient Software for the Data Center

In physical science the first essential step in the direction of learning any subject is to find principles of numerical reckoning and practicable methods for measuring some quality connected with it. I often say that when you can measure what you are speaking about, and express it in numbers, you know something about it; but when you cannot measure it, when you cannot express it in numbers, your knowledge is of a meagre and unsatisfactory kind; it may be the beginning of knowledge, but you have scarcely in your thoughts advanced to the state of Science, whatever the matter may be.

—William Thomson, Lord Kelvin (1824–1907)

Energy efficiency is a major concern in the data center. From fine-tuning the servers by selecting the most energy efficient parts, to the optimization of the cooling systems using thermal scheduling, techniques available to administrators are numerous and capable of improving the data center energy efficiency. The book *Energy Efficiency for Information Technology* (Ellison, 2010) presents a comprehensive survey of these techniques and methods. However, very little is known and done about the software itself. This is unexpected since hardware in general is bought solely to run software. Nevertheless, for a long time, software was simply excluded from the energy efficiency effort. Developers, keen to offload their responsibilities to the operating system vendors and hardware manufacturers, at best were optimizing their code to run as fast as possible, so the system could sleep earlier and longer, allowing the hardware to reach deep sleep states, and therefore save energy. This approach is great, but it omits the most important span of the software life cycle: when the software runs and generates useful work.

In this chapter, we present and discuss various techniques software developers can adopt to write energy-aware and energy-efficient software for the data center. Two detailed case studies are presented to illustrate this new approach focusing on software energy efficiency. The objective is to empower the software developers so they can bring their unique and indispensable expertise to the global energy efficiency effort in general and into the data center in particular.

Software Energy Efficiency

We define *software energy efficiency* as the ratio between the amount of useful work generated by the software and the amount of energy consumed by the system(s) required to generate that useful work.

$$SW\ Energy\ Efficiency = \frac{Useful\ work}{Energy}$$

The following list provides a few examples of software energy efficiency metrics. Note that inverse metrics can be used when the work done is not null, in other words, when the software is not idle but productive.

- SQL transactions executed per joule

- Video frames encoded per joule

- E-mails sent per joule

- E-mail bytes sent per joule

Since software is unique, and because there are no universal proxies to measure the useful work, we decided not to simplify the problem to avoid denaturing it. Therefore, we let the software define what the useful work it does is. As a consequence, some sort of instrumentation is required to account for and to expose this very important quantity. Other than the amount of useful work done, nothing else is required to measure the software energy efficiency when using the Intel® Energy Checker Software Development Kit.

The Intel® Energy Checker

The Intel® Energy Checker Software Development Kit (SDK) was developed to help software developers measure software energy efficiency and to write energy-aware software. Energy-aware software is capable of measuring and reporting its energy efficiency metrics dynamically. The SDK was designed to simplify this task, so the software vendor can focus on developing the heuristics required to save energy. These heuristics—a real added value for the company— can use many different inputs, including the energy efficiency metrics.

The tools provided in the SDK also allow data center managers to better understand and measure facility productivity using metrics that really matter to the end user, while hardware is running the end user's software, crunching the users' data.

In this chapter, only the first use model is exercised. Readers interested in the other use models of the SDK can consult the documentation.

SDK Lingo

At the core of the SDK is a very simple application programming interface (API) allowing unidirectional data exchanges between applications. It is composed of five functions (`pl_open`, `pl_attach`, `pl_read`, `pl_write`, and `pl_close`), which can be used from most programming languages (C/C++, Java, C#, Objective-C). In addition, a scripting version of these functions is provided so they can be called from scripts and batch files.

The exchanged data is called *counter*. These counters are software counters and should not be confused with hardware counters like the ones found in modern processors' performance monitoring units (PMUs).

Counters are eight-byte unsigned integers (`unsigned long long` in C) and are designed to count events or processes such as SQL transactions executed, gigabytes of data written to storage, or video frames encoded. A good analogy for a counter is the odometer counting miles or kilometers traversed by a vehicle.

Counters can also be used to signal remarkable conditions or software states. Such *state counters* (or state variables) may be used, for example, to signal in which software phase the code is running, what is the code performance, or even whether the software meets or does not meet its QoS (quality of service) agreement. Figure 10.1 shows a recording over time of several counters defined in the scope of an image rendering software application. Note that state counters become handy when the data is processed post-mortem. The *Software Phase* counter in Figure 10.1 clearly delimits when the application was rendering an image and when it was active idle.

These counters are logically regrouped into *productivity links* (PLs), and can be *exposed* (written) and *imported* (read) between applications.

Last but not least, the SDK encourages the use of *integral counters*. Integral counters hold the sum over time of a counter's value. For example, energy is the integral counter of power. Integral counters are useful to ease the task of software using them (the data consumer—such as management middleware or an experimentation framework). Indeed, it allows running multiple, even overlapping measurements in parallel with a minimal processing requirement from the consumers. For instance, by measuring the elapsed time between two arbitrary run points of interest, it is possible to compute the average power drawn by a system executing a single subtraction and a single division.

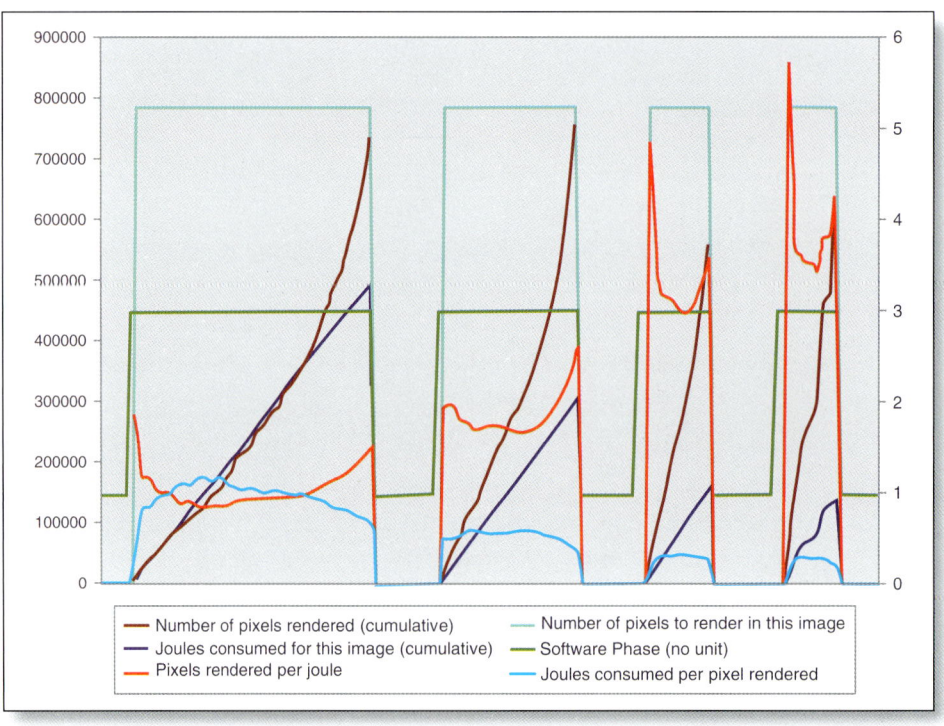

Figure 10.1 Several counters and state variables of an image renderer recorded over time. The *Software Phase*, the square blue curve, is a state counter used to represent applications activity: 0 = not running, 1 = active idle, and 3 = rendering.

ESRV the Energy Server

Besides the core API, the SDK is shipped with several useful tools, among which is ESRV (Energy SeRVer). This module uses the SDK API to expose, via a set of counters, key metrics related to energy and power. As a consequence, the software developer can focus on adding energy-saving heuristics to their code without having to spend resources in managing communications with a mixture of power measurement devices. Figure 10.2 lists the counters exposed by ESRV. These counters are directly accessible by applications using the API. The SDK documentation can be consulted for a list of supported measurement devices. Note that ESRV also maintains a set of MIN and MAX counters to simplify the monitoring of over and under loads.

```
Energy (Joule)
Energy (kWh)
Energy Overflows (no unit)
Power (Watt)
Power (Watt)--Max
Power (Watt)--Min
Current (Ampere)
Current (Ampere)--Max
Current (Ampere)--Min
Current (Ampere seconds)
Voltage (Volt)
Voltage (Volt)--Max
Voltage (Volt)--Min
Voltage (Volt seconds)
Power Factor (no unit)
Power Factor (no unit)--Max
Power Factor (no unit)--Min
Power Factor (no unit seconds)
Current Frequency (Hertz)--Max
Current Frequency (Hertz)--Min
Current Frequency (Hertz seconds)
Voltage Frequency (Hertz)
Voltage Frequency (Hertz)--Max
Voltage Frequency (Hertz)--Min
Voltage Frequency (Hertz seconds)
Channel(s)
Status
Version
```

Figure 10.2 Listing of the key counters exposed by ESRV. Note that not all measurements are provided by all power meters. Only counters in bold are always available. Integral counters are marked in italic.

The Intel Energy Checker SDK supports a wide range of operating systems and hardware platforms. The source code of the core API and of several of its components is shipped.

Making PostgreSQL and TPCC-UVA Energy Aware

The Intel Energy Checker SDK can be used to instrument any kind of application running on most systems. However, in this chapter, a typical data center application was chosen and instrumented: a database engine and a transactional workload. The PostgreSQL (PostgreSQL, 2010) data base and the TPCC-UVa (Llanos, 2010) benchmark were instrumented and are used in the two case studies presented in this chapter. Similar instrumentation can be performed on other data bases.

One recommendation the SDK documentation suggests to developers is to limit the impact of the instrumentation to the existing source code. This can often be achieved by adding a dedicated *metric thread* to the application (Figure 10.3). This metric thread is then responsible for collecting the useful work data from the worker thread(s), importing the energy readings from the right instance of ESRV, and computing and exporting the energy efficiency metrics. The SDK documentation has sample code demonstrating these tasks and more. Note that even if it is not required to export energy efficiency metrics, it is a good suggestion to take, so it can be monitored by tools and used by management middleware.

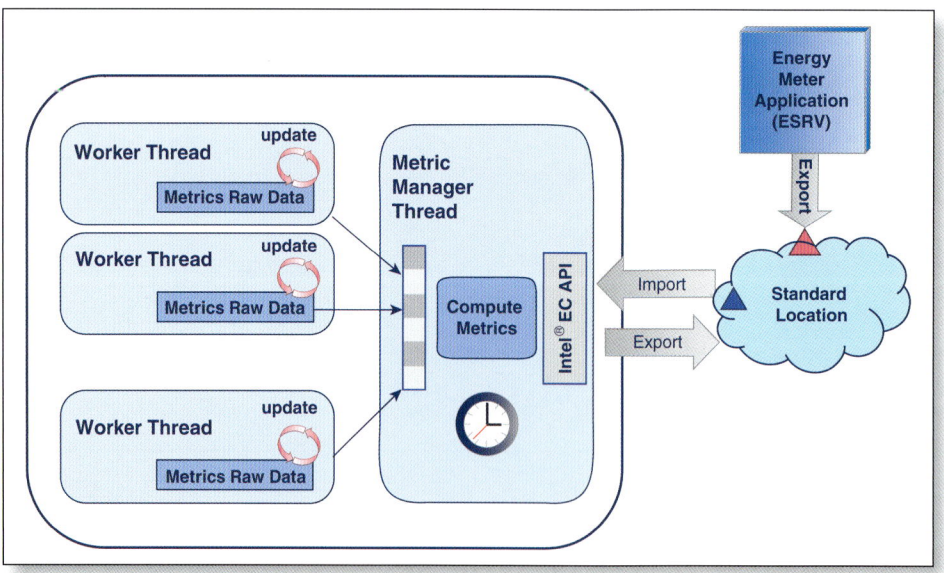

Figure 10.3 Adding a dedicated metric thread makes it possible to limit the impact of the instrumentation in existing code.

Nonetheless, with a database engine such as PostgreSQL, we can completely avoid touching the software's source code and simply rely on the database's existing statistics gathering mechanism to extract the amount of useful work done. For PostgreSQL, useful work was simply defined as the number of SQL statements executed. Proceeding this way, we can devise a set of dedicated processes, called *loggers,* which communicate with the database backend using the PostgreSQL native interface (version 8.4.4). A similar approach is taken when it comes to instrumenting the workload, which is a transactional benchmark in this case (TPCC-UVa). Logs generated on the fly by the frontend are parsed by a logger and the extracted data is used to compute and expose energy efficiency metrics and benchmark results using the SDK API. Figure 10.4 represents the basic data exchange flows between the database and the main logger.

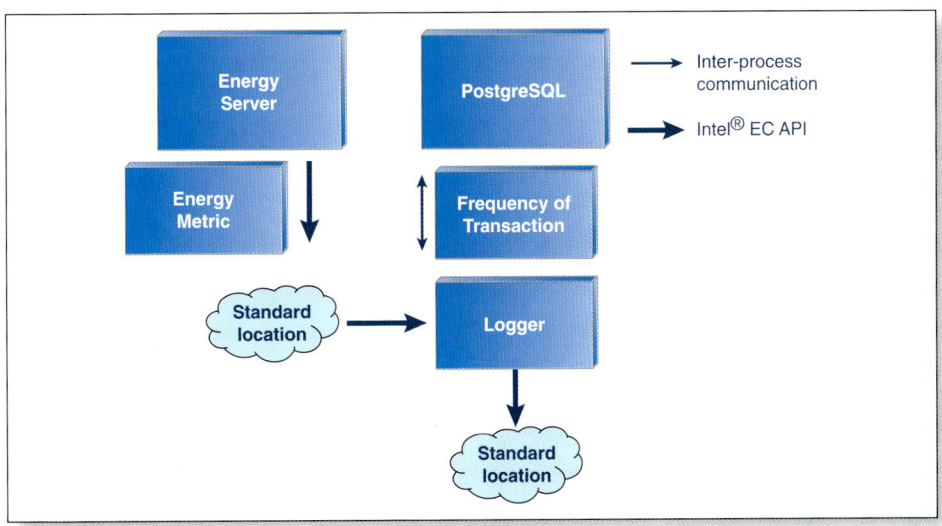

Figure 10.4 Flow of data exchanges occurring between the database backend and the main logger.

Figures 10.5 and 10.6 represent in more detail the overall experimental setup architecture and the added instrumentations. In addition to the dynamic logger, a static logger is added for run validation, so it can report final TPCC-UVa results and statistics in a dedicated PL.

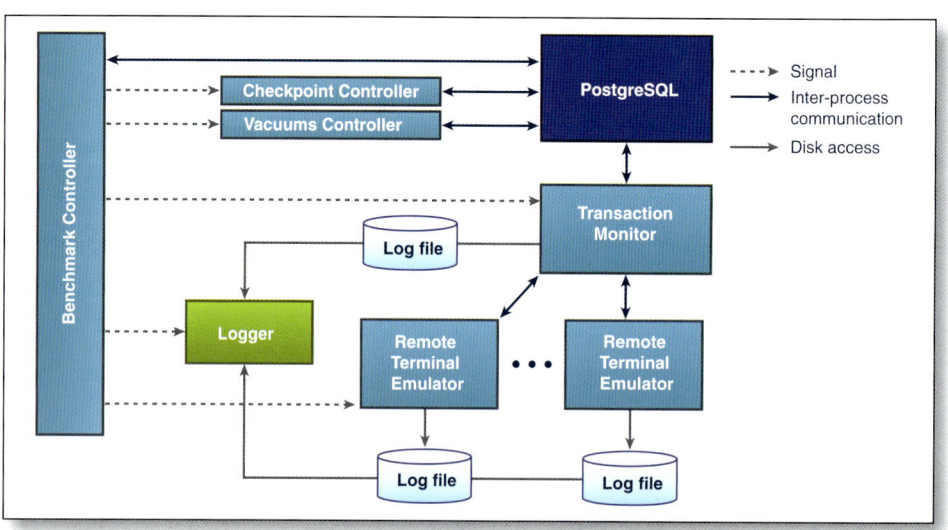

Figure 10.5 PostgreSQL and TPCC-UVa overall architecture without instrumentation.

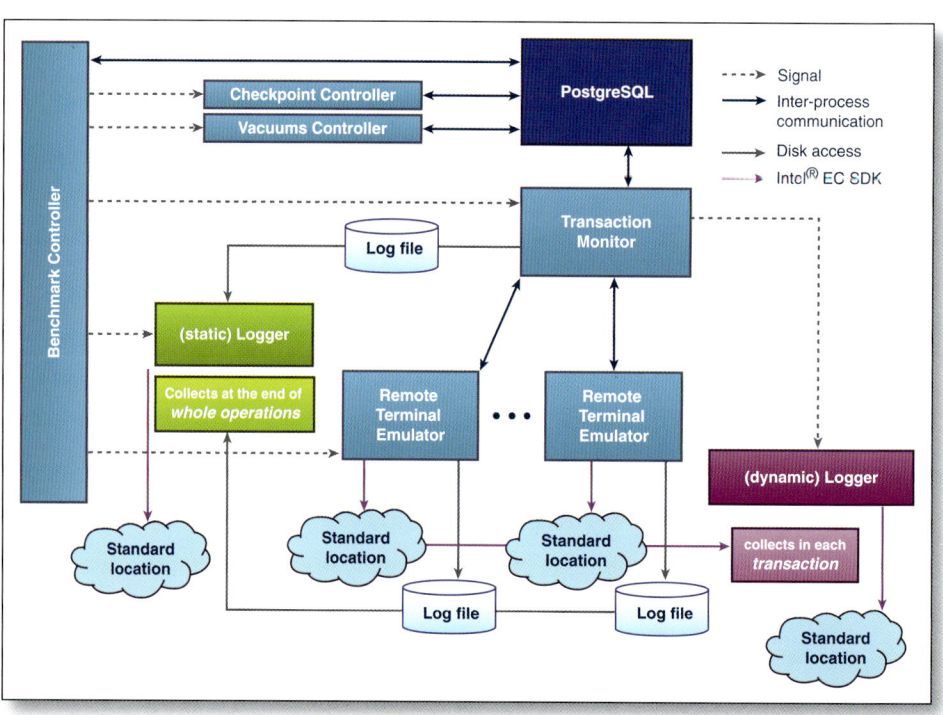

Figure 10.6 PostgreSQL and TPCC-UVa overall architecture with instrumentation.

Each PL generated by an application instrumented with the Intel Energy Checker SDK has a configuration file (`pl_config.ini`). This ASCII file contains the description of the counters exposed with various additional data. Figure 10.7 shows the content of the dynamic logger's PL. The energy efficiency counters are highlighted in bold. Readers interested in the meaning and the function of other elements present in the PL configuration file can refer to the SDK user guides.

```
iec_pgsql
4b5e9aa1-5733-42e8-8380-d29d52299776
/opt/productivity_link/iec_pgsql_4b5e9aa1-5733-42e8-8380-
d29d52299776/
26
/opt/productivity_link/iec_pgsql_4b5e9aa1-5733-42e8-8380-
d29d52299776/Total Number of Transactions (PGSQL)
/opt/productivity_link/iec_pgsql_4b5e9aa1-5733-42e8-8380-
d29d52299776/Total Number of Transactions in recent 5
seconds (PGSQL)
/opt/productivity_link/iec_pgsql_4b5e9aa1-5733-42e8-8380-
d29d52299776/Heap Allocations in Bytes (PGSQL)
/opt/productivity_link/iec_pgsql_4b5e9aa1-5733-42e8-8380-
d29d52299776/Heap Allocations in Bytes (PGSQL) in recent 5
seconds
/opt/productivity_link/iec_pgsql_4b5e9aa1-5733-42e8-8380-
d29d52299776/Measurement Time in second
/opt/productivity_link/iec_pgsql_4b5e9aa1-5733-42e8-8380-
d29d52299776/Measurement Time in second.decimals
/opt/productivity_link/iec_pgsql_4b5e9aa1-5733-42e8-8380-
d29d52299776/System Energy Consumption in joule
/opt/productivity_link/iec_pgsql_4b5e9aa1-5733-42e8-8380-
d29d52299776/System Energy Consumption in joule.decimals
/opt/productivity_link/iec_pgsql_4b5e9aa1-5733-42e8-8380-
d29d52299776/System Energy Consumption in Wh
/opt/productivity_link/iec_pgsql_4b5e9aa1-5733-42e8-8380-
d29d52299776/System Energy Consumption in Wh.decimals
/opt/productivity_link/iec_pgsql_4b5e9aa1-5733-42e8-8380-
d29d52299776/System Energy Consumption in joule in recent
5 seconds
/opt/productivity_link/iec_pgsql_4b5e9aa1-5733-42e8-8380-
d29d52299776/System Energy Consumption in joule in recent
5 seconds.decimals
```

Figure 10.7 Listing of the instrumented PostgrseSQL PL's configuration file. Energy efficiency counters are highlighted in bold.

(Continued on next page)

```
/opt/productivity_link/iec_pgsql_4b5e9aa1-5733-42e8-8380-
d29d52299776/System Energy Consumption in Wh in recent 5
seconds
/opt/productivity_link/iec_pgsql_4b5e9aa1-5733-42e8-8380-
d29d52299776/System Energy Consumption in Wh in recent 5
seconds.decimals
/opt/productivity_link/iec_pgsql_4b5e9aa1-5733-42e8-8380-
d29d52299776/Number of Transactions per joule
/opt/productivity_link/iec_pgsql_4b5e9aa1-5733-42e8-8380-
d29d52299776/Number of Transactions per joule.decimals
/opt/productivity_link/iec_pgsql_4b5e9aa1-5733-42e8-8380-
d29d52299776/Number of Transactions per Wh
/opt/productivity_link/iec_pgsql_4b5e9aa1-5733-42e8-8380-
d29d52299776/Number of Transactions per Wh.decimals
/opt/productivity_link/iec_pgsql_4b5e9aa1-5733-42e8-8380-
d29d52299776/Number of Transactions per seconds (PGSQL)
/opt/productivity_link/iec_pgsql_4b5e9aa1-5733-42e8-8380-
d29d52299776/Number of Transactions per seconds.decimals
(PGSQL)
/opt/productivity_link/iec_pgsql_4b5e9aa1-5733-42e8-8380-
d29d52299776/Number of Transactions per joule in recent 5
seconds
/opt/productivity_link/iec_pgsql_4b5e9aa1-5733-42e8-8380-
d29d52299776/Number of Transactions per joule in recent 5
seconds.decimals
/opt/productivity_link/iec_pgsql_4b5e9aa1-5733-42e8-8380-
d29d52299776/Number of Transactions per Wh in recent 5
seconds
/opt/productivity_link/iec_pgsql_4b5e9aa1-5733-42e8-8380-
d29d52299776/Number of Transactions per Wh in recent 5
seconds.decimals
/opt/productivity_link/iec_pgsql_4b5e9aa1-5733-42e8-8380-
d29d52299776/Number of Transactions per seconds in recent
5 seconds(PGSQL)
/opt/productivity_link/iec_pgsql_4b5e9aa1-5733-42e8-8380-
d29d52299776/Number of Transactions per seconds in recent
5 seconds.decimals (PGSQL)
2010.01.18(L)
__PL_LINUX__
__PL_GENERATE_INI__
__PL_GENERATE_INI_VERSION_TAGGING__
__PL_GENERATE_INI_BUILD_TAGGING__
__PL_GENERATE_INI_DATE_AND_TIME_TAGGING__
__PL_BLOCKING_COUNTER_FILE_LOCK__
PL created on Fri Sep 17 06:19:35 2010
```

Figure 10.7 (Continued)

Outfitted with these energy efficiency counters, it is now possible to add innovative energy saving heuristics into PostgreSQL so it can save energy without compromising performance or sacrificing functionality.

Memory Usage–Aware Energy Saving: An Autonomous Approach

While the Intel Energy Checker SDK can be used under many operating systems and virtually any architecture, the energy saving heuristics are likely to be very system-specific. Indeed, to save energy, software can easily leverage its intimate knowledge of the work it does and the data it is processing, but it still requires means—often provided by the hardware—to act upon the host systems' power draw. We call these hardware features *actuators*.

In many cases, power-saving hardware feature logic, the firmware, cannot make any sense of what is happening in an application and must therefore rely on measurements to search opportunities to kick in and save some power. Whatever the hardware detects through its measurements, the software action at the origin has already elapsed.

Luckily, the software has this essential knowledge right when it happens and in some cases it can project its future actions using some form of modeling. Memory utilization is one of these key knowledge points that the application knows best.

Memory Energy Saving Actuator

The Intel® codenamed Nehalem EX platform offers a feature called dynamic memory power management (code named Monroe technology). Systems having this technology can manage their physical dual inline memory modules' (DIMMs') power draw. In the short, the BIOS and the hardware allow the positioning of the DIMMs power draw to various levels, including an unpowered state. Even so, there are two catches when this feature is used. The first catch is the performance hit taken when a DIMM in low-power state is first accessed. Indeed, the hardware needs to power up the DIMM to its operational power state and this injects a slight deterministic delay. In our transactional workload, this delay is insignificant and doesn't translate in performance degradation. The second catch is related to the abstraction introduced by the virtual address space visible to used space processes. Undeniably, this requires either a mean for the application to map virtual addresses to physical addresses, using for example a page table walk mechanism in a kernel module/driver, or to amend the operating system's page allocator to allocate memory pages linearly in the physical DIMMs associated to a nonuniform memory architecture (NUMA) node. In other words, this means that for a given NUMA node, consecutive memory allocations are made linearly in the physical address space by the amended operating system. The second path was taken in this example and the Linux[†] kernel was modified to expose such behavior (kernel version 2.6.28.8).

Energy-Saving Heuristic

Since in PostgreSQL it is possible to monitor the database memory usage, and since the amount of memory buffers maintained by the software to store table data is proportional to the database size, a simple energy-saving heuristic can be implemented.

Two key metrics (`buffer_hit` and `buffer_usage`) were defined for this purpose. The first metric, similar to the processor cache hit/miss ratio, indicates the percentage of successful lookup in the buffers for requested data (the higher, the better). The second reflects the use of the buffer pools (the higher, the better). The Intel Energy Checker API is used to dynamically expose these counters so they can be monitored and used as inputs to the energy-saving heuristic. Figure 10.8 shows the associated PL's configuration file. Note that this instrumentation required modifying several source files of PostgreSQL.

```
pgsql
1124f161-773f-4da9-abfe-fa02688e19ab
/opt/productivity_link/pqsql_1124f161-773f-4da9-abfe-
fa02688e19ab/
3
/opt/productivity_link/pgsql_1124f161-773f-4da9-abfe-
fa02688e19ab/buffer_hit
/opt/productivity_link/pgsql_1124f161-773f-4da9-abfe-
fa02688e19ab/buffer_usage
/opt/productivity_link/pgsql_1124f161-773f-4da9-abfe-
fa02688e19ab/buffer_state
2010.01.18(L)
__PL_LINUX__
__PL_GENERATE_INI__
__PL_GENERATE_INI_VERSION_TAGGING__
__PL_GENERATE_INI_BUILD_TAGGING__
__PL_GENERATE_INI_DATE_AND_TIME_TAGGING__
__PL_BLOCKING_COUNTER_FILE_LOCK__
PL created on Fri Sep 17 06:18:00 2010
```

Figure 10.8 Listing of the instrumented PostgrseSQL memory usage PL's configuration file.

By monitoring these two counters and by varying the data set size while running the workload, we can identify several interesting domains and thresholds valued for the counters. In particular, it allows us to note that the buffer hit percentage can be reliably used to detect when the database backend is expanding its buffers pool.

Two memory use cases where defined (*lightweight 0* and *1* and *heavyweight*). Figures 10.9 and 10.10 show the evolution over time of both memory counters while running the TPCC-UVa workload and varying the data set size. In addition to revealing a few unstable transitional intervals that must be provisioned for in the final energy-saving heuristic, Figure 10.9 shows how the buffer hit percentage metric can be used to detect the increase of the buffer pool size when transitioning from a lightweight data set to a heavyweight data set. It also shows that this same metric cannot be used to detect a situation where the buffer pool size could or should be reduced so the associated DIMMs could be powered off.

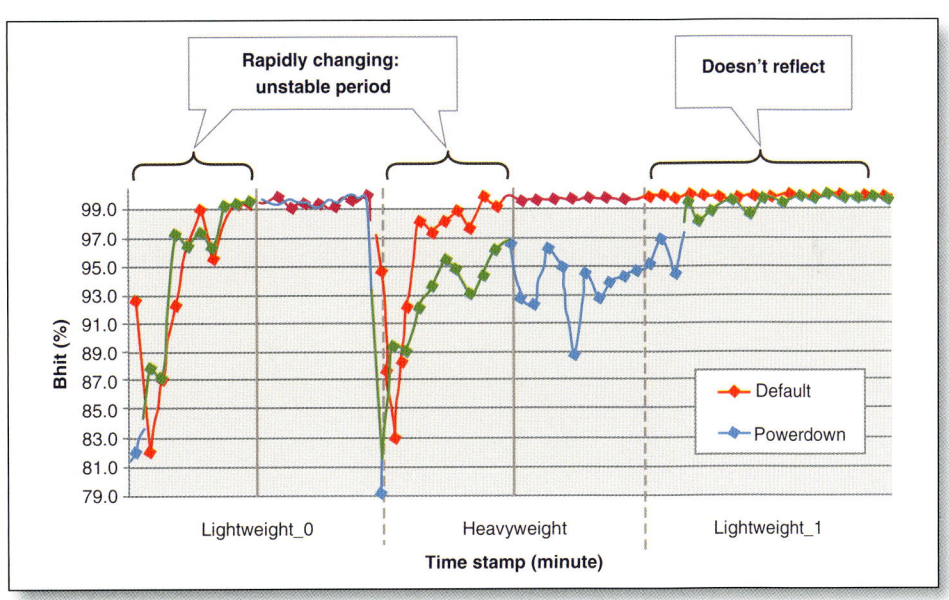

Figure 10.9 Evolutions over time of the buffer hit percentage while running the workload using different data set sizes.

This is where the buffer utilization metric fills the gap as shown in Figure 10.10. Indeed, this metric can inform us of a situation where the buffer pool is not fully used anymore and unused memory could free and powered down.

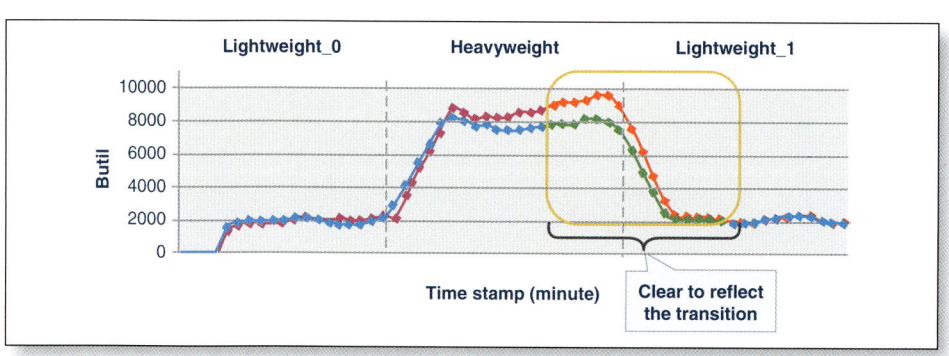

Figure 10.10 Evolutions over time of the buffer utilization while running the workload using different data set sizes.

Since the version of PostgreSQL used in this study is capable of expanding dynamically its buffers pool, but cannot shrink it, we amended its buffer management routines to add this required feature. This work was done by modifying a limited number of source code files and at a very reasonable development cost.

The knowledge gained by this study, and the two memory utilization metrics associated with the new buffer pool shrinking feature, allows the definition of a third counter (`buffer_state`), which is used to provide a hint from the software to signal which memory domains are not used and can therefore be powered down. Note that the control of the actuator (the physical DIMMs power level) is not performed directly from the database. Though it could be done autonomously, especially in the scope of an enterprise application likely running on dedicated nodes, we decided to present an indirect management path. This way, a management middleware application, or even the operating system if it was aware of this, could use this counter to marshal the memory power draw setting. This way, multiple instances of the same application or different memory-aware applications could share the same platform harmoniously.

Figure 10.11 shows the state machine implemented to drive the memory usage–based energy-saving heuristic using the two memory metrics defined earlier.

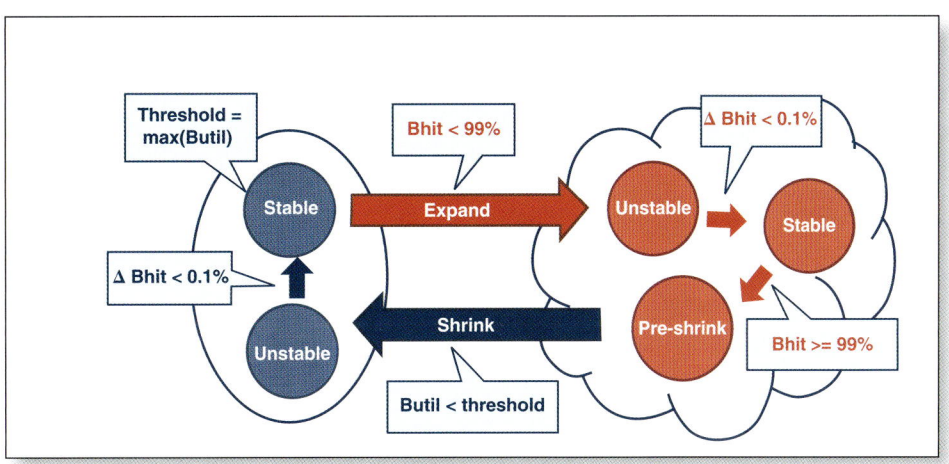

Figure 10.11 State machine used to drive the memory usage based energy saving heuristic added to PostgreSQL. The system usually starts in the stable state shown in the blue domain.

Experimental Results

To measure the energy savings performed while applying the energy saving heuristics presented previously, we ran the TPCC-UVa benchmark with two data set sizes in two different cases. The first case was not using the memory power management feature of the Nehalem EX platform; it was not supported anyway by the used operating system version (*default* case). The second case was using the memory module power manager developed in the scope of this experiment (*adaptive* case). Both cases were running on the same hardware with the same version of the operating system. The data set sizes where selected so they guarantee two memory configurations where one (*lightweight*) fits in one half of a memory module and the other doesn't (*heavyweight*). The expansion of the data set size was done following the TPCC-UVa rules, adding warehouses and terminals to the problem rather than increasing the size of the data handled by each warehouse. Data collected during unsuccessful runs were rejected.

Since the performance between the lightweight and heavyweight test cases are naturally different, the average response time is used to measure the system's performance. In addition to being independent from the data set size, the average response time is a good metric because it directly influences the user experience.

In the next sections, we first describe the experimental setup with detailed configurations and settings, and then present the experimental results.

Experimental Settings

A high-end server, an Intel® Software Development Platform (Intel SDP), was used to run the experiments. Table 10.1 summarizes the SDP's key features and characteristics. Figures 10.12 and 10.13 shows the memory architecture of the server and depicts how memory modules are physically implemented. Each memory module's power draw can be controlled independently by using the power management technology of the Nehalem EX platform.

A Yokogawa[†] WT210 Power Analyzer is used to measure the server's energy consumption. An instance of ESRV is started at the beginning of the test.

PostgreSQL is started and the TPCC-UVa benchmark is run implementing the lightweight, heavyweight, and lightweight cases in this order without interruption. The database and the workload energy efficiency metrics are computed and exposed, as described earlier in this chapter, by the loggers. In addition, the buffer utilization and buffer hit percentage metrics are computed and exposed along with the requested memory module power settings as deduced from the database backend's memory utilization. The memory power management module, a simple independent process importing the memory counters, uses the state machine to dynamically set the server's memory modules' power state. Note that the lowest nonzero power level was used in these experiments.

Figure 10.12   Eight memory modules are installed in the test server. Each memory module's power draw can be setup using the memory power saving feature of the platform codenamed Nehalem EX.

Figure 10.13   Each memory module can hold up to eight DIMMs. The test configuration used 128 GB of memory. By fully populating the modules, up to 1 TB of memory can be used.

Table 10.1   Test System Configuration Details

CPU and Chipset	Model/Speed/Cache: X7560 - Q3X4- 2.26 GHz
	64 cores/4 chips/16 cores per chip
	4 sockets
	Chipset: Codenamed Emerald Ridge Gold
	System bus: Intel® QuickPath Interconnect - 6.4 GT/s
Platform	Intel Software Development Platform
	Chassis: Boxboro - 4U rack mount
	Baseboard: Quanta QSSC-S4R
	Board revision: "Silver" (equivalent to "qual")
	BIOS: BIOS 26, BMC 17, FRU 10, HSC 2.14, ME 1.83
	DIMM slots: 64 (8 on each of 8 memory risers)
	PCI slots: 9 - PCIe; 1 - PCI
	Drive controller: Intel SRCSASBB8I RAID controller
	Power supply: 2x - 850W - Delta DPS-850FB A Rev S3F
	NIC: 2x Intel® 82576 Gigabit Dual Port
Memory	Memory Size: (n GB ((n x XGB)) 128 GB - 32 x 4 GB
	Brand/model: Hynix/HMT151R7BFR4C-G7
	DIMMs: 4 GB - 2Rx8 - PC3 - 8500R
Mass storage	Spindles: 2ea 146 GB SAS

Experimental Results

Figure 10.14 shows the experimental results of response time reported by TPCC-UVa during the running of the benchmark for both the baseline and memory utilization-aware power saving. Table 10.2 shows the energy savings data.

From the experimental results, we see that, comparing with no memory power saving in the operating system, more than 8 percent energy reduction is achieved with memory utilization–aware energy saving, while the average response time of the benchmark gets little impact.

The experiment demonstrates that comparing with no insight and support on the application's memory utilization in the operating system, additional energy can be saved with little performance impact by incorporating application level memory utilization feedback into power management software.

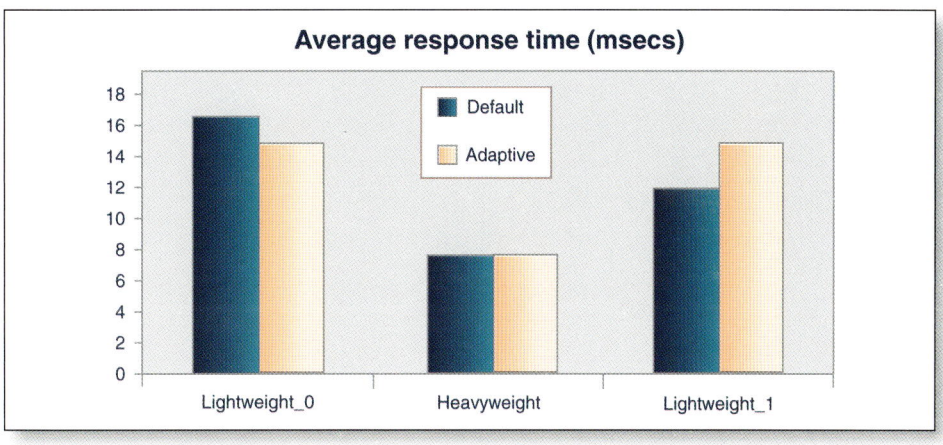

Figure 10.14 Response time between default and the adaptive test cases.

Table 10.2 Experimental Results of Energy Saving on TPCC-UVa
(Default versus Adaptive)

Dataset Size	Energy Savings
Lightweight_x	+8.25%
Heavyweight	+4.12%

Performance-Aware Energy Saving: A Coordinated Approach

In addition to driving the energy saving from the memory sub-system with memory utilization information, we conducted another experiment by taking the application level performance information into consideration, in which the coordination among hardware, middleware, and application is performed.

In a typical online transaction processing configuration, a power-saving application is built. The application monitors the performance counters of transaction processing from both the frontend and the backend, and checks whether the performance is affected or not. The information is provided to the middleware component, which learns and updates the optimal power limiting policy on the system. At the lowest level, a firmware component provides the basic building block to cap the system's power for energy reduction, acting as the policy executer.

The experimental results demonstrate that significant energy reduction is achieved without performance impact.

Performance-Aware Power Saving

Various power-saving policies are commonly provided by the power management module in operating systems. For example, several CPU utilization counters are considered by the power management module in Windows[†] when the balanced power plan is chosen. When CPU utilization is low, the power management module regulates the CPU to a P-state with lower performance for reduction of power consumption. When CPU utilization is high, the power management module regulates the CPU to a P-state with higher performance, to avoid the impact on user or application experiences. Although such an approach provides the generic power-saving functionality that is widely applicable to a large variety of scenarios, the room for energy reduction is not fully exploited because the power management module does not gain the visibility of application performance.

Recently there has been a growing interest for performance-aware power saving, where application-level performance indicators are taken into consideration by intelligent power controllers. Figure 10.15 depicts the high-level system diagram of a typical setting of performance-aware power saving. The job scheduler is responsible for scheduling workloads to computing systems and acts as the performance manager to monitor the application-level performance. The information is provided to the power controller, with which the intelligent power policy is computed. The power policy is then executed to reduce the power consumption of the computing systems.

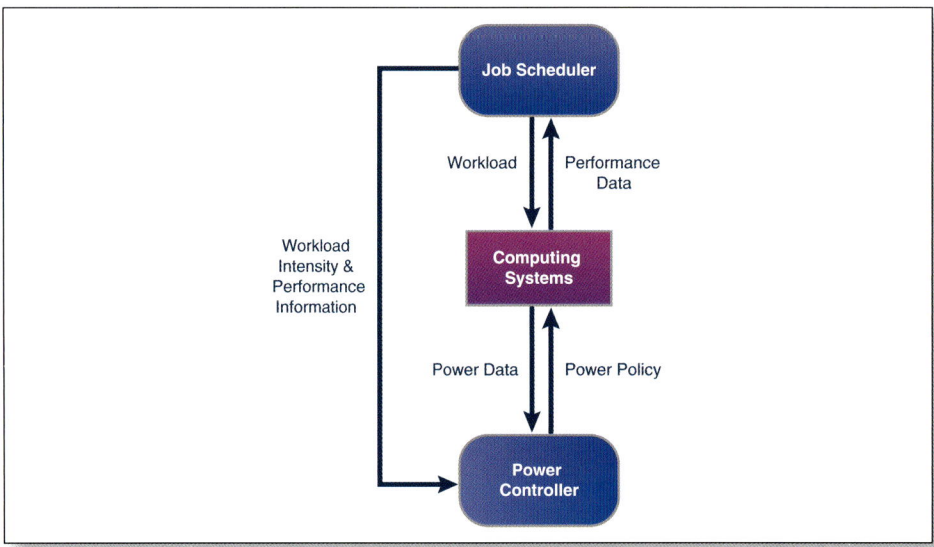

Figure 10.15 High-level system diagram of a typical setting of performance-aware power saving

Power Saving on TPCC-UVa

We adapt performance-aware power saving to the benchmark of TPCC-UVa, in which a coordinated approach among different components is proposed. Figure 10.16 shows the system diagram of performance-aware power saving adapted to the benchmark.

There are several components in the system. The centralized coordinator power-saving application reads the performance information from the benchmark through Intel Energy Checker's instrumentation and provides the information on workload activity, as well as performance impacts to Intel® Data Center Manager. Intel Data Center Manager is the power management middleware that provides the building block for performance-aware power saving. Inside Intel Data Center Manager, a utility learner collects the performance feedback and builds the utility functions on how well the power-saving task is performed, considering both the power reduced and the performance impact. The policy calculator then uses the utility functions to generate the decision on the best power policy, which is a power limit on the entire server. The power limit is enforced by Intel® Node Manager, a firmware component, which is responsible for *capping* the server's power below the power limit, with a control loop of retrieving power readings from the power supply unit and regulating the CPU P-state. The process is repeated over time.

The components are described in details in the next sections.

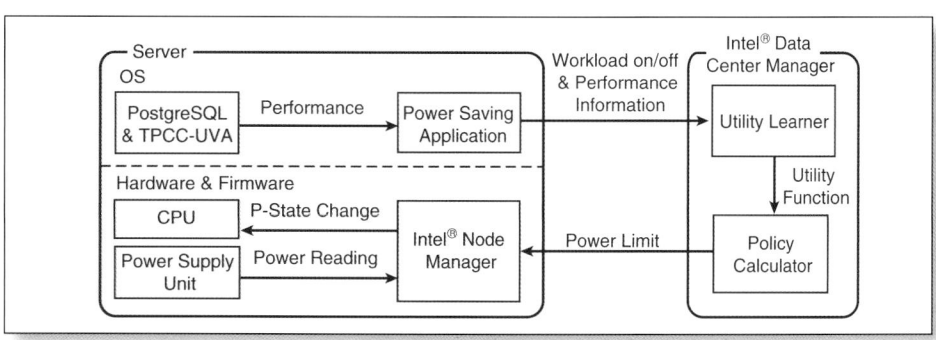

Figure 10.16 System Diagram of Power Saving on TPCC-UVa

Intel® Node Manager

Intel® Node Manager is a firmware component providing platform level power management capabilities among which *power capping* is one of the key features.

Power capping (or budgeting) limits the power consumption of a certain server below a configurable threshold under varying workload intensity. This enables the implementation of a variety of advanced usage models, such as protecting the platform under failures in part of the power supply units, maintaining a global power cap on a rack of servers given the increase of server density with power budgeting and shifting among them to minimize the performance impact, and, as we show in the experiment, reducing the power consumption of the platform with little performance impact.

Intel Node Manager receives the desired power limit from high level power management software and employs a feedback controller to cap the platform power. In power capping, the highest P-state of CPU configurable by the operating system is taken as the control knob. For a fine-grain control of the platform power, Intel Node Manager cycles the highest P-state between two adjacent options at different time lengths. It measures the platform power consumption given the current highest P-state from the power supply unit and aggregates the average power consumption over a slightly longer period. Intel Node Manager then compares the average power consumption with the desire power limit enforced and regulates the two adjacent options for cycling as well as the time lengths to stay at the two options according to the error measured.

Given such a mechanism, Intel Node Manager is able to maintain the platform power consumption close to the desired threshold, providing fast correction for power bursts under changing workload and maintaining the best possible performance.

Intel® Data Center Manager

Intel® Data Center Manager is a middleware solution addressing the power and cooling challenges emerging in data centers. It leverages the platform power management capabilities, builds advanced usages at the data center level from the perspective of software interaction, and exposes the web service interface for ease of integration with data center management software or cloud operating environment.

Intel Data Center Manager provides the building block for performance-aware power saving. APIs are exposed for management software to hint power optimization with the current workload intensity and the performance impact. Inside Intel Data Center Manager, the optimal power limit policy is sought by maximizing the utility of the power capping decision under the workload intensity.

Considering the background noise, such as background processes and minor randomness of workload, whether the performance gets impacted or not given the workload intensity and the power capping decision is not considered as deterministic. A probabilistic approach is proposed to evaluate the utility of a certain power limiting decision. Let w denote the current workload intensity and c denote the power capping decision of Intel Data Center Manager. Let $R \in \{-1,1\}$ denote the random variable on whether performance gets impacted or not. The utility of the power capping decision under the workload intensity is calculated as

$$ U\left(w,\, c\right) \overset{\text{def}}{=} P\left(R = 1 \mid w,\, c\right) \frac{c_{max} - c}{c_{max}} - k \cdot P\left(R = -1 \mid w,\, c\right) $$

Where c_{max} is the maximum power capping allowed and k is a constant giving the weight for tradeoff between the reward of power saved without performance impact and the penalty with performance impact.

In Intel Data Center Manager, the probability of whether performance gets impact or not is estimated online by referring to the performance feedback from the management software. Before estimating the probabilities with maximum likelihood estimation, a heuristic is employed to augment the training set with some *pseudo samples* derived from the existing ones. The idea is that if at time t, the performance gets impacted given the workload intensity w_t and the power capping c_t, we regard that with the unknown noise at that time, the performance is also affected given a larger workload intensity ($w > w_t$) or a smaller power capping ($c < c_t$). Similarly, if at time t, the performance is not affected given the workload intensity w_t and the power capping c_t, we regard that with the unknown noise at that time, the performance will not be affected as well given a smaller workload intensity ($w < w_t$) or a larger power capping ($c > c_t$). The heuristic balances exploration and exploitation in the typical online learning paradigm and smoothes the probabilities estimated.

The pseudo code of performance-aware power saving is outlined in Figure 10.17.

```
Initialize T ← ∅
Repeat
    If workload intensity w_t is updated
        c_t ← argmax_c U(w_t, c)
        Enforce power capping decision c_t
    End If
    If performance feedback r_t is updated
        If r_t = 1
            T ← T ∪{ (r_t, w, c) | w ≤ w_t & c ≥ c_t}
        End If
        If r_t = -1
            T ← T ∪{ (r_t, w, c) | w ≥ w_t & c ≤ c_t}
        End If
        Estimate probability distribution P(R = *|W = *,C = *)
          with T
        c_t ← argmax_c U(w_t, c)
        Enforce power capping decision c_t
    End If
End Repeat
```

Figure 10.17 Pseudo code of performance-aware power saving in Intel® Data Center Manager

Power-Saving Application

The power-saving application acts as a coordinator bridging TPCC-UVa benchmark with the power-saving building block in Intel Data Center Manager. It provides the 0–1 workload intensity information to Intel Data Center Manager indicating whether the benchmark is running or not. The application also reads the performance counters output by Intel Energy Checker in TPCC-UVa and judges whether the performance gets impacted or not. The performance feedback is provided to Intel Data Center Manager for updating the utility of power capping decisions.

In judging whether the performance is affected or not, the application first checks the frontend counters of each of the client terminals periodically. The number of transactions processed and the number of transactions regarded as well-done for each of the five transaction types within the period are collected. The data is aggregated across all the client terminals and the percentage that the transactions are processed as well-done ones is calculated. By comparing the percentage values of each of the five transaction types with a predefined threshold, the application judges whether the client side experiences are affected.

The application also monitors the performance counter of the backend database. The number of transactions completed in the recent five seconds is sampled periodically. Before we start saving power, we perform a preliminary run of the benchmark without power saving kicked in, collecting a set of samples. During the run with power saving, the application collects a few samples within a interval and compares the running samples with the original sample set. Welch's t-test is performed to test whether the difference of the mean number of transactions completed from the two sample sets are statistically significant or not. Specifically, it computes the t value as

$$t = \frac{\overline{X}_1 - \overline{X}_2}{\sqrt{\dfrac{s_1^2}{N_1} + \dfrac{s_2^2}{N_2}}}$$

where $\overline{X}_i$, s_i^2, and N_i are the ith sample mean, sample variance, and sample size. The Welch-Satterthwaite Equation is used to approximate the degrees of freedom associated with the variance as

$$\upsilon \approx \frac{\left(\dfrac{s_1^2}{N_1} + \dfrac{s_2^2}{N_2}\right)^2}{\dfrac{s_1^4}{N_1^2(N_1 - 1)} + \dfrac{s_2^4}{N_2^2(N_2 - 1)}}$$

Once t and υ are computed, the values are used with the t-distribution to test whether the difference of the means is statistically significant or not in terms of comparing the p-value with a predefined significance level.

For the power-saving application to provide the feedback that the performance is not affected, it requires that both the frontend performance and the backend performance pass the check.

Experimental Results

Experiments were conducted for a comparative study on the TPCC-UVa benchmark, investigating the effects of performance-aware power saving versus power saving with the power management module in the operating system.

In the next sections, we first describe the experimental setup with detail configurations and settings and then present the experimental results.

Experimental Settings

We used a server with two Intel® Xeon® X5570 CPUs and 12 GB memory in the experiment of running the benchmark. Each of the CPUs has four cores and has Intel Hyper-Threading Technology enabled. The operating system of the server is Red Hat Enterprise 5.2. Throughout the experiment, we enabled the on-demand governor in the operating system, which provides the functionality of P-state regulation based on CPU utilization. We regard the configuration as the baseline.

TPCC-UVa benchmark is set up on the server. Before running the experiments, we tried different configurations of the benchmark as a preliminary step to maximize the throughput, reaching the settings of 24 warehouses and 10 terminals per warehouse. In our experiments, we kept the ramp up period of TPCC-UVa to be 10 minutes and the measurement period to be four hours.

In performance-aware power saving with a coordinated approach, the power saving application locates on the same server running TPCC-UVa. The middleware, Intel Data Center Manager v2.1, however, is set up on a different server simulating the deployment scenario that the power management middleware locates on a centralized node managing the others in the entire data center. Intel Node Manager v1.5 is enabled on the server running the benchmark and is managed by the instance of Intel Data Center Manager.

The power-saving application judges whether the performance is affected every minute. To check whether the frontend performance is affected, 99 percent is used as the threshold for the values of percentage of well-done transactions for each of the five transaction types in the minute. To check whether the backend performance is affected, we first ran the benchmark for one hour and every 15 seconds we looked into the performance counter of number of transactions completed in recent 5 seconds reported using the Intel Energy Checker SDK, resulting in a static sample set of 240 samples without power saving. During performance-aware power saving, in every minute, the power saving application samples the performance counter four times, resulting in a running sample set with four samples. The Welch t-test is then applied to the two data sets with a significance level of 0.005 to judge whether the backend performance is affected.

In Intel Data Center Manager, the weight for penalizing with the performance impact in utility calculation is set to 1.

Experimental Results

We ran TPCC-UVa benchmark with power saving of on-demand governor in Red Hat Enterprise 5.2 and with performance-aware power saving respectively. Table 10.3 shows the experimental results of performance reported by TPCC-UVA and average power during the running of the benchmark for both the baseline and performance-aware power saving.

From the experimental results, we see that, compared to power saving of the power management module in the operating system, more than 10 percent power reduction is achieved with performance-aware power saving, while the performance of the benchmark is not significantly affected.

The experiment demonstrates that, compared to power saving of the power management module in operating systems, which refers to the resource utilization counters, additional energy can be saved with little performance impact by incorporating application-level performance feedback into power management software through a coordination of multiple components.

Table 10.3 Experimental Results of Power Saving on TPCC-UVa

Power Saving Method	Performance	Average Power
Baseline	300 tpmC	183 W
Performance-Aware	300 tpmC	*164 W*

Need One More Heuristic to Get Started?

Let us consider an additional software-driven energy saving heuristic: the *dynamic migration* (see Figure 10.18). In this heuristic, basic software knowledge and virtualization technology are leveraged.

Virtualization is often used in the data center to consolidate applications hosted by several older servers on a newer and more energy-efficient system. Even if this approach yields measurable energy savings, in this heuristic, virtualization is exclusively used as a convenient method to shuffle energy-aware applications among various servers.

To describe the dynamic migration energy-saving heuristic, the previously instrumented PostgreSQL is showcased. Of course, any other application can be used, assuming it is instrumented to expose (at minimum) the amount of useful work it does.

The main PostgreSQL monitoring process dynamically computes the energy efficiency metrics of the database. To handle manageable values, we add the transactions per kilowatt-hour energy efficiency metric to the existing counters (TPkWh—the higher the better). The Intel Energy Checker SDK is used as-is in a virtual machine. The sole difference with previous case studies is that a distributed setup must be used. Refer to the SDK manuals for details on how to use the Intel Energy Checker SDK in a distributed configuration.

Once the energy efficiency metrics are known, it is possible for the database engine to use the virtual machine in which it runs, associated with the hypervisor's VM migration mechanism, to autonomously—or in a middleware assisted way—initiate a migration to a different server. Table 10.4 summarizes the various values used during the following discussion.

The dynamic migration heuristics can be described as follows. It is Monday morning, and as usual, the customers are actively placing their orders. Thus, a considerable amount of useful work is done by the database backend. The server running the VM hosting the PostgreSQL instance is powerful enough to allow the application to process 100,000 transactions every second. The TPkWh metric is then equal to 27.78.

As the day goes on, the closer we get to noon, the number of customer orders is dropping. The related transactions count is then 20,000. Even if the operating system and the hardware compensates for the system's utilization drop by activating several power saving features, the TPkWh metric drops to 6.78. Since this value is less than an arbitrary threshold—say 9—the backend can autonomously initiate or request a migration toward a less powerful server. Sure, that server has less horsepower to process customer requests, but since only 20,000 transactions are executed the TPkWh metric rises to 18.52.

Another important part of the heuristic consists in monitoring the utilization of the system by the customers over time. Based on this historical data, the application can identify periods of time where spikes in demand usually happen. In addition to a self-learning system, policies input by a database administrator can be added to override the autonomous mechanism.

In our scenario, this second part of the heuristics has learned over the last months of operation that around five o'clock in the afternoon, a huge demand rise happens during weekdays. Therefore, few minutes prior to this time, the backend can request or initiate its migration back to a powerful server. In this case, it can also request the deactivation of some performance-limiting power-saving features of the operating system and/or the hardware. In these conditions, the platform can squeeze out a few additional thousands of transactions, reaching a peak of 106,000 for a power draw of 1050 watts. The TPkWh metric rises to 28.04. And so on... .

This simple scenario can be easily implemented, since all the building blocks are available: the Intel Energy Checked SDK can be used to compute and exchange dynamically the TPkWh metric, likely using a power sensor (based on a power supply unit) readable via Intelligent Platform Management Interface (IPMI), and hypervisors offering VM migration capabilities are commonly available.

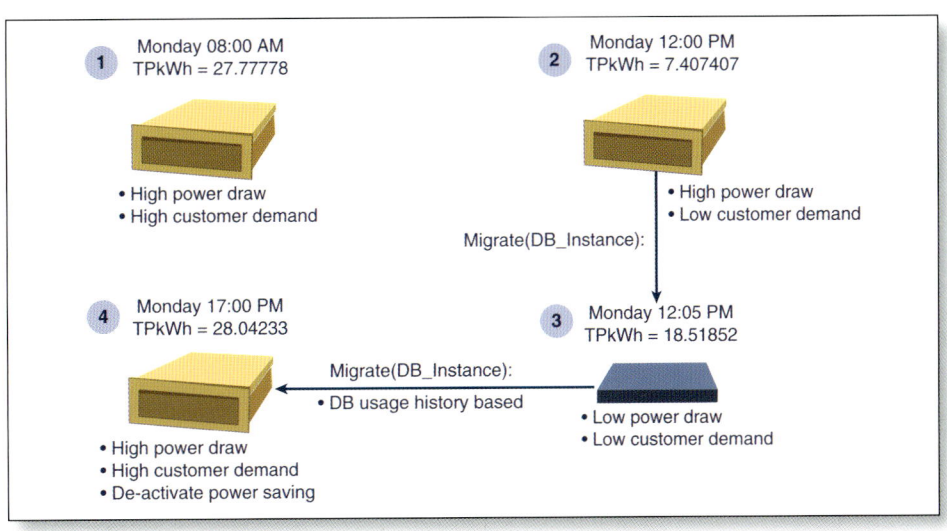

Figure 10.18 Four steps of the dynamic migration scenario

Table 10.4 Summary of Useful Work, Power Draw, and Energy Efficiency Metrics

Transactions per second	Power Draw per second	TPkWh
100,000	1000 W	27.77778
20,000	820 W	6.775068
20,000	300 W	18.51852
106,000	1050 W	28.04233

Summary

When it comes to saving energy, software developers and data center managers have a wide array of options available to them, from the hard, low-level code optimizations to the easy heuristic-driven optimizations. Between these two ends of the spectrum lies the grey area usually explored, where energy savings are traded for performance or functionalities.

Some of the low-level options encompass optimized code generation by a static compiler or a just-in-time (JIT) compiler, instruction fusion, co-scheduling, or even data type demotions. Algorithm optimizations could also find a home in this class, but one might argue that energy savings measured are in fact due to better performance. Anyway, these optimizations are difficult to implement and yield very little energy savings when considering the whole server and not just an isolated sub-system.

The tradeoff approach provides generally good and sometimes measurable energy savings, but has an intrinsic drawback: the end user looses either performance or functionality.

As demonstrated with our two cases studies, the heuristic-driven approach has the benefit of rejecting performance or functionality losses while generating substantial energy savings by focusing on the server's key energy-hungry components. In addition, these heuristics don't require deep hardware knowledge or subtle operating system tweaking, since they leverage existing potent hardware energy-saving mechanisms.

We strongly encourage the reader to focus first on this research area since it provides the best result with little effort. Only a good understanding of the application is really required, and this is exactly where the software developer can make the difference.

References

ACPI. 2004. "ACPI Overview." http://www.acpi.info/presentations/ACPI_Overview.pdf

Android Open Source Project. 2011. Web site. http://source.android.com/

Android (operating system). 2011. Web site. http://en.wikipedia.org/wiki/Android_operating_system

Android—Power Management. 2011. Web site. http://www.netmite.com/android/mydroid/development/pdk/docs/power_management.html

Android—PowerManager Class. 2011. Web site. http://developer.android.com/reference/android/os/PowerManager.html

Android Memory Usage. 2011. Web site. http://elinux.org/Android_Memory_Usage

Android Debbugging—Using DDMS. 2011. Web site. http://developer.android.com/guide/developing/debugging/ddms.html

Android Developers—Debugging from Eclipse with ADT. 2011. Web site. http://developer.android.com/guide/developing/debugging/debugging-projects.html

Android Debugging. 2011. Web site. http://www.omappedia.org/wiki/Android_Debugging

Android Developers—Profiling with Traceview and dmtracedump. 2011. Web site. http://developer.android.com/guide/developing/debugging/debugging-tracing.html

Apple Instruments. 2011. Apple Energy Instruments. Working Paper. http://developer.apple.com/library/ios/#DOCUMENTATION/ DeveloperTools/Conceptual/InstrumentsUserGuide/Built-InInstruments/ Built-InInstruments.html

Apple Xcode. 2011. Apple Xcode4. Working Paper. http://developer.apple.com/xcode/

Barkhuus, Louise, and Ainind Dey. 2003. "Is Context-Aware Computing Taking Control Away from the User? Three Levels of Interactivity Examined." *Proceedings of UbiComp*, pp. 150–156, Springer.

Bray, T. 2010. Android Developers—Traceview War Story. http://android-developers.blogspot.com/2010/10/traceview-war-story.html?utm_source=feedburner&utm_medium=feed&utm_campaign=Feed:+blogspot/ hsDu+%28Android+Developers+Blog%29

Cameron, Kirk, and Wu-chun FGeng. 2011. The Green 500, Web site. http://www.green500.org/about.php

Chabukswar, R., Jun De Vega, Karthikeyan Krishnan, Bob Steigerwald. 2010. "Creating Energy Efficient Software," http://software.intel.com/en-us/ articles/creating-energy-efficient-software-part-1/

Chynoweth, M. and Lee, M. 2009. "Implementing Scalable Atomic Locks for Multi-core Intel® EM64T and IA32 Architectures," Intel Corporation Web site, http://software.intel.com/en-us/articles/implementing-scalable-atomic-locks-for-multi-core-intel-em64t-and-ia32-architectures/

Climate Savers. 2011. Climate Savers Computing Initiative. Web site. http://www.climatesaverscomputing.org/

Dey, A. K., et al. 1999. "Towards a Better Understanding of Context and Context-Awareness," Technical Report 99-22, Georgia Institute of Technology.

Farag, Sharif and Cooper, Barnes. 2008. "Advancing the Platform", Microsoft WinHEC 2008. http://download.microsoft.com/download/5/e/6/.../ mbl-t541_wh08.pptx

FEMP. 2000. "How to Buy an Energy-Efficient Personal Computer: Why Agencies Should Buy Efficient Office Equipment," http://www1.eere.energy.gov/femp/pdfs/computer.pdf

Gilchrist, Jeff. 2002. Web site, http://www.compression.ca/act/act-files.html

Gordon, M., Zhang, L., Yang, L. 2010. PowerTutor—A Power Monitor for Android-Based Mobile Platforms. http://ziyang.eecs.umich.edu/projects/powertutor/

Google. 2011. Google Green Web site. http://www.google.com/intl/en/corporate/green/

Heger, D.A. 2011. "Mobile Devices — An Introduction to the Android Operating Environment — Design, Architecture, and Performance Implications," CMG.

IBM. 2011. "Boost application performance using asynchronous I/O," Working Paper, IBM Corp., http://www.ibm.com/developerworks/linux/library/l-async/

Intel Corporation. 2003. "Serial ATA II Native Command Queuing Overview," Working Paper, http://www.intel.com/assets/pdf/whitepaper/252664.pdf

Intel Corporation. 2008. Web site. http://software.intel.com/sites/products/documentation/hpc/compilerpro/en-us/fortran/win/compiler_f/optaps/fortran/optaps_prg_io_f.htm

Intel Corporation. 2008. Web site. http://software.intel.com/en-us/articles/power-analysis-of-disk-io-methodologies

Intel Corporation. 2008. Web site. http://software.intel.com/en-us/articles/data-transfer-over-wireless-lan-power-consumption-analysis

Intel Corporation. 2009. "Using CPUID to Detect the presence of SSE 4.1 and SSE 4.2 Instruction Sets," http://software.intel.com/en-us/articles/using-cpuid-to-detect-the-presence-of-sse-41-and-sse-42-instruction-sets/

Intel Corporation. 2009. "Enhanced Intel SpeedStep® Technology and Demand-Based Switching on Linux*," http://software.intel.com/en-us/articles/enhanced-intel-speedstepr-technology-and-demand-based-switching-on-linux/

Intel Corporation. 2009. "Intel Active Management Technology," http://edc.intel.com/Intel-Product-Technologies/AMT/

Intel Corporation. 2011. Web site. "In-Vehicle Infotainment," http://www.intel.com/p/en_US/embedded/applications/in-vehicle-infotainment

Intel Corporation. 2011. Web site. LessWatts.org, http://lesswatts.org/

Intel Corporation. 2011. Web site. Military, Aerospace & Government, http://www.intel.com/p/en_US/embedded/applications/military#fragment-a-1

Intel Corporation. 2011. Tools Evaluation Web site. http://software.intel.com/en-us/articles/intel-software-evaluation-center/

Intel Corporation. 2011. Military, Aerospace, Government (MAG) Case studies, http://www.intel.com/p/en_US/embedded/applications/military#fragment-a-1

Intel Corporation. 2011, Web site (VTune). "Intel Performance Analysis Tools," http://software.intel.com/en-us/intel-sdp-home/

Jeyaseelan, Jaya, Arai, Susumu, and Cooper, Barnes. 2011. "Energy-Efficient Platforms–Considerations for Application Software and Services". Intel Working Paper. http://download.intel.com/technology/pdf/Green_Hill_Software.pdf

Kuulusa, Mika. 2006. Multiprocessors in Wireless Multimedia Terminals. In-depth presentations, Sixth International Forum on Application-Specific Multi-Processor SoC (MPSoC'06), August 2006. [Online] Available: http://www.mpsoc-forum.org/2006/slides/Kuulusa.pdf

Larsson, Petter. 2010. "Energy-Efficient Software Guidelines," Working Paper, Intel Corporation. http://software.intel.com/en-us/articles/energy-efficient-software-guidelines/

Larsson, Petter. 2010. "Energy-Efficient Software Checklist," Working Paper, Intel Corporation. http://software.intel.com/en-us/articles/energy-efficient-software-checklist/

Llanos, D. R. 2010. "TPCC-UVa: A free, open-source implementation of the TPC-C Benchmark," http://www.infor.uva.es/~diego/tpcc-uva.html

Maker, F. and Chan, Y.-H. 2009. "A Survey on Android vs. Linux," University of California, Davis.

Microsoft. 2004. Web site. http://research.microsoft.com/apps/pubs/default.aspx?id=64538

Microsoft. 2007. "Application Power Management Best Practices for Windows Vista," Working Paper, Microsoft Corp. http://www.microsoft.com/whdc/system/pnppwr/powermgmt/pm_apps.mspx

Microsoft. 2007. "Optimizing Windows Vista Platforms for Energy Efficiency," http://msdn.microsoft.com/en-us/windows/hardware/gg463233

Microsoft. 2007. "PPM in Windows Vista and Windows Server 2008," http://www.microsoft.com/whdc/system/pnppwr/powermgmt/ProcPowerMgmt.mspx

Microsoft. 2009. "Mobile Battery Life Solutions for Windows 7", Working Paper, Microsoft Corp. http://msdn.microsoft.com/en-us/windows/hardware/gg487547.aspx

Microsoft. 2009. "Windows Timer Coalescing," Working Paper, http://msdn.microsoft.com/en-us/windows/hardware/gg463269.aspx

Microsoft. 2010. "Introduction to Windows Performance Analyzer (WPA)," Working Paper, http://msdn.microsoft.com/en-us/library/ff190932.aspx

Microsoft. 2010. "Timers, Timer Resolution, and Development of Efficient Code", Working Paper, Microsoft Corp. http://msdn.microsoft.com/en-us/windows/hardware/gg463266.aspx

Microsoft. 2010. "Using PowerCfg to Evaluate System Energy Efficiency". Working Paper, Microsoft Corp. http://msdn.microsoft.com/en-us/windows/hardware/gg463250

Microsoft. 2011. Web site. Process Explorer v15.01 http://technet.microsoft.com/en-us/sysinternals/bb896653.aspx

Microsoft. 2011. MSDN article on Windows Perfmon. http://msdn.microsoft.com/en-us/library/ms803998.aspx

Microsoft. 2011. "PowerSettingAccessCheck Function," http://msdn.microsoft.com/en-us/library/aa372761(v=VS.85).aspx

Microsoft. 2011. "RegisterPowerSettingNotification Function," http://msdn.microsoft.com/en-us/library/aa373196(VS.85).aspx

Microsoft. 2011. "Accessing System Power and Network Status Using SENS", http://msdn.microsoft.com/en-us/library/aa480679.aspx

Microsoft. 2011. "Synchronous & Asynchronous I/O," Working Paper, Microsoft Corp., http://msdn.microsoft.com/en-us/library/aa365683(v=vs.85).aspx

Microsoft. 2011. Web site. http://technet.microsoft.com/en-us/sysinternals/bb896653.aspx

Microsoft. 2011. "Powercfg Command-Line Options," Working Paper, http:// technet.microsoft.com/en-us/library/cc748940(WS.10).aspx

Microsoft. 2011. Microsoft Energy Smart. Working Paper, Microsoft Corp. http://msdn.microsoft.com/en-us/windows/ff944599.aspx

Minas, Lauri and Ellison, Brad. 2009. *Energy Efficiency for Information Technology*. Intel Press.

Murugesan, San. 2008. "Harnessing Green IT: Principles and Practices," *IEEE IT Professional*, January–February 2008. http://software.intel.com/en-us/ intel-sdp-home/

Newton, Tim. 2008. "Two Minute Drill: Introduction to Xperf", http:// blogs.technet.com/b/askperf/archive/2008/06/27/an-intro-to-xperf. aspx

Nokia. 2011. "Nokia Energy Profiler quick start", http://www.developer.nokia. com/Resources/Tools_and_downloads/Other/Nokia_Energy_Profiler/ Quick_start.xhtml

Oprofile Open Source Project. 2011. Web site. http://oprofile.sourceforge.net/

PostgreSQL. 2010. PostgreSQL. http://www.postgresql.org/

PowerTop. 2007. Intel Working Paper, http://www.lesswatts.org/projects/ powertop/powertop.php

Sabharwal, Manuj and Chang, Eunice. 2010. "Impact of "Idle" Software on Battery Life". Intel Developer Forum, http://www.intel.com/content/dam/ doc/guide/idle-software-battery-life-idf2010-presentation.pdf

Sabharwal, Manuj. 2011. "Fine-Grained Application Analysis for Energy-Aware Computing". Intel Working Paper. http://software.intel.com/ partner/assets/pdf/misc/Fine-Grained_Application_Analysis_for_Energy_ Aware_Computing_WP_v3_4_14_11.pdf

Schmidt, Albrecht. 2005. "Interactive Context-Aware Systems Interacting with Ambient Intelligence," Chapter 9 from *Ambient Intelligence* by G. Riva, F. Vatalaro, F. Davide, M. Alcañiz (Eds.) IOS Press, http://www. ambientintelligence.org

Sharma, S., Chung-Hsing Hsu, and Wu-chun Feng. 2006. "Making a Case for a Green500 List," IEEE IPDPS Workshop on High-Performance, Power-Aware Computing, http://www.green500.org/docs/pubs/hp-pac2006.pdf

Steigerwald, B., Rajshree Chabukswar, Jun De Vega, Karthikeyan Krishnan. 2010. "Creating Energy Efficient Software," http://software.intel.com/en-us/articles/creating-energy-efficient-software-part-1/

Steigerwald, B. and Agrawal, A. 2011. "Developing Green Software", Working Paper, Intel Corporation. http://software.intel.com/en-us/articles/developing-green-software/

TLDP. 2011. Web site. Battery Powered Linux Mini-HOWTO, http://tldp.org/HOWTO/Battery-Powered/powermgm.html

Top—display Linux tasks. 2011. Web site. http://linux.die.net/man/1/top

Top500. 2011. Top 500 Supercomputer Sites, Web site, http://www.top500.org/

Vaddagiri, S., Santhanam, A.K, Sukthankar, V. and Iyer, M. 2004. Power Management in Linux-Based Systems, http://www.linuxjournal.com/article/6699

ZDNet. 2008. "Google makes waves and may have solved the data center conundrum," http://www.zdnet.com/blog/btl/google-makes-waves-and-may-have-solved-the-data-center-conundrum/9937

Zhang, J. 2010. Linux Kernel and Android Suspend/Resume. http://kzjblog.appspot.com/2010/11/20/suspend-en.html#sec-6

Zhang, L., Tiwana, B., Qian, Z., Wang, Z., Dick, R.P., Mao, Z.M., et al. 2010. "Accurate Online Power Estimation and Automatic Battery Behavior Based Power Model Generation for Smartphones," Hardware/Software Codesign and System Synthesis.

Index

Page numbers followed by f and t indicate figures and tables, respectively.

Display Power Saving Technology (DPST)
feature, 38–39
embedded gaming, 187–188
energy efficiency designs, 32
energy-efficient optimization, 32–33
following failure of a thermal solution, 32
HEMS, 181
in Linux, 41–46
in Windows, 47–48
in-vehicle infotainment, 179
Industrial Control Systems, 185
Intel® Intelligent Power Node Manager, 36–37
MAG markets, 177
medical-grade computing systems, 186
memory power, 39
overview, 31–32
performance per watt, 40–41
sleep states (S-states), 35–36
Standard Linux Power Management,
198–199
system configurations, 35–41
virtualization, 37–38
Power management integrated circuit
(PMIC), 194
Power management multichannel integrated circuits
(PMIC), 17–18
Power management test tool (PwrTest), 136–139,
137f, 138f, 139f
Power measurement, 21
system AC, 21–24
system DC, 24–30
Power planes, 13
Power policy
802.11 wireless power-save mode policy, 118
defined, 116
display brightness policy, 117
display idle timeout policy, 117
impact of, 116–118
Power sensor, 241
Power supplies, 12–13, 13–21
20- and 24-pin connectors, 15
80-plus-certified, 16–17, 17
at facility level, 12
ATX, 13–15
color coding, 15
efficiency, 15–17

efficiency of, 15–17
graphics cards, 15
level, 12–13
PCIe cards, 15
printed circuit boards (PCBs), 14
voltage regulator, 17–21
Power, defined, 2
Power-saving application, 236–237, 238
Powercfg -list, 48
PowerCfg command-line tool, 130–131, 131f
detected problems, 132t
timer resolution change request,
155–156, 156f
PowerCfg utility, 116, 117, 121
PowerInformer, 141, 142f
PowerTop, 139–141, 140f
PowerTutor, for Android, 205–206, 205f
PPM. *See* Processor power management (PPM)
PPM states. *See* Processor Power Management
(PPM) states
Printed circuit boards (PCBs), 14
Process Explorer, 80–81
Process Monitor (ProcMon)
disk I/O analysis and, 167, 168f
network I/O activities and, 168, 169f
Processor counters, 81
Processor power management (PPM), 116
states, 137f
sampling, 138f
Procrank program, for Android, 202–203, 203f
Pulse width modulation, 21
PwrTest. *See* Power management test tool (PwrTest)

R

RAM, 67
Real-life switching voltage regulator circuit, 20
Red Hat Enterprise 5.2, 238, 239
Remote procedure calls (RPCs), 106
Retail embedded systems, 181–182, 182f, 188t.
See also Embedded systems
RPCs. *See* Remote procedure calls (RPCs)

S

S0 idle, 115
S3 resume testing, 139f

Continuing Education is Essential

It's a challenge we all face—keeping pace with constant change in information technology. Whether our formal training was recent or long ago, we must all find time to keep ourselves educated and up to date in spite of the daily time pressures of our profession.

Intel produces technical books to help the industry learn about the latest technologies. The focus of these publications spans the basic motivation and origin for a technology through its practical application.

Right books, right time, from the experts

These technical books are planned to synchronize with roadmaps for technology and platforms, in order to give the industry a head-start. They provide new insights, in an engineer-to-engineer voice, from named experts. Sharing proven insights and design methods is intended to make it more practical for you to embrace the latest technology with greater design freedom and reduced risks.

I encourage you to take full advantage of Intel Press books as a way to dive deeper into the latest technologies, as you plan and develop your next generation products. They are an essential tool for every practicing engineer or programmer. I hope you will make them a part of your continuing education tool box.

Sincerely,

Senior Fellow and Chief Technology Officer Intel Corporation

Turn the page to learn about titles
from Intel Press for system developers

Creating the Infrastructure for Cloud Computing

An Essential Handbook for IT Professionals
By Enrique Castro-Leon, Bernard Golden, Miguel Gomez, Raghu Yeluri, and Charles G. Sheridan

Cloud computing is a logical extension of the technology of virtualization, integrated with application group self-provisioning, enormous scalability, and agile responsiveness borne of a no need to make long-term commitments for compute resources. It promises to make the efficient data center agile enough to meet today's chaotic business environment. However, despite its obvious benefits, cloud computing imposes challenges as well—translating manual processes to automated one is often difficult and always expensive. It remains to be seen which "flavor" of cloud computing—internal, external, public, private—becomes the widest used; there is no doubt at all that the conditions dictating cloud computing will engender its success.

Written for the professional IT engineer "*Creating the Infrastructure for Enterprise Cloud Computing*" is a hands on must-have guide to the theory, practice and implementation of Virtual Service Grids. The book is organized into separate sections that focus on: Virtualization & Cloud technology, General Architecture, Solution Architecture and Reference Implementations. This structure allows the reader to quickly access the information needed to plan and implement a cloud computing project.

"The authors appear to have leveraged Intel's latest nanoscale fabrication technology to achieve unprecedented density of ideas, information, and insight into the theory and practice of cloud computing. In a balanced treatment richly detailed with case studies, process charts, screen captures, and quantitative engineering data, they bring the cloud—which is still hazy to some—to life."

—Joe Weinman,
Vice President,
Strategic and Business
Development, AT&T

Energy Efficiency for Information Technology

How to Reduce Power Consumption in Servers and Data Centers
By Lauri Minas and Brad Ellison

ISBN 978-1-934053-20-1

Minimizing power consumption is one of the primary technical challenges that today's IT organizations face. In Energy Efficiency for Information Technology, Lauri Minas and Brad Ellison point out, that the overall consumption of electrical power by data centers can be reduced by understanding the several sources of power consumption and minimizing each one. Drawing on their engineering experience within Intel Corporation and with the industry, they break down power consumption into its constituent parts and explain each in a bottom-up fashion. With energy consumption well defined, Minas and Ellison systematically provide guidance for minimizing each draw on electrical power.

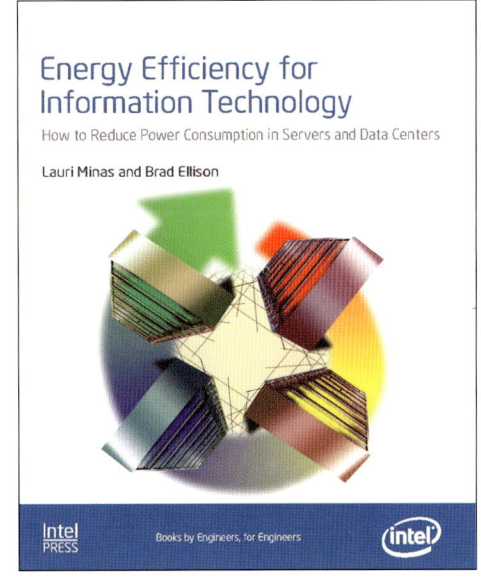

"Throughout my global travels, I hear increasing concern for the issues of power consumption by data centers, both due to the costs and also harm to the planet. *Energy Efficiency for Information Technology* addresses a critical issue for IT suppliers and consumers alike." Vernon Turner, Senior Vice President & General Manager, Enterprise Computing, Network, Consumer, and Infrastructure, IDC

"In *Energy Efficiency for Information Technology* Minas and Ellison underscore the magnitude of increases in power consumption, they systematically suggest ways to minimize consumption and provide checklists and assessments tables that are particularly useful to gather or summarize the right information for the planning. This is a multidimensional book that addresses a serious challenge to IT departments around the globe." YY Chow, Managing Director, Systems and Securities Services, Mitsubishi-UFJ Securities

"*Energy Efficiency for Information Technology* is a remarkable compilation of cutting-edge technical knowledge for addressing the critical issue of power and cooling in data centers. It shows how your data center can compute more but cost less, while also reducing energy use and environmental impacts". Jonathan Koomey, Ph.D., Project Scientist, Lawrence Berkeley National Laboratory

Beyond BIOS 2nd Edition

Developing with the Unified Extensible Firmware Interface
By Vincent Zimmer, Michael Rothman, and Suresh Marisetty

ISBN 978-1-934053-29-4

In *Beyond BIOS: Developing with the Unified Extensible Firmware Interface* the authors have updated the successful first edition to include the latest UEFI specifications and have expanded the scope of the book to include support of embedded and SOC platform designs.

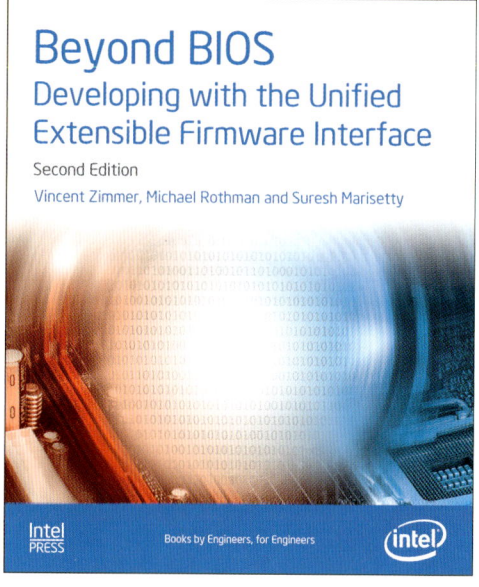

"In just a few days, a programmer familiar with C should have a good understanding of how to get started writing UEFI drivers and applications. For those who haven't developed PC BIOS firmware, *Beyond BIOS 2nd Edition* presents an opportunity to ramp up on the industry standard firmware platform for PCs and start writing UEFI apps as they do apps for today's mobile operating systems."

—Steve Jones, Chief Technology Officer, Phoenix Technologies Ltd.

". . . highly recommend this book as a "deep dive" into the UEFI specifications and the flexibility these standards give to those who choose them. This publication is full of practical information and real-world examples for system designers and can empower them to get and keep a competitive edge in their designs. I would like to commend Intel for compiling such a valuable resource."

—S. Shankar, President and CEO, American Megatrends Inc. (AMI)

"Our customers were able to gain efficiency and time-to-market advantage from legacy BIOS to Framework and EFI . . . *Beyond BIOS 2nd Edition* provides an extremely thorough yet lucid explanation of UEFI and PI that should be helpful to anyone that wants to understand or use this modern firmware environment."

—Jonathan Joseph, Executive Vice President, Insyde Software

Break Away with Intel® Atom™ Processors

A Guide to Architecture Migration
By Lori Matassa and Max Domeika

ISBN 978-1-934053-37-9

Break Away with Intel® Atom™ Processors: A Guide to Architecture Migration provides insight into architecture migration discussing real world software migration issues and highlighting them with case studies. The book covers pertinent topics that are at the heart of the software migration, such as techniques to port code originally written for other processor architectures, as well as capturing the benefits of Intel® Atom™ platform technologies. The reality is that architecture migration is not a one-size-fits-all activity and developers must understand all of the decisions that comprise a successful migration. The authors deliver this information as a handbook to your software migration plan and project activities.

"This is an essential guide to working with the Intel® Atom™ processors that should be read by anyone who wants to understand how to use the platform effectively. The book covers key concepts including power management, parallel applications, and machine virtualization, while providing a clear explanation of the system architecture and how to use it to its fullest advantage."

—Paul Krzyzanowski, CTO, OpenPeak Inc.

"This isn't just a book about Intel extending its reach into the embedded market. In a way that is fresh and exciting, the authors have really understood that it is a powerful software methodology and tools eco-system that is needed for developers to make best use of the multicore and multithreaded world we now live in. The style of this Atom book will be the standard against which all processor architecture books are measured from now on."

—David Stewart, CEO, CriticalBlue

A Vision for Platform Autonomy

Robust Frameworks for Systems
By Rahul Khanna and Mohan J. Kumari

A Vision for Platform Autonomy provides the holistic overview and the solution to the platform autonomics related to power, thermal, RAS, locality, and resource monitoring.

In addition to providing the theoretical basis of autonomics features, this book introduces the current state of the art in Intel platforms. It also covers the software based models and industry standards relevant to each autonomics feature. Additionally, the emerging concept of low speed wireless interconnects to achieve better platform autonomics is introduced.

The bottom line is that the system is able to maintain the stable equilibrium while hiding the complexity of the autonomics system from the users. It is similar to what its biological inspiration—the autonomic nervous system—does in our bodies.

"Driven by nearly a billion people online and a trillion connected objects, the scale of computing technology has exploded over the last decade, mandating the need for autonomic capabilities in IT systems and systems components. *A Vision for Platform Autonomy: Robust Frameworks for Systems* reveals the concepts, architectures, and core methodologies enabling the underlying elements essential to achieve autonomic computing."

—Alan G. Ganek, Chief Technology Officer & Vice President, Strategy and Technology,
   IBM Software Group

"I would highly recommend *A Vision for Platform Autonomy* for data center managers, enterprise management professionals, and platform architects. The authors have made significant contributions to the field of autonomics by providing an implementation framework and real life examples of how various feature and capabilities of modern compute platforms can contribute to a robust solution for autonomics."

—Professor Mariette Awad, Assistant Professor, Electrical and Computer Engineering Department,
   American University of Beirut

Special Deals, Special Prices!

To ensure you have all the latest books
and enjoy aggressively priced discounts,
please go to this Web site:

www.intel.com/intelpress/bookbundles.htm

Bundles of our books are available,
selected especially to address the needs
of the developer. The bundles place
important complementary topics at
your fingertips, and the price for a
bundle is substantially less than
buying all the books individually.

About Intel Press

Intel Press is the authoritative source of timely, technical books to help software and hardware developers speed up their development process. We collaborate only with leading industry experts to deliver reliable, first-to-market information about the latest technologies, processes, and strategies.

Our products are planned with the help of many people in the developer community and we encourage you to consider becoming a customer advisor. If you would like to help us and gain additional advance insight to the latest technologies, we encourage you to consider the Intel Press Customer Advisor Program. You can **register** here:

www.intel.com/intelpress/register.htm

For information about bulk orders or corporate sales, please send email to
bulkbooksales@intel.com

Other Developer Resources from Intel

At these Web sites you can also find valuable technical information and resources for developers:

www.intel.com/technology/rr	Recommended Reading list for books of interest to developers
www.intel.com/technology/itj	Intel Technology Journal
developer.intel.com	General information for developers
www.intel.com/software	Content, tools, training, and the Intel Early Access Program for software developers
www.intel.com/software/products	Programming tools to help you develop high-performance applications
www.intel.com/embedded	Solutions and resources for embedded and communications

IMPORTANT

You can access the companion Web site for this book
on the Internet at:

www.intel.com/intelpress/tmip

Use the serial number located in the upper-right hand
corner of this page to register your book and access
additional material, including the *Digital Edition* of
this book.